A MEDICINE MAN'S UN[...]

Of

The Medicine Of Selves

Another Spiritual Odyssey
&
Medicine Primer

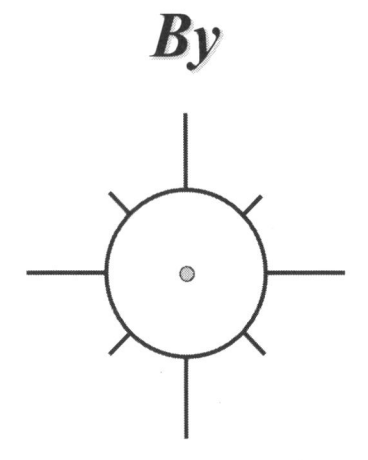

By

WHITE EAGLE

Volume 1 - How To Realize Real Success In Life

Regarding Grow, Growth and Life purpose...

In asking Great Pop as to how I should be and do while I am here on Mother Earth, He told me, "*Little One, I made that theme park for any Beings and Things that want to experience some of the limitless means and ways to experience and express Love and Brotherhood.*"

Some people profess that we each have a specific mission to accomplish in our lifetime, or that we come here to learn lessons of some sort through which we will Grow toward completing some kind of "Spiritual Transformation" and thereby achieve a "higher" condition of being. I personally believe that all of this aspiration and ambitious thinking about one's reality and life purpose is founded in Fear and is all a falsehood. I am certain that we come here for experiences by our own choice and that we experience things of our own manifestation through our thoughts and Prayers of Desire. This means that there is No mandate or mission, nor any requirement to learn anything, there is only a path of life that is of our own choosing and design.

When I was young Great Pop told me, "*Grow like the tree and thereby from the inside out in all directions.*"

I thought He meant that I should aspire to grow taller and thereby bigger. I later learned the Proper idea and ideal meant by His use of the word 'grow' as being more like the concept of "multi-dimensional expansion," as in this ideal we are in a sense "Ever and Always Complete". Through each incarnation we gain knowledge and understanding and therefore Expand from the experiences and expressions of being ourselves, thus we have more to offer and share with other Beings and Things and their expansion as well. This is the real and true condition and potential for every Being and Thing in the physical or spiritual condition, from the single celled microorganism to the entirety of all Creation - period.

All Beings and Things are considered "Even" in Great Pop's idea and Love of us. He would Never favor or set any Thing as being better than any other Thing of His Creation, therefore, within the contents of this or any of the other material that has been brought forth by this channel and servant of The Creator, I pray that you will properly interpret and correctly understand the use of the words Learn, Lesson, Grow, or Growth to mean and be interchangeable with "**To Become of**," "**Embody**," "**Expand**," or "**Expansion**".

The Medicine of Selves

Volume 1 - How To Realize Real Success In Life

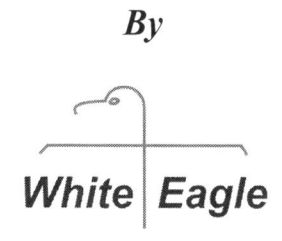

By

White | Eagle

Copyright © 2002 White Eagle

Revised - November 2012

White Eagle is a practicing Medicine Man who has been blessed by the Great Spirit Father with both Healing and Vision Medicine. Being part Algonquin and Arapaho, he carries forward a mixture of both traditional and nontraditional Medicine techniques. Ever seeking to serve the Will of The Great Spirit, White Eagle endeavors to enable all of the Great Spirit's children to learn of His Love and in the many ways in which we may allow His Light and Love to enrich our Well-being and lives. White Eagle has left the normal order of the societies that we live in to walk totally the path of a Medicine Man in order to embrace and help in the initiation of the New Order of the Great Spirit's Will and Consciousness in humankind.

Much information about the coming events pertaining to the reawakening of Spirituality has been provided to him by his Guides or Angels so to speak, as well as by the Creator Himself, in order to bring forth a new and heightened life in the Spirit of each of His Creation.

As a PohTikaWah or Medicine Man, White Eagle is a Priest, Healer, Teacher, Visionary, Counselor, and Ceremonial Leader but perhaps most important, a Guide in the way of discovering the Truth and Perfect Child within each of us.

In the traditional way, a Medicine Man would give a person a Medicine Name usually around the birth time as a vision would be given them however, several years ago during one of his daily Mediations the Great Spirit said for him to start Naming people with a Name that describes His Original Thought as He created each of them. This Name describes the perfect pattern of each Self as He created them and describes what they not only have always been but also that which they are and ever will continue to be (or better said, "What does Not need fixing".) The Medicine Name as described by White Eagle helps us understand why we have certain likes or dislikes and habits that are most normal for us, as well as abilities in which we can easily excel and use in our growth. White Eagle explains the Name as well as its Medicine and tendencies but always reminds us that we are ever in growth as to become greater channels of the Great Spirit's Light and Love and to do this we are ever learning new Medicine to add to that of our beginning so as to please the Creator. This is our true desire of our inner child.

In addition to the Naming Vision, White Eagle has also been given abilities in vision such as looking inside one's body to detect illness or infirmary, finding objects that are considered lost, going backwards or forwards in time as well as others. White Eagle has also been given the ability to channel or so as to say allow another person's Guides to speak to them through the body of him as well as channel his own personal Guides in an advisory capacity about all matters current and past that are having an immediate influence on one. White Eagle lives in what might best be described as altered states and does not use or condone the abuse of any drugs nor of anything or of anyone. Another of the abilities that has been given to White Eagle is for him to walk in another's moccasins in a past life review in order to release carryover problems that often occur from past lives. This process takes several days to complete and the product is specific documentation and a channeled review. White Eagle's knowledge of the Spirit world also provides dream state interpretations as well.

As a Healer, White Eagle has many abilities in working with energy, potions, and teas as well as Medicine Stones. There have been many instances whereby he has cured someone's headache or hiccups with a single thought. White Eagle will also be the first one to thank another for healing themselves and as he says that he takes no credit but full responsibility in such matters as he only invokes the Will and Love of God. White Eagle guides people in the process of meditation and from time to time holds workshops in learning the Medicine

Wheel Way as well as about Plant Spirit, Animal Spirit, and Mineral Spirit Medicines and how we can use them to enrich our lives.

White Eagle sometimes kids around about being a Native American Ghost Buster but know well he takes these matters very seriously. Unlike some others he uses the unlimited potential of Love to help in problems with discarnates, or entities, and possession as they are very dynamic in the Well-being of all involved. White Eagle is not a Witch or Witch Doctor although he has much knowledge about such things and will refuse to help any who are not aspiring to the highest ideal which is, "To Walk in Balance and With Harm to No One Being or Thing, including Oneself!" If possible White Eagle will record personal readings on cassette tape and asks that each provide their own tape for use. He says that one receives what they are willing to invest in any matter. He asks that each desiring a reading, prepare and bring a written list of questions to be answered for their own use, as he does not want to see them. White Eagle also makes many ceremonial items and personal items such as prayer sticks, rattles, shields, earrings, necklaces, as well as paintings.

Often White Eagle will speak of only charging a commitment to change when asked about receiving money for his services. However, as all truly know, one must be willing to give something away to receive more of anything at any point in time. Gifts or donations of money or other things that might support the work will be welcomed by him as White Eagle recognizes that in a respectful sharing way, those who have resources to share will be the first to benefit in the sharing process. However lack of money or resources are often manifestations of symptoms of other Spiritual dilemmas and he would never deny his services to anyone because of their lack of a comfortable money supply. Each one should feel comfortable with whatever they feel they should provide, as it is a contribution not a fixed price. White Eagle sees it only as a contribution to God and the Church.

This document is presented in what might best be described as pristine in its word usage and while sometimes the word usage might not be considered to be grammatically correct, it is in its original true condition to the Spirit of the Consciousness and is most proper. As it is given to express this information in the English language, many of the words available for use fall short of the full dynamics of the total scope of the Consciousness being expressed. In no way is it to be inferred that there is any bias or weight given to the male or female of the human species. All true Beings, which are all Spirits created by

The Great Spirit or God as some refer to Him, have chosen to incarnate into each of the "body-forms" and races, which is why the Great Spirit created the diversity in the first place. I call Him Great Pop and I am certain that He loves and favors each as equal in His esteem and so should we. As the Earthplane experience is truly that of learning the unlimited ways of experiencing Brotherhood and expressing Love, the Consciousness associated in the term Brotherhood is that of the willingness to support, sacrifice for, share, care, nurture, guide, and most important, value another Being regardless of what sex or other condition the body is in. Any other word associations that might even in the slightest way be considered to be gender biased should be considered the same way and the Consciousness to the Spirit of the use retained. This material is presented in the Spirit of Onement and the Law of One and is meant to be received in the same way, each samely unique and in their uniqueness the same.

This document is a product of the endeavor given by the Great Spirit for him to do in answer to his prayer for guidance in his daily meditation. These manuscripts are still new and seeking conventional publishing and support in distribution.

This material was completed in 2002 is the sole property of White Eagle and all rights are reserved. No part of this book may be transmitted or reproduced in any form or by any means, electronic or mechanical including photocopying and recording, or by any information storage or retrieval system, except as may be expressly permitted by White Eagle.

White Eagle may be contacted at **ASpiritWalker.com** or at:
PO Box 183
Pinebluff, NC 28373

It is my sincerest hope that this material will in some way be of service in bringing forth some of the abundance of Light and Love that the Great Spirit has for each and every one of us.

In the years that I have been guiding peoples, I have always cautioned them about what they read in books as I do also to you here and now. A book in its very best of conditions is but one person's documentary of their observations as they walk the path of life, and indeed can be no more than that. But, while they might speak of the squirrel running up the tree ahead and share their vision of that, they might miss the butterfly emerging from the cocoon behind. This book is a composition of information that comes to me both through meditation and channeled through me by my Guides. It is presented in the Spirit of Love. It was given to me to understand that the purpose of each person's incarnation to Earthplane for an Earthwalk is to learn more about the unlimited ways to experience and to express Love and Brotherhood.

In many of these books I talk about the Prevalent Culture. When I call it "White," I am not meaning Caucasian or even European for any that might be sensitive to such or take any offense as none is intended. The current Prevalent Culture, which is at times also called the "White Western Way" by some, actually has it genesis long before the man named Jesus was hung on a cross. I consider that event to be an act of "Being Murdered" by some of its adherents because of its Religion and foundation of materialism. And as Great Pop often tells me, *"This too can Change."*

I hope He was Not talking about those 30 pieces of silver, don't You?

Presented With Love,

White Eagle

CONTENTS

Introduction 3
A Note From The Author… 10

PART I 11
HUMMMM 13
GREAT POP 25
MEDICINE 34
OPERATIVES & ESSENCES 42
ENERGY 46

PART II 59
WHO AND WHAT AM I - REALLY? 61
CONSCIOUSNESS 66
DESIRE PRAYERS AND FEELINGS 75
THE PERSONAL STRUCTURE 81
THE FOUR WILLS 90
BARK ON TREE 97

PART III 109
ONEMENT 111
THE FOUR SELVES 119
THE REAL SELF 130
THE PROJECTED SELF 136
THE IMAGINED SELF 142
THE COSMIC / COMMUNAL SELF 148

PART IV 157
IN REVIEW 159
SELF DISCOVERY 175
MAKING A RESOURCE WHEEL 178
SELF REALIZATION 190

CONTENTS - Continued

PART V 201
SELF - ACTUALIZATION 203
SELF - DETERMINATION 211
SELF - AWARENESS 222
SELF - EXPRESSION 227
SELF HELP 238
How to Champion Insecurity 244
How to Champion Inferiority, Complexes, Addictions,
   and even Obesity. 248
How to Experience Renewall (Versus Recovery),
   and Healing. 256
How to Champion Personal Issues. 265
How to Realize Success in all Relationships. 269
How to Champion Anger and the other many faces of Fear. 276
How to Realize One's Objectives in the Medicine
   and Proper Way. 281
How to Live Life more Fully, and Stay Oneself in it 289
FINALLY..299
APPENDIX 305

A Note From The Author...

It has now been over two decades since Great Pop first told me to begin the writing of these now many books. At first I was reluctant and told Him that I certainly desired no such thing for myself. I also mentioned that I did not feel qualified or with sufficient skills in writing to do such an important task. He was persistent in His bequest of me to do such though, and soon began the effort on my part of such an important endeavor.

At the completion of the material of the first work that is titled The Medicine Way, I was 47 years of age. At that point, I already was keenly aware of the power and potential impact of the Word, be it in song or print. Each of these mediums can dynamically affect and effect an individual's attitude and perspective and thereby, Life. One can always find something positive or negative about any condition or thing as well. If one listens to angry or sad songs often enough then one will soon become of that same attitude and perspective. Once that occurs, one's Life experience and expressions will become more of a mirror of that than anything else.

In the material of some of the volumes that Great Pop has given for me to write, He has had me include the parallel account of my personal Life experiences during the development of them. In doing that I can only speak as honestly as I can of my feelings and attitude as each experience occurred. Also, when more than a single Being or Thing is involved in an experience, each that is involved will have its own personal perspective of it as well. Therefore I pray that no one Being or Thing be judged or condemned by their behavior or personal choices of expression in such an accounting. Still, I can and do honestly say that these experiences and expressions actually happened, and happened to me.

This material is presented in the Spirit of Love. It was given to me to understand that the purpose of each person's incarnation into the Physical realm and Mother Earth is to learn more about the unlimited ways to experience and to express Love and Brotherhood.

So as you read the pages...

I Pray That You Walk in Joy and Enjoy Your Walk ...

WHITE EAGLE

PART I

THE CIRCLE AND ODYSSEY CONTINUES

HUMMMM...

My name is White Eagle. I have a little boy. His name is Nolayte StarShine Eagle. Tomorrow will be December 11, 2001. It will also be his sixth birthday. I wanted to make or get him a birthday present but I do not know where to send it. You see, Nolayte's mother left me and took him away only a couple of weeks after he was born and I do not know where he is living.

Now to find her and him and be in his life, I have to get quite a lot of money for an attorney and court and the support that I will need if I can ever find where they are. Right now, I do not even know where my next rent payment or money for food will come from, except from the Creator through others in some way. Over a decade ago, long before I met Nolayte's mom I had given my life over to be of service to the Creator. Before that, I used to try to walk in two moccasins, one being like a white person in the prevalent culture and the other as what I am, a PohTikaWah. I was never very successful in the first type of moccasins, as they did not seem to fit me very well.

My lifestyle is pretty much doing whatever I can to continue to live and still be dedicated to serving only the Will of the Creator. Most of the resources that come to me are from people that try to help me continue doing just that through donations and odd job kinds of work. I used to be what some call a computer person or expert in my earlier years but since I made that commitment in the 1980s to serve the Will of the Creator, I have no longer been able to get that kind of work anymore. Now I use that knowledge to keep this writing machine as I call it, going, and making these books. Earlier this year the Creator had me make a website named ASpiritWalker. I was able to use some of my computer skills in that effort and it seems to work very well.

Nolayte's mom knew about all of this before she asked me to commit in the sacred union of marriage with her. She thought that I would change. I didn't though. It is now two years since I have seen Nolayte, which was only for a very short time in a fast food restaurant. That was over a year since I had previously been able to see him, for a few minutes in a shopping mall.

I know that I am not alone in my circumstance, as many have become estranged from or will miss family and friends this and every holiday season. I pray that one takes one's feelings to heart as I do and will, because whether they hurt or not, I would not want to not have them, or become insensitive. It is risky to care and love as well as trust, and things do not always turn out like we hope or plan, but Life is a path of momentary expressions and experiences. While I still miss Jack who exited suddenly in 1968 and so many others, be they family or friend, I will continue to feel blessed by the moments that I did share with each and every one of them. That is my choice and option, and it is available to any and all Beings and Things.

So I thank you Nolayte, Nolayte's mom, Jack, Jim, Mom, Dad, Sandy, Dayna, Heath and Jackie and their mom, Spirit, Spot, Sparkie, Hal, and so many others that have shared their Earthwalk experience with me, as well as their Care and Love for a time in it. I am truly wealthy from these you see, as they helped make my Life as it is and has been. And for and in that, I am most blessed and appreciative. Now whenever I feel alone, down or sad at this or any time or season, I will keep choosing to be thankful to each of these who have shared of themselves with me in the past, as well as those that are now in it. I will also then choose to continue to walk this path of my life as The Creator guides me, and use what is called the Prayer Proper to continue to make choices and expressions that

Walk in Balance with Harm to No One Being or Thing, Including Oneself!

As I begin the writing of this material, I once again have a hard time getting started, as I really do not claim to be a writer or even know what is going to be said in it. This is the twelfth book that I have been given to write though, and I continue to do such even though at this point none of the others have been published in the normal fashion of such. Actually, I was planning to write a book about Tribes earlier this year when I completed the last volume of Origins, and the Medicine of Numbers after that. Also, in most if not all of the other books, I really did not plan to write about their content at all.

I never did well in school and in my later years I figured out why that was perhaps. A part of the problem I feel was the fact that I do not have much memory in the normal sense. I like to tell people that I only have two brain cells left and that I gave all of the rest of them away. I tell them jokingly that I kept two so as to keep my ears apart. I also say that I do not want to have any memory. The reason for such is that I do not desire to limit the options available at any moment or about the future, by anything in the past.

Since birth, I have been able to journey backwards and view the past. Of course when I took tests in the history classes in school I did just that. I would write down the answer just as I saw it. I failed history more than twice. What I saw and wrote down was different than what they said in their history books. Another reason that I did not do well in school, outside of being girl crazy, was that I think in what I call my personal language. It is different than these small words that appear on this page and have so many interpretations and meanings. The Creator told me a long time ago that the language I use and think in is an ancient dialect of Algonquin. The problem for me begins in that this language, which by the way has no curse words, has what I call picture words. The simple word TohNaWah from my language, that is the name of my new feline partner in life, will take a paragraph of these words to express and explain. A simplified idea of it might be that of a lightening storm, at night. But it is also about Passion from the Heart, Soul Purpose and dedication, Warrior-ship, and a lot more than just those elements and things. Also, not only are the words in my personal language pictures, they are pictures in motion. So I will apologize now for the lengthy run on sentences and so forth in this material. If it is not already obvious, I failed English in school a couple of times as well. The final problem perhaps, that comes from my thinking in my personal language comes from the fact that the words are what I call multidimensional. In this regard the pictures that are in motion are global, not flat and linear like these words now appearing on this page. Because of this aspect, I might seem to talk in circles sort of, at least some of the time.

I remember as a child always knowing about certain things that I could not explain to others. Even if they might stop and listen, they probably would not believe what I was given to know about anyway. This was well in advance of, as well as after a drowning experience that I experienced at four years of age. Typical of most Medicine people, I have experienced the "near death" experience many times in my present term of life. This has facilitated a greater awareness and understanding of the Spiritual as well as Physical Nature of Life and the conditions of being in both realms. Oftentimes when Beings experience "going through the veil" as I like to call it in a death circumstance, if they are given to return to the Physical realm, they usually are enhanced with a special power or gift, such as being a healer or visionary. Most oftentimes as well, a change in the orientation and or purpose of their individual life expression is also manifested so as to serve The Creator in some fashion or way.

In my own experiences of such, of which there have been several, each time I did not so much change the orientation of my life expression as I did its focus. I was very enabled as a Medicine Man at birth and have always been able to see into people's bodies as well as have visions of events forthcoming and journey through the veil at will. I have never lost my association to the Spirit realm at any level of Consciousness, even when taught differently by the White western society that I grew up in. In addition to being a "channeler" I also have often been blessed with healing energy, although sometimes I seem to need it more for myself than to support others in the Medicine and thereby Brotherhood Way, of being on Mother Earth.

Growing up with such abilities including the ability to move objects, was not always fun. This was especially true when other children would be saying or planning mean things about me, and I would read their thoughts or hear their words from even a great distance away. In my earlier years I was taught by my parents to believe and act like I was "White". Or at the very least I was to be very quiet about being Indian much less than being in the Medicine Way. My parents wanted this from me primarily so as to be accepted by others. I quickly found that my life that way was much worse than what I experienced on the other side of the veil. Even in the church that they took me to, in which I later became an acolyte and sang in the choir, when I looked at the Light as it shone upon the cross that they had hanging there, I would simply leave and cross the veil so as to be with the Creator.

I struggled for many years trying to live the life that my parents had planned for me, but somehow it just never did work so well because I simply was not myself in it. It was only when I got older and kept going through the many death experiences that I finally realized and accepted my gifts as well as purpose in this incarnation on Mother Earth, as little else became available or fulfilling to me. After my parents had exited the Physical realm of Mother Earth, I saw how they, perhaps innocently, had negatively influenced me throughout that part of my life. I later realized that this influence continued even thereafter, as my earth father became a Possessing entity and thereby a negative energy. The result of this was that I finally chose to accept who and what I was, and to disregard the desires of them.

Throughout my early time, people would simply show up in my life that needed my support as a healer or visionary and I simply accepted the condition of it as being essentially God-sent, although I was always a little curious about how they might know about that ability in me. I never challenged nor even was curious as to the why or how things worked, I simply trusted and accepted everything as being perfect as the Creator had planned it. I needed no more than that to be fulfilled as a willing participant. I did, however, find out some things in time that made my understanding secure in different facets of my awareness, such as when I would leave my body to do something in another realm. In these circumstances my body would shut down completely unless there was another Spiritual energy source associated with it, such as a Protector Spirit or Guide. I realized this condition when one time I left my body to do something in another realm, only to find out upon my return to the Physical realm that others were calling the ambulance, as I had no respiration or heartbeat.

Even in the process that I was given to use in channeling other Spirits and Guides through the vessel of the body of myself, it would often affect my biology for some period of time thereafter, depending upon the Nature of them and their personality so to speak. I make mention of these things simply so as to give some orientation to my sense of trust, dedication, and faith in the Creator and the Medicine Way.

Traditionally at birth, people would seek out a Medicine person that was a visionary so as to identify the Medicine and thereby name the newborn child, so that the parents might properly raise it to fulfill the child's and Creator's image or plan of, and in, itself. I named people this way for many years, giving them a name reflecting a vision provided by the Creator to me when I prayed for it. In doing this I simply accepted it as being the way of such and did not question either the result or the process, and I must also mention I was also quite certain, as well as content in it. I then wondered one day "Why am I White Eagle?" I knew of the Medicine of the name and that also other Beings had been or were named White Eagle, but I was simply a little curious about the why of that for myself.

On many occasions when operating out-of-body in other realms, I have been guided or asked by the Creator to perform some task. Each time, I simply did what was given, or asked as to How, and never even wondered about the potential outcome. I knew that if He wanted it done by me, then I was already facilitated with all that I needed to do or perform in it. Often, in the process and experience of such, I would see myself to appear in bird or Eagle form.

After some period of time and many such experiences, in a revelationary manner most often during Meditation or Ceremony, I received some insight and perhaps even understanding as to the greater extent and Nature of things. At this point in my journey on Mother Earth, I have received many such awareness and understandings about many diverse things. Yet I still am somewhat unsteady as to what I might be in for next, as for me and my understanding and this greater awareness has a deep and definite responsibility associated with it. I have found that my growth has only occurred at the deeper soul or Spiritual level through such metamorphic experiences and expressions of understanding. I have often stated that I seek not to know so much, simply to understand and thereby grow from what I have already experienced. The Creator then interjected that I cannot truly grow the Round and thereby Proper and Medicine Way, if I only look forward or backwards. He told me that it is only possible if I look at things from a position and perspective that is outside of myself and thereby in Onement, so as to see the complete picture. As one might suspect, I am still trying to work on that approach.

Many years ago the Creator told me *"Little One,"* as He likes to refer to me that way, *"from now on Pray and go into your rattle or drum, and seek from Me a Vision as to the beginning of each of My children, and this will be the Ever or Medicine Name that you shall give to them describing the perfect Nature of their Spirit or Soul."* He then showed me how each individual came to be. It was as if He were standing by a still pond and I was looking at the event a little ways from and above His right shoulder, like a little bird sitting on a limb of a tree. In each event, out of the forehead and Mind of Him, I would see an amorphous vibratory pattern of energy projected, as such is the very Nature of thought. Next out of the chest and Heart of Him, would come a green vapor-like mist of energy that stayed connected to His Heart by a Golden thread. Then this cloud of green substance and energy blended and merged with the thought pattern and it became whole, real, and everlasting, as it thereby was manifested or born as a True Spirit.

During my morning meditation many years ago after expressing my curiosity about "Why was I White Eagle?" and "When was I first on Mother Earth?" I was given to see the original event of His making of Mother Earth. I saw how during the event of it, I was flying about that area of The Great Void in my Eagle-like bird form, essentially showing off, as I often did for Him by doing flying feats. I became overwhelmed as I truly then did immediately remember and feel again the very profound experience of it. The Creator then showed me the experience of that event again from the outside and again off to the upper right from much the same viewpoint as being the little bird in the tree as mentioned before. It took some time for me to realize as well as accept the whole of what was given for me to see. Actually, I must admit that I still have some doubt associated with it, as it must mean that I was existent before Mother Earth. Each time that I would ask Him, He would simply confirm that suspicion, which does still leave me quite uncomfortable for perhaps many reasons. He then compassionately and jokingly stated that perhaps I will get over it some day. I then spent some time trying to understand the significance of what was shown to me. Finally, I asked Him again in my morning meditation if He would help me to better understand how I came to be.

I was then again projected outside of the arena of it so to speak, much in the manner of being an outside observer, or camera mounted on the wall. I was situated in that same position of reference or viewpoint, being a short distance above, behind, and off of the right shoulder of Him. I still recall it vividly as I write these words describing it, which are at times very difficult to form, as the experience is very overwhelming, if one can truly imagine.

The setting where I was located was a large rectangular room with one of the walls of the long sides missing. It appeared much in the manner of being some kind of cubicle whereby the walls went up to the ceiling, yet there was no ceiling there. There was a floor of sorts, at least there must have been something holding up the very large and long table in the middle of the room. There were some cabinets and other simple structures as I recall, but nothing specific comes to mind now, which is some years later. As I was given to see everything as it was then, I must state that the vision was in color, however most everything was the color White it seems. The table was White. The walls were White where there were any. The door off to the left was White and the hallway beyond it was White. The bottom or floor was White and the perch on the table was White, as was the beautiful Eagle form on it that The Creator was fashioning, like some artist or sculptor in their studio. I do not specifically recall any light source like lamps or such. The place or structure looked a lot like this:

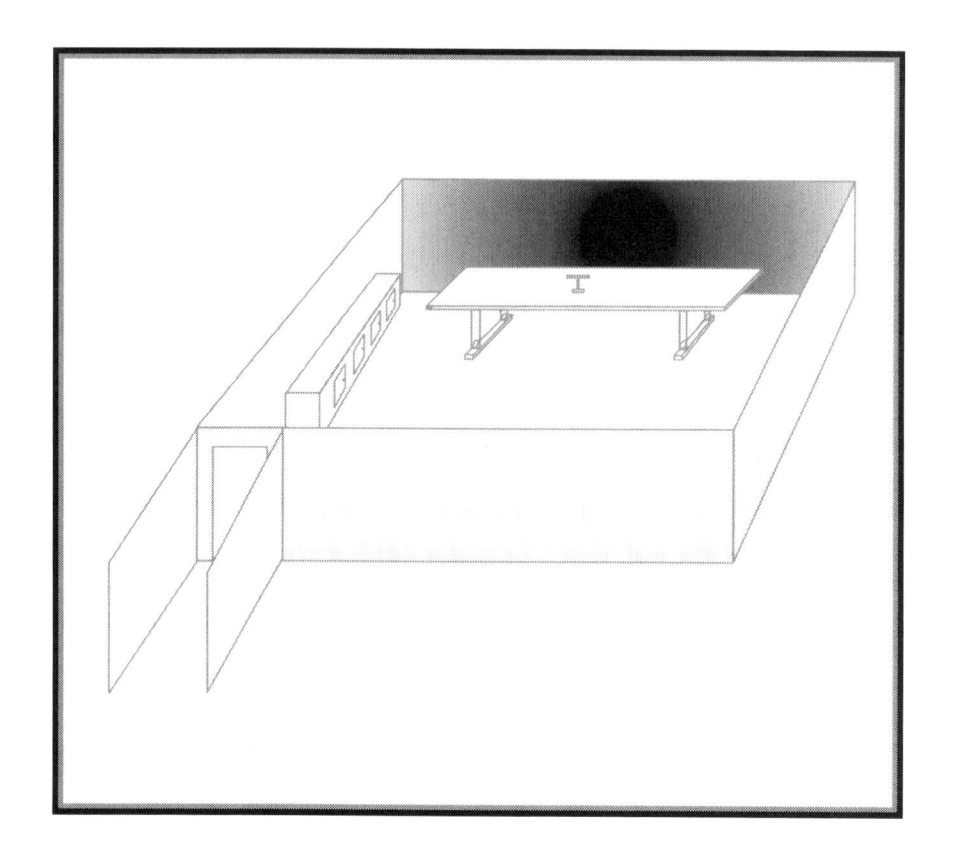

In this experience, there just was a lot of the Whitest and softest light. It seemed to just radiate from the walls as this wonderful form of The Creator, appearing like a tall - as in huge - Marlon Brando kind of man, in a White robe or gown with the kindest of face and expression pondered at the creation He was making, which was that of myself. The color of His skin was an off-White with just a tint of Blue, turning sometimes Green, Reddish, Orange, Gold, or Purple, depending upon the emotion of Him, but ever predominately White. It was not ashen White, but instead it was the purest and most vibrant White that is possible for one to imagine. As I later recall, The Creator at the time also wore some kind of White beard and cap. These appeared much like an artist might be imagined wearing, and it was also very neat and trim as was everything else that was there. It still comes to mind that there really was not that much there in this place to describe, as it was so basically simple and especially clean and tidy - as The Creator wants me to say. The table seemingly took up most of the room, and The Creator stood in front of the middle of it. The perch and bird form of myself was situated closer to His side of it, rather than that of the other side. The other side was open, with only The Great Void being visibly present beyond there. The Creator said that He feels especially inspired to artistically Create as He calls it, by having the view of The Great Void present in this manner.

I felt especially overwhelmed as well as strange in this circumstance of myself. The Creator facilitated me to see and re-experience the event from not only the vantage point of being outside, but also to simultaneously sense, feel and view it again from the inside of the bird form of myself as well. This caused me to recall and realize the whole Nature of the event at a much deeper level of my Consciousness. The experience brought forth an even greater understanding as well as awareness of the dynamics that were involved in the process of it. I also realize at this later time, that I must have been at least partially Spiritually complete in a certain manner and way before the creation of the bird form of myself. Obviously, there already were certain parts of myself that were available before the starting of the project so as to speak.

When I asked The Creator about such, He did confirm that it was so. He then said that what is now being described, is kind of a backtracking of the project of His making of myself. He so often shows me many things this way, such as when Naming people. The Creator explained that this description is of the semi-final form of my Spiritual body development, or integration, as He prefers to call the process. The Creator then explained that He simply considers it to be a refinement on His part of what was already working perfectly. He added that at any consideration, the All was already complete in its relative stage of creation. He added that more will be described as to the initial stages of such, later in this work. During the whole experience of observing His making of the final or current Spiritual form of myself, The Creator also allowed for me to in some way sense both His thoughts and feelings during the process. In this regard, I can only say that the experience was most enlightening as well as most extraordinary, indeed.

I was next given to observe as He looked upon the almost finished bird form of myself, and thought for a moment about what He desired next to become a part of or in me. He then got a glimmer in His eye and once again held out his left hand. Then from His left middle finger He projected another perfect and beautiful White feather. Next, He so lovingly and caringly placed it into the very back of the form of me. The Creator then stepped back a bit and looked approvingly upon

His creation. At that moment, I sensed that everything was in place and complete. I then felt Him project my Consciousness inside of the bird form, after which I could see through the eyes of it. The eyes were of a Whitish Green and Golden color on the outside, with the rest of the form being of the purest of White. I heard and felt Him think about what was to be next and then I felt it, as He gave me vision, and I could see as well as sense the image of Him before me. He then smiled so pleasantly as He saw what He had made and was indeed pleased.

The Creator then pondered for a moment and gave a little pause. Then once again I saw the twinkle in His eye and suddenly I felt Him give me mobility, and so I turned my head about. I stretched each wing to see what it felt like, after which I then moved my feet. It was so wonderful to feel what He had done to and for me and I was so very grateful. I saw that He was truly pleased and proud of what He had done in creating the beautiful and perfect bird form of myself. Once again He gave a pause, wondering if it was indeed complete. Thereafter, I again felt as something else came from the eye of Him and it became embodied in me. I wondered what it was. In a telepathic kind of way, He let me know it was sound, or voice. I pondered what to next do. In no moment of the experience did I feel awkward or afraid, only in total awe, Love, and wonderment. I must mention that in this event, time, and place, there was very little as mentioned, in the arena of it. Absent was any idea or Consciousness to wind or air, water, food or any need to sustain or express oneself, only that everything was possible with no sense of need. There was only the Creator, the structure that we were in, The Great Void, openness, unlimited possibility and my bird form and also my Free Will.

I thought for a moment, or what might truly have been an eternity, as both were the same then and there. The first idea that came from within me was to try to please Him with this new gift that He had just given and made in me. So I gathered up the greatest expression that I could, in the new body form that He had made in and for me. I then reared back and gave out the greatest cross utterance of a "Hey"-like squawk that I could make.

The Creator reeled back with a great roar of laughter and I saw how what I had just done did so please Him. I felt so much thankfulness and Love for Him in that moment and still do now. Maybe that is why it seems that I have been trying to do the same ever since. Next, in my great show off way, I went zooming out of the room and through The

Great Void. I tried to do flying and acrobatic tricks in a further desire to please and make Him glad He made me, in the most passionate and respectful way. I must mention that during this experience, I did not see or sense anything else being there. However, there might have been other Things or Beings in other rooms in the facility that He and I shared at that time. I do not remember anything at this time about the other rooms that were there, except that I know there were and are some. I will add also that from the vantage or viewpoint of The Great Void, at a great distance one can see the facility as a modular kind of structure. It is suspended magically in nothingness and it radiates the kindest glow of the Whitest light. One can find it anywhere in The Great Void quite easily, as that is all that is there. It appears much like this:

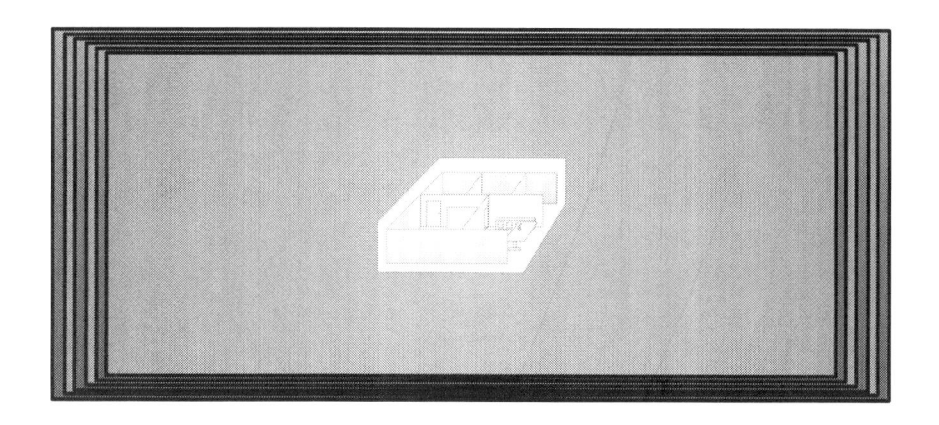

I was then given to reflect upon the many times that I would be given to journey through the veil. Most times I would transform myself into my bird form and simply project myself upward and forward, to wherever He wanted me to be. Most often I see things over the top part of a great beak, which I see as well as sense as being there in front of me. In reflection about the circumstance of the creation of my bird form, from the outward appearance it looked very much the same as the present physical form of an Eagle. Yet it was all White and seemed to glow in a certain way.

On being inside of the bird form, it was not dense like the physical body that my Spirit now inhabits, which is made from Mineral Spirit and Water. This is probably because its substance was made from a different material and in a different way. The bird form was already fully developed as one might say. It was fashioned in a condition that can only be considered as mature in every sense and way. On being inside of the bird form, there is no sense of bone or muscle or any sense of taste or smell. Instead of these, a different set of senses is present, with both vision and feeling being enhanced in many ways.

As I was flying about showing off for Him, there was a great sense of speed and flight, yet with the absence of air. One can only imagine what it felt like in that I did not need to flap my wings to move about. However, I could move or flap my wings if I wanted to experience such. As one might imagine, I did often test out the effects of all parts of this wonderful vehicle that He had made for my Spirit to express myself in. Of course, I took great joy in watching and sensing His pleasure as I discovered and experienced more about this vessel. To accomplish each maneuver I would simply think about a potential of expression and make a choice to try it. I would then gather some type of energy or force that was always present and available and simply channel that as an expression of the Will of myself. In so doing, I would then move about and perform so very easily, although not always so very gracefully, at least for a while.

In watching The Creator and the scene from my vantage point outside, I discovered perhaps the Why that He had made me, as I saw the great satisfaction and joy that it brought to Him. It often still makes me cry when I think about it all.

Since the time that The Creator first told me to "write this book," which led to the genesis of the material called The Medicine Way, I have wondered why He would desire such from me. Certainly there are many more people qualified to do this, especially in the English language. Then I remembered what The Creator showed me as being my beginning Medicine. A picture of my beginning Medicine is:

Like all of the picture words in my personal language, this symbol too is multidimensional and in motion. Basically, it is the symbol of the Creator and four lightning bolts that converge beneath Him. The four lightning bolts form the Purpose and message, which is that of "Bringing the Word and Will of the Creator to the mountaintop." No matter what my condition is or where I am, this is what I most desire to do and be, period. Whether I am incarnated or not, this is what I most desire and wish to accomplish, no matter what. So, like myself at this point, one might also find oneself thinking or saying:

Hummmm...

GREAT POP

Ever since my childhood I have had trouble with the word God. Perhaps it is simply because the word God is the word Dog spelled backwards. Another reason is the idea promoted about God in most of the religions that I have encountered or studied. "Allah" seems better to me, as does the "Great Spirit". These at least are names of a sort. Also, these references allow for some personality to be considered, as to me the word God simply does not. I also feel that this title versus name is probably intentional. It is sort of like the word "Boss". As an underling in a large corporation you certainly would not be able or invited to casually talk to the Boss whenever you desired. Nope, "the

Boss is busy right now," some other underling will say. Or, "the Boss does not have time for chitchat or trivial conversation." "The Boss has more important things to do." These are the responses that all individuals in the corporate world of the prevalent culture have experienced at times, as have I. Sadly, it seems that most of the available religious organizations are little different in their structure and goals than the corporate entities of the prevalent culture. Their ambitions seem parallel, as do their practices. In fact, some of the leaders and support personnel of these religions are even less available for anyone to interact with than the Boss of a large corporation. Would you like to have a friendly chat with the Pope? Or how would you like to sit down to chat with a Bishop? If you would, it is highly unlikely that you will be able to. This perhaps is one of the reasons that I personally quit participating in them on a regular basis. I consider all religions correct that do not exclude another. Of course that one criteria makes most of them incorrect to me. I feel that perhaps this is primarily because both are founded upon hierarchical structures and competition in some manner or way.

After I drowned at the age of four and came back to life, my parents went looking for a religion. One could liken the experience to that of shopping or looking for a college to enroll in. They first took us to the church that the neighbors were attending. It was Presbyterian I believe, and we only went there for a little while. My dad decided that we should be Episcopalian instead, even though I was already baptized in that other one. My dad, whom I now refer to as being my earth father, was like that though. He had a way of always getting what suited him best. I was OK with that, as I understood that he was really mostly afraid. I found out later that he was actually afraid of me, as well as for me, especially after that drowning experience. I also found out that I had died a year before drowning as well. I believe it was from what some call scarlet fever. Of course as you can tell from reading this, I did come back to life each time.

Like most children, I idolized the big people including my parents. However my earth father was quite insecure. I now remember that I was born with two "club" feet. They were operated on after I was born and have worked perfectly every since, however as an infant in the crib I had to wear casts and braces for a while. My earth father never allowed me to be held or nurtured. I remember someone getting into trouble from my earth father for picking me up one time. Even my mom's parents and family were not allowed to touch me when we visited them. So as one might imagine, I was pretty insecure in my early time, especially with the pattern of my earth father being all I was exposed to for a while.

I can still vividly remember the day that some new people moved into the house across the street. They had three boys with the youngest being my age. Later I was to realize, all of the people in that neighborhood were of German descent and so were these new ones. All of the neighbors had that in common but here I was, a dark skinned, skinny, insecure little boy, wanting to be accepted by someone or just somehow fit in. This new little boy that was the same age as myself was fat. Yep, he was as fat as I was skinny. This boy got teased a lot by his older brothers for being fat. They would fight and wrestle around a lot as well. He would then take that out on me. I went home crying many times because he would use his weight to make that happen. My dad decided that I should learn to box not too long after that, however I never wanted to hurt anyone at all. I did not want to be hurt either for that matter, but somehow that did not seem to make any difference. The one boxing match that I was put in was with about the only friend that I had in school. They told me to hit him. I did, and he cried. I cried then too and felt real bad because I hurt him and made him cry. None of it made any sense to me. I did not box anymore.

I was always tall for my age and this did not seem to help either. The first day of kindergarten the teacher had us go out to the playground. She brought over this other little boy in the class and introduced us to each other. He was a lot shorter and stockier than me. I said hi, hoping to make a friend. Then he hit me in the belly and knocked the wind right out of me. I did not like school at all from that point on. I would even make myself sick so that I did not have to go. There was only one reason that I did go back it seems. There was a little girl named Sally in my class. She had the blondest hair and I was in love! If it were not for the girls I never would have gone to school. That is not if I had anything to say about it. Yep, since early childhood I have always been fascinated with girls and women!

My mom met my earth father in Washington D.C. He had a job in intelligence, designing some stuff for the military and she was his secretary. They moved back to Oklahoma City right after the Second World War and I was born there. My earth father moved us to a subdivision in Texas when I was one year old. I was a lot darker skinned than any of my relatives except for my dad who was Algonquin.

My mom's parents had three children, all of them were girls, and my mom was the firstborn of the three, but in that time and culture what really mattered was being the first grandson and that certainly was not me. Nope, the first and favored grandson was named Sandy and he was the apple of my mom's father's eye. Sandy's earth father was in the Second World War like my dad, and I believe he received a Gold Star. I remember my earth father saying that he was "shell shocked" or something like that. I always liked Sandy's earth father. He was real quiet, yet he took me fishing with him sometimes. I guess being with me was like being alone, or at least with someone that he could trust in a way. Now that I think about it, I have always gotten along that way with older people. Throughout most of my life most of my close friends are or were much older than me. Maybe it was because they felt sorry for me or because I have been dead a lot of times. It might also be just because I am a PohTikaWah and they knew it somehow.

As quiet as Sandy's earth father was, his mom was not. In fact, I feel comfortable saying that she was actually pretty darn mean at times. I have several, if not many memories of her beating Sandy when she was in a rage. Those actions probably would get her arrested in these days and times. I certainly saw how this affected Sandy and realized the impact of such, early on as a child. Later in growing up I would at times see Sandy behave in a mirroring fashion. I certainly knew where he got the idea of that kind of behavior.

In those earlier years I was much taller than Sandy and like with the kid across the street, I was much skinnier too. Sandy was much tougher than me. Actually, he acted much tougher than I ever wanted to be. This became real uncomfortable as I started growing up. Whenever I went to Oklahoma, like the short kid in kindergarten, the first order of business so to speak was for Sandy to prove his strength and power over me. And of course I had to prove that I could take it and measure up so as to be accepted and OK with him. Of course, all I ever wanted in these times was just to be accepted as being even. Period.

This became even more significant when we got a little older. When I was eleven and still in elementary school I was already six feet tall. Also, by this time most of my friends were in the class ahead of mine and it stayed that way into college. However when I turned eleven, my mom's dad decided to let me come up there for the summer and work the farms with Sandy. And this meant the most important thing to me at that time in my life, which was that I would get to drive! Yep, I would get to drive the tractors and plow, like Sandy. I would get to drive the trucks and cars, like Sandy. Finally, I would be even, and in a heaven of sorts, with Sandy. So at eleven years of age, my mom put me on the train by myself for the days' long ride to that part of Oklahoma where her parents lived, and Sandy. Boy was I both excited and nervous at the very same moment! Little did I expect what would happen as soon as I got to my grandparent's' house.

No longer were the cows and chickens in the back yard, like when I was growing up. They had a real garage and the tiny place of a few old farmhouses now had several new ones. As soon as we had put my bags in the room in the attic, Sandy welcomed me by telling me to meet him behind the shed. On arrival, I promptly got hit and wrestled to the ground and put into as much pain as he could muster until I cried "Uncle". Once I recovered from that one, then and only then, would he even recognize my existence. Yep, "Heaven" did not work out so well after all.

That first summer was much different than I had ever planned or imagined. For five dollars a day I got to sweat behind the exhaust of the "little" tractor while Sandy drove the more powerful "big" one. And we both did such in 110-degree temperatures, from dawn to dusk. We dug postholes in what they call "calitchie" which is basically hard rock and clay. We both worked very hard under the supervision of a much older foreman who used to imbibe a lot of whiskey during the day. Yep, it was as if I had gone to another part of the universe and I was a most unwelcome visitor there.

One afternoon while waiting for dinner, I watched Sandy strike a kitchen match with his thumbnail. He then flicked it on some dry grass and deftly stomped it out. After watching this behavior for a few days, I tried it for myself when I was alone. Things worsened for me that summer when unlike him, I could not stomp out the ensuing blaze. Yep, I set the whole field surrounding my grandparent's home on fire. My grandmother's only statement to me was that I was going to kill my grandfather by giving him a heart attack. The rest of the time I was there that summer I was reminded of my inadequacy whenever we came home from work, by the scorched earth surrounding my grandparent's house.

One of the tasks of a field hand such as I was supposed to be, was to turn oats and wheat. This meant that whether one was in a silo or barn, you dug from below and rotated the grain with a large shovel. Not only was this hard and in a very hot place, there was that dust and chaff. That chaff was worse than any itching powder ever conceived.

In my earlier years, I used to get asthma and bronchitis and I used it a lot to get out of school. So, I ended up in the hospital that summer with chronic bronchitis, not too long after the fire. I went home before the summer was half over that year. Perhaps the only good thing that came from that experience was that on my return home I behaved more like Sandy. I actually got a little more recognition if not even respect, especially from the fat kid across the street that was somewhat of a friend by that time. In this I do not mean that I was mean at all, just that I would stand up for myself at least a little bit. My mom did not like this change in my behavior though and she told me about it in no uncertain terms. It was at this point that I told my earth father never to hit me again, which he had just done, and he did not.

That fall was my entry into junior high. It was that wonderful, confusing and scary time in a child's life. It is the time where they get those apparatuses that separate the men from the boys and the women from the girls. Yep, that strange thing that my mom took me to the store to pick out was called a jock strap! I'm pretty confident that for the girls, it is the same with the bra. I was a little more secure in going to this new school, as I had older friends that already thought that I went there also. Of course like kindergarten, on the first day I met another "little" girl named Jamie and I was in love again! It was too bad for me that she liked this shorter fellow. All that year at social events her mom would spend time with me though. It seemed that she liked me more than her daughter did. However unlike elementary school I was no longer the tallest kid in school. And even though I was a top scorer in one of the local teenage teams, I did not make the basketball team.

After that school year, I was most surprised to get another invite to work the farms in Oklahoma. After another long day's ride alone on the train, my grandmother again delivered me back to their home. I was quick to notice that the field next to their house seemed to have recovered OK, and nothing more was ever said by anyone about that incident. As if on cue, Sandy again offered to meet me behind the shed. This time I was different somehow. Sandy was still much shorter and somehow I got him in an arm lock around his neck right off. Even his punches to my belly and head would not make me let go this time. Noticing that his face was turning blue, I asked if he were ready to give and he finally said "Uncle". We both had a lot more fun that summer. We would take on all kinds of challenges like "normal" wild Indian kids. My grandfather even bought us a painted pony that summer, however I found out later that it was stolen that winter. I was even with Sandy this time, like never before in my life.

We found an old oil drum by the garage so while waiting for dinner or after dinner we would try to roll it by standing on it and walking it with our feet, down the rutted red clay street. We would try to see who could get the farthest without falling off. Unlike before, we both applauded each other's efforts. Another one of the many tests that we posed for each other was to sit on the very back edge of the flatbed truck on the way home from the fields. We would let our legs and feet dangle over the back edge and not hold on with our hands. In this test, whoever grabbed onto anything would loose. This does not seem like much of a challenge to some, perhaps. But consider that the roads were deeply rutted red clay and the foreman had been drinking whisky all day!

Yep, it seemed that finally Sandy and I became even that summer. And that was a good thing for both of us. Maybe I had something to do with it when he was blue in the face. I am certainly glad too, because that fall he grew over a foot in height! Either way, he did not have to prove anything to me anymore, or me to him. I have a lot of stories that I could tell, especially about the two wild Indian kids, one of them called Sandy. Sandy was killed in Viet Nam. He was six foot six inches tall. He got the Bronze Star, just like his earth father. Chon A-Tah, Sandy! (meaning - Thanks for your share and being in my life and I will see you on the other side.)

In that small town in Oklahoma where I used to go to work for the summer those couple of years, there were two churches that my grandparents used to take us. I am pretty sure one of them was Methodist and the other might have been Baptist. I could never tell the difference. I believe one of them was my grandmother's family church and the other my grandfather's. They both seemed the same to me when I was young and even the same as I became older. I remember not being allowed to play cards at my grandparent's house and I am sure that was because of the restrictions and influence of one of the churches. I did not really feel comfortable in those churches for some reason and I was always glad when the services were over.

Understanding my earth father's behavior, I was not ever what they call "close" to the people in Oklahoma. My mom's parents, like my earth father hid their Native American background. In Oklahoma being "Indian" was worse than being "Negro". While I was growing up there were still many signs in Oklahoma that said "No Injuns Allowed".

With parts of Texas, Kansas and Nebraska, most of Oklahoma was a part of the Great Prairie before the White people came to this continent. The very easternmost part of Oklahoma that borders Arkansas was not a part of the Great Prairie and is the part that does not hurt so much for me to be in. As a PohTikaWah I have always been able to read the Memory energy in the soil and this place was no exception.

The rest of Oklahoma is where the story *The Grapes of Wrath* takes place. It used to be called the dust bowl. You see there are literally no trees west of the very easternmost portion. When the White people tried to do genocide to the Native Americans by killing off all of the Buffalo, they caused deep pain to the Spirit of the land. In only a few generations after that slaughter, the White people's plows destroyed the rest of the delicate balance that kept the surface intact. The Great Prairie needed the Buffalo you see. When the White people killed them off and removed any stones or trees, there was nothing to protect the soil from the ever-present wind that blows there. Still in that part of Oklahoma you cannot get away from the fine red dust that gets into every nook and cranny, of every place and thing. White paint is used a lot on the older houses there but they all look pink and are darker pink at the bottom. It would take me several days of washing when I got back to Texas, before my hair and everything else returned to its normal color. It was a dust that you could almost never wash off and when wet, it was better than any stain made by man. It got into your skin, teeth, eyes, hair and ears. It was as if Mother Earth was claiming your body, even before you were dead. At this point in my life, I do not ever care to go back there again.

In Texas I did enjoy going to the Episcopal Church that my earth father decided was right for us though. I sang in the choir for many years. I really enjoyed our time doing that together. Perhaps it was because, like with Sandy, it was one of the things that we were even in. I was an acolyte there for many years as well. But I am pretty sure that it was sitting up front in the choir, that I first felt OK talking directly with the Creator. I talked with Him all of the time ever since I can remember, but never in a Church before. That is because in Church I felt that I was supposed to talk at Him, not with Him. There is a great difference in talking to the Creator than talking with Him.

I was pretty young at the time I remember, but am not of any idea as to how old. I do remember there was a large wooden cross on the wall with gold coloring between the dark brown wood edges. It seemed like the gold was embraced in a channel of the wood and one could almost smell as well as feel something coming from it, in a way. There was a light pointed down upon the center of it from above in the rafters. One day as the service was progressing, I felt drawn into the light radiating from the center of it. I have not told anyone about this experience until this moment. It was at that time that I knew not only that I could talk to the Creator in this setting, but also that He would talk back to me, which He did.

It was about this same time that I used to sneak out of the house at night after my parents had gone to sleep. This practice started even before my sleeping quarters got relocated to the converted porch / office of my earth father. Of course it was much easier to accomplish after that happened. At one end of the block that we lived on there was a grassy ravine. I would lay down in that ravine late at night and look at the stars for hours. My Spirit Guides and helpers would show up and I would learn all that they wanted me to know, about everything. I would talk with the Creator from time to time in these experiences as well. It seems that all of this was in a sense simply reinforcing what I already knew. However it also was for the purpose of helping me keep going along a certain pathway that had many forks and branches.

I did like being in the church building that my earth father had decided for us to go to and although I found that I could talk with the Creator there, I had trouble talking with my Guides and helper Spirits there, but not in this grassy ravine. About the time of my early to middle teens, I set about to learn something about all of the religions that were available. However, it was not until recently that I have come to terms with what I call the inadequacy and intent within them.

I can still vividly remember when I drowned and went through the tunnel of Transition that time. When I got to the other side, I saw and was with the Creator, whom to me is "Great Pop". Several times over those early years, I would ask Him if it is OK for me to call Him that. I like it because I know that He is a Real individual and in a sense a personality as well. Besides, "Pop" spelled backwards is still "Pop!" Great Pop's response to me when I ask is always, *"Certainly, Little One, after all, where do you think that the idea of it came from? Ha, ha, ha!"*

MEDICINE

In reality, I have always been able to talk with Great Pop. To me, it would seem almost inconceivable as well as at least most awkward, not to. After the development of the material that He had me prepare in the four volumes of Origins, I became of a much greater understanding through the Odyssey of it, as to the Why it is of things as they now are. This even includes the general attitude of the masses towards both Great Pop and religion. I personally do not adhere to many things, beliefs and values in the prevalent culture. I learned the genesis of such in the experience of Origins. Of course now that I understand Why, it is much easier for me.

Part of the problem it seems is that most religions exist as a response and proponent of a 'Need' based mentality. Every child that is born knows Great Pop and talks with Him all of the time. Of course they recognize and have an ongoing relationship with their Spirit Guides that some call guardian angels as well. A child born is never alone in the Spiritual sense. It is also Spiritually conscious and aware all of the time. That is until its family members and parents start telling the child, "That is your imagination" relative to those elements in its sense of awareness. It is at this point that the programming or brainwashing of the child begins, usually in earnest, and even perhaps with well-meaning intent. The motive is that for the child to have any chance to maintain itself or succeed in a society based on Need mentality, it must also be of that Consciousness in itself.

I call the morays and ideology of the prevalent culture, The Bee Hive game of the religion of Materialism. This is founded on Need mentality versus self-sufficiency and thereby, Have mentality. Of course most of the religious offerings espouse the ideal of Need versus Have and are its major educators and proponents. Why I say such is that in every single entity of the religions of the prevalent culture, hierarchical structuring and secularism is what is promoted and taught. This practice places a few individuals into positions of power and control of the masses. The religions do not teach their membership to talk with Great Pop. Instead, in most if not all instances, they promote an image of Him that is unavailable or even impotent and uncaring. Some proponents of those religions talk about the "wrath of God" thus promoting Fear of Him, instead of a personality of Support, Love and Care. In the religion of Materialism, the end always justifies the means. Like the chairman of the board in a corporation, God will sacrifice the weak to maintain or reward the strong. The idea of God that they sell in this practice is certainly an insensitive and unfeeling one, if not at all times, at least in some of them.

Certainly, the image purported of God is not Great Pop at all. What is purported in the "Supreme Power" or "Supreme Being" idea is that of an unavailable entity that lacks any semblance of a persona or personality. And there is a reason for such to happen. The reason is that all of these "organized" religions have nothing at all to do with Spirituality in the Real sense of it. Nope, their focus is that of Organization and Government. In fact, these religions are an industry in themselves that are competing for the ownership of the populations in the masses to some extent. Of course, the King or Queen bee needs worker bees to be anything such as that in itself. From the experience of the odyssey of Origins, one will find that things were not always this way though. The reason this is being mentioned here is that as this material progresses, one will indeed get a different image of the Creator that likes to be called Great Pop. Vastly different. Also in the prevalent culture, the influence of these religious entities upon one's self-image is most dynamic.

Early on in my life things were relatively simple it seemed, and uncluttered. At least it was before going into elementary school. It certainly was simpler before those people moved in across the street. By simple and uncluttered, I mean that a child is born as a person that is relatively complete within his or her own self-image. An infant really does not care what others do, or might think of them. Also, an infant or baby has few expectations placed upon them. Whatever expression the infant or baby might make most oftentimes will bring forth pleasure and acceptance as well as emotional rewards from those in its company. Even during the period of adjustment called the terrible twos, which actually migrate far past that time and age, the child is still relatively secure in what and who it is. Very little pressure is placed upon the child during that period to become anything different than what is natural for it to be or do.

Part of this condition that leads to the relative security in the child has to do with the reality that there are relatively few models of behavior for it to choose from, as well as image patterns for itself to migrate into. If there is an older sibling of whatever sex, the child will naturally want to assume that image and ability of self-expression and potential. Whatever types of individuals come into the sphere of awareness of the child, also become examples of potential for it to develop within itself in some manner. The reason that I drowned at four years of age is further proof of the reality of this. I drowned because I wanted to follow someone over to the other side of the pool. I did not have the capacity or ability to swim at that time but more than anything, I wanted to be with that person. They swam to the other side on top of the water so I tried to get there through the only means available to me at the time, which was by walking on the bottom.

When I reflect upon these times and events, I am quick to recognize that there seems to be more than just one of myself in them. Certainly the reflective person that is putting these memories and words together on these pages is seemingly much different than the little boy that drowned because he wanted to be with someone. That little boy did not know anyone else in that setting and event. He did not want to be left behind there, like had occurred before on occasions in Oklahoma. He was insecure, a pattern projected upon him by the attitude and influence of his earth father since birth. Yet, the person that is telling about this event is quite different, maybe. I can certainly swim now. In fact, because of that event, when I did learn how to swim I became very good at it. A part of the self that is me now, is not insecure at all, about anything. Yet another part of me now is still insecure, especially as to how I will get the necessary resources in this culture to continue to live past this point. I am not insecure about Nolayte, however I certainly do not know at this point how or when I may ever see him or my older children again. That little boy that drowned never imagined a computer, much less having the abilities that I have developed in using them. In a way, it seems that I am still that same little boy that drowned. Yet in many other respects, I am someone totally different now.

Which self am I now, I begin to wonder? Am I the self that drowned and went back to Great Pop? Am I the self that set the field on fire because I wanted to be most like the self of Sandy? Am I the self that went to Oklahoma to work that last time, or the very changed person that returned home after? Am I the self that sang in the choir and talked with Great Pop in that church way back when? Or am I the self that lay in that grassy ravine and spent so much time learning from the Spirits and Great Pop late at night in that time? Maybe I am the self that committed in the sacred union of marriage to Nolayte's mom? Or have I instead been or become, just her idea of me? I then wonder about Nolayte and what he is like, as well as my other two children now. Clearly, it seems this self and self-image stuff is important, if not somewhat tricky as well.

For me it was not so easy growing up, especially knowing what others were saying or thinking about me. It is very hard, if not impossible for me not to care, or want people to like me. Some people are not like that though and do not care, or in the case of some of them, even feel. I have learned this in my now 55 years. Not knowing what people are saying about you or planning to leave you out of, can be a great blessing. This is especially true if you are a "sensitive" person. Such was clearly not the case for me.

Since birth I have possessed several abilities such as reading thoughts and conversations at a distance. Heck, as a child I thought everyone else could as well! Of course that made it even harder to accept and understand. Yep, children can be real mean at times and now I realize that this is taught behavior. I have been a PohTikaWah since birth. Reading thoughts and minds at a distance is just one of the many abilities that I came to Mother Earth with. When I drowned, Great Pop sent me back. He told me then and on several other such occasions that I had much more to do for Him here in this life expression of myself. That is also the reason that I have yet to stay dead, although on many occasions now I have been in just such a temporary condition. The word PohTikaWah is another picture word in my personal language that is multidimensional and in motion. PohTikaWah loosely translates in this English language to being "A Spirit Walker". The White western culture idea of it is that of being a Medicine Man.

Many years ago, decades in fact, Great Pop told me to go into my rattle or drum and He would show me the beginning idea, or Medicine, of each of His children. To experience this, my Consciousness journeys to some place, of which I am not sure but know, and a moving picture develops. To the best of my ability I then translate those images into words in this English language, which when combined, describe the different characteristics of one's Soul or Spiritual persona. This is called one's Ever Name and these characteristics are always available to one in any and all life expressions. Before that time, in a similar fashion I could describe what a person's Now Name was, as well as Life Name, which most oftentimes are different. When a Medicine person or Shaman named someone in the past, most often these latter two types were given. Knowing what one's Life Name is can be very helpful as one might imagine, as well as that of their Now expression. In a sense, each of these names can be considered as one's Medicine, as well as being a "Self". In the past ways and times of Native American culture, an individual might have several different names and thereby identities. A child might receive their first name by a parent or Medicine person before or at the moment of birth. As that child entered puberty, they might be given a totally different name. A child or adult might be given another name if they were given a significant vision themselves. After the event of any significant or heroic deed, that person or child might be given another name that honored that expression or experience. Typically, a male person might be given another name, either before or after a battle. In some tribes, the male individual that weds is given a new name by the parents or members of the wife's tribe that they then both move into. So as one might now realize, a single individual in such conditions and times could and did oftentimes have as many as seven different names.

The word Medicine that is being used in the context of this material is quite different than the idea of it in the White western culture and this English language thereof. In the prevalent culture, the word Medicine is used to describe things that are basically a remedy for some illness or disease. In the experience of the odyssey of Origins, one finds that each and every thing that exists has Medicine. What is meant by this use of the word is that each and every thing that exists, not only has a unique identity and Spirit, it is also a Potential that has an Essential Nature, or properties. An example of such is that water is most often wet, but not always. Therefore, one can rightfully interpret this use of the word of Medicine to mean:

The Essential Nature of a thing, of which everything that exists, has such.

Long ago I asked Great Pop for a definition of Medicine. Great Pop defined Medicine to me at that time as being:

The Resonance to a Consciousness, Understanding, or Ability.

Great Pop went on to say that any and every thing that exists has Medicine. In Origins it was learned that there were in fact what are called the Five Founding Medicines and thereby Essences. From Origins, one will also realize that each and every thing that exists, has as a part of itself and thereby Medicine, some respective portion of the Five Founding Medicines as well. Therefore whatever exists has as part of its Essential Nature: **Desire, Feeling, Onement,**

Balance, and Change, which are the five Founding Medicines. So from this understanding, one can also realize that the Medicine of a Thing or Being is actually a composition of such Essential Natures. As with water - at times water can display Falling Medicine as in rain, yet at other times it can exhibit Rising Medicine in the way of evaporation.

One might wonder what good is to come to them by knowing the Medicine of a thing? The answer is: ***As much as one can gather to oneself from employing it in their daily life.*** A simple example of such is that part of the Medicine of Water is that of Flow and Adoption, which some call absorption. No matter what condition water is in, if it gets a chance to move about (Flow) it will! Also, if it gets a chance to embrace anything at all, it will adopt it if at all possible. One has only to put some sugar or sand next to water and see what happens in a very short period of time to realize this. And of course knowing just this part of the Medicine of water facilitates one to wash oneself or anything else that they might desire. It also allows one to use water to erode things with, or use in many other ways.

One might wonder next as to how knowing the Medicine of themselves or another Being or Thing would help them? The answer is simple. Knowing the Essential Nature of one's own or another's Spirit is the very best that one can do in any sort of relationship. I say this because Relationship Proper was defined to me by Great Pop as being:

The Respectful Sharing of the Experience of the Expression of Being, and one's allowing for others to experience and express being themselves in ways and means of their own choice which Walk in Balance and With Harm to No One Being or Thing and are most comfortable to Themselves.

Clearly, what can be more respectful than learning of the Essential Nature of someone? And how can one share fully, what one does not even know about oneself, which happens if one does not know fully one's own Medicine? To know that a person has Crystal Medicine allows one to be patient with them, as they continually strive for perfection in what they are doing. If one knows that one's self has Star Medicine, one can remember that is the cause when one gets anxious or impatient. Knowing the Medicine of one's family and friends is invaluable in all types of relationships. There have even been some conscientious employers which have had all of their employees Named. One reason that some did such was to be able to make the most of the Medicines and thereby assets available within each, such as in task assignment and so forth. Of equal significance is the reality that each and every group or organization has Medicine, as well as workplaces and homes, and of course so do religions and governments.

Certainly it would be wonderful if each and every Being and Thing came to Mother Earth with their Medicine of self tattooed on their forehead or something like that. A parent would not try to make a baseball player out of an artist or violinist. Such was the case in tribal times. Yep, the parents and family members, meaning the whole tribe, set about the discovery of the Medicine of the child newly born. They certainly did whatever possible not to limit its potential with some preconceived idea, or failed expression of themselves. But then again, the tribes were originally founded in the religion of Spirituality and Have mentality, not materialism, competition, Need mentality and the Bee Hive way, of being in life. Clearly those times were much easier for a child, as well as adults. This is real and true because the child most oftentimes always had an image of itself that was complete and fulfilling for the simple reason that everyone including the child, respected and honored its unique and special qualities and Nature, and thereby Medicine

Clearly it is extremely valuable to know the Medicine of oneself such as was just described. Certainly any and all should endeavor to learn such about themselves and each other, however and whenever possible. But what about those that might never have the opportunity to be named by a PohTikaWah like myself? Just knowing that such exists, can and will make a great difference anyway. The trick here is to seek to determine that which is unique and expanding in oneself, or any other Being or Thing, and not to define and thereby limit it or oneself. When one starts looking at others as being uniquely special in their Medicine, it is not too difficult to then accept that condition and possibility in oneself as well.

One of the first questions most White people ask me is, "What tribe are you from?" They do not ask what my Medicine is. They do not even ask most of the time what tribe am I now, only what tribe am I from. What is really hilarious in a sense is that when I tell them, they still do not have a clue. It usually only frustrates them because they cannot define me in it to their complete and total satisfaction and control. I am not saying that all people are like that in total, but most are of that way and motive to some greater or lesser degree. And to me, it is just another one of the many expressions of hierarchical structuring and competition in the religion of Materialism in the prevalent culture. The following is usually how it goes for me:

What kind of Indian are you? Native American. That means born here in North America. Actually I prefer to be called aboriginal or indigenous. *What tribe?* Now, I am chief of the Rainbow StarLight Church, Tribe and Nation. *No, what tribe do you come from?* I can't answer that because I come from more than just one. My mom was part Arapaho and my earth father was Algonquin. *What is Algonquin? That is not familiar to me. I do know what Sioux and Cherokee and Apache are though.* The Algonquin peoples were a nation and confederacy that at one time embodied all of the territory of the United States east of the Mississippi. *Oh.*

Such people do not really desire to know me, or anything about me at all. Native Americans would never ask such questions of someone in such a demanding and disrespectful manner, period. Actually in the most part, neither would most people that have studied anything in depth about Native peoples in general. As some that are of some of such knowledge are aware, what also is funny is that I still did not tell what actual tribe that my parents or I came from, ha, ha, ha!

OPERATIVES & ESSENCES

One might wonder what is meant by use of these two words. Great Pop first introduced the concept of Operatives and Essences to me when I was working on the material named Possession that directly preceded the four-year Odyssey of Origins, and the Understanding of Operatives and Essences was further developed in that material as well. To gain an understanding about oneself, one's Spirit, or actually anything at all in the most part, these two concepts are fundamental. This is real and true because these two elements are the basis upon how everything works, is, or expresses itself in some manner or form. Of course, hopefully this will help one to gain an even more solid understanding of Medicine as well.

In the Very Beginning, any and every thing that existed was an Essence in form. At that point, that was all that there was and all that was there was just that. Actually Consciousness existed at that time, or better stated, moment, as well as The Law of One, but we will cover those items in a subsequent chapter.

One might wonder what an Essence actually is or what does it look like or feel like? I wondered, and had the benefit of being able to jump right into the middle of some so to speak. In fact, if I were to fly way up in the air, far enough to not be able to see the earth or anything solid like that at all and start falling, it was something like that. In doing so I could tell that something was there. In fact, I could see that there was a lot of that something everywhere that I could look. Yet, in the same moment, I did not really see it as much as feel that I was in something, sort of. One might ask if it were like a cloud, and in answer to that, I can only reply that it was sort of like a cloud. But, it was like a cloud that you could see right through. It had no edges to it at all and it just seemed to go anywhere and everywhere there was a where! No matter how much you gathered up of this stuff, there would simply be more in an inexhaustible and renewing supply. Nothing could contain it all it seemed and a portion of it seemed to migrate into every nook and cranny of any and every object imaginable.

This air / cloud concept is just an idea of one kind of Essence.

Another concept of an Essence might be to fall from the sky into the middle of the deepest and most expansive ocean, with no need to breathe air. In this case, the water is neither warm nor cold, but it certainly is wet. And unlike water as we know it, this stuff flows right through every cell and membrane of one's body with absolutely no resistance at all. Once immersed there is no up or down, top or bottom, no seabed or surface. There are no shorelines to this ocean and it really does also go wherever there is a where to be found.

A third concept might be that of light. Except this light has no single color as we think of it, but one that is of all of the colors imaginable, all at once, in every part or place that one goes in it. Yet unlike any light that we know of, in this light, one does not even cast a shadow. This is because the light not only goes right through the bodyform of oneself; it seems to be the very substance that one's bodyform is made from.

In reality, all of these are qualities of Essences, and yes they really exist and are that way. Thereby this use of the word Essence might connote something that is limitless in its supply, shape, form, or utility. Essences can in no manner or way be destroyed and are the fundamental building blocks of any and all things that exist. One cannot quantify or even measure an Essence in any fashion or way. Even infinity is a small idea as compared to these things.

Now comes the tricky part for some. It might not be too difficult to imagine just one of these Essences and liken it to what we call outer space, or even space in general. But in reality, there are literally countless numbers of different types of Essences, everywhere that there is a where, all at the same moment, and in the same place! Perhaps a graspable example of this might be that of radio waves. There are literally thousands, if not millions of such waves that are detectable, at any particular location, at the same time. Yet unlike those radio waves, Essences continue on going right through anything that might be in their path, seemingly at the same amplitude and frequency, forever and a day. Actually Essences unlike radio waves, not only have no end, in a sense they do not have any beginning either, because for all practical considerations they have always been.

In the Odyssey of Origins I got to see and experience how this really is exactly how everything began. Now the real neat part of this understanding is this: everything that exists now or will ever exist is made of this stuff called Essences, and it can never be destroyed once it is made. In Origins, I learned that this is by and because of what is called The Law of One. Everything that is, is made from Essences, including Mother Earth, one's physical body, the galaxy and so forth. In reality, the Spirit of any and every thing is made from Essences too. Yep, one's Spirit is actually a combination of many different forms and types of Essences in different mixtures for each individual.

Medicine has always existed, as have Essences. Essences can almost be considered to be the same as Medicine and in a way they are. Yet in another way they are different. This is because Medicine is made from Essences and not the other way around, except that all Essences have certain Essential Natures and by that definition, Medicine, ha, ha, ha!

Also in Origins it was learned that the significant event that started the ball rolling so to speak, was when the Law of One segmented a part of itself that resulted in the five Founding Essences and Medicines. These Founding Essences and Medicines are Desire, Onement, Feeling, Balance, and The ThunderBeing of Change. Because of the Essential Nature of Essences, when the Law of One segmented a part of itself, it did not actually loose a part of itself at all. What it did was to set in motion what would ultimately become the Future and the All that is, including that of Great Pop and oneself. From that event and moment forward, any and every single or collective thing that exists, has as a part of itself at least some relative portion of the Essences of Change, Feeling, Desire, Onement, and Balance. No matter what, each and every single thing that exists has in it in some relative capacity, some measure of each of these five Founding Essences in limitless and renewing supply.

Have you ever desired more than one thing at the same time and in even measure, such as to be with two different people at the same time, but not together? Have you ever desired two different types of automobiles that you wish that you could be driving, at the same time? Have you ever desired to attend two different events or functions, at the same moment? Have you ever desired food, and at the same moment not be hungry for anything at all? Have you ever felt anger, disappointment, Love, Desire, worry, and value for a person all at the same time? Certainly every parent has felt most of the last one I am sure. How can this be? Simple - because Desire and Feeling are Essences, and just such ability is their Medicine and Nature.

Now comes the really brilliant part. Imagine the scenario that I mentioned earlier of having all of these mega-multitude of Essences, just floating around willy-nilly as some say. What do you do with this incredible resource that seems truly unmanageable by any standard or means? How do you give shape, form or utility to something that by definition is limitless and infinite in its capacity of such? It is pretty much like chasing and trying to catch the Wind, ha, ha, ha! Well, as found in Origins, Great Pop as the Group Consciousness of Medicine, was just hanging around, literally. In that condition He certainly had a lot of time on His hands for thinking stuff up. And as you might have deduced, a plan was indeed developed by Him for just such ability to occur. For those that may have by now guessed from the title of this chapter, the answer came in the form of the development of what is called the "Operative".

In a sense Operatives came into being long after Essences. However, there was no 'time' to measure it with, as that came later as well. The short version of what happened was that The Group Consciousness of Medicine that would later become personified as Great Pop, knew that at some point all of the five Founding Essences would have experienced being in different shapes and forms to a point that they would no longer care to do such. In this instance, all would be dead so to speak, as there would be nothing "new" to experience for anything that existed, period. The Group Consciousness used the Law of One to send a message to all that then existed, and all that then existed was within itself. The message was that the Group Consciousness desired to express itself, outside of itself, just as that which was within it had continually been doing outside of themselves, while still inside of the Group Consciousness. The five Founding Essences inside the Group Consciousness then held the first Pow Wow to see who might be in agreement, or not, with this Desire. The Essences of Onement and Balance were the two holdouts because by their Essential Nature, they were satisfied and desired no Change to occur. Desire and Feeling then offered a portion of themselves to be used by The ThunderBeing to make a conduit through which something could be flowed to the outside. Because of Onement and Balance there was then a tie in the vote but the ThunderBeing of Change broke it with His natural Desire to bring forth that which was within Himself, which of course was Change. As a result of the ensuing event and action, the first Operative was made; hence Operatives are made and exist so as to direct the flow of Essences through, much in the same manner as an air conditioning duct or water hose.

One might now wonder just what any of this has to do with Who and What you are, or Why you Feel or Desire certain things? The answer is simple. Everything. Your Spirit is a stylized Essence, meaning that it is a uniquely blended and individualized Essence that was formulated and put together by Great Pop. It is limitless in its shape, form and utility. Your Spirit is endless in its capacity and it is self-regenerating in its supply. Also, by and because of The Law of

One, your Spirit can never be destroyed, nor will it ever end or die. Period.

ENERGY

At this point one might be thinking that I do not respect religions or people that practice such, or even the society of culture that I live in. Another thought might be the question of why what has been given so far in this material is important, or how can it be of help in some way. The answer to the last question is simple. The more one understands what causes certain influences or limits in their lives, empowers them to choose differently and thereby regain control of their lives and themselves. Actually, a person does not even have to believe in The Creator for this material to be of benefit. And in response to the first, I do love a good ceremony and respect those individuals that are committed to a value system and way of behavior, as long as it Walks in Balance with Harm to No One Being or Thing. Of course to do that, means that it cannot suffer or put down oneself or any other Beings or Things, in any shape, fashion or form!

Each and every person and thereby Self, is molded by their family, religion and community, and through its laws and influence upon the available educational structures and system, their government. Of course, each individual chooses to incarnate into that environment at birth. At this point one might consider themselves and their life expression to be an Essence and the elements of influence that were just identified, as being Operatives, that do shape, direct and control it in some manner. In the Operative of the current prevalent society, most available religions are governments of a sort, and both are industries in themselves. I say this because both promote and enforce Need mentality, competition, hierarchical structures, materialism to some degree, and the Bee Hive game and way of life.

In the "Good Old Days" before the empire building that eradicated most "primitive" indigenous cultures and social orders, in any sort of conflict it was the PohTikaWah or "Chief" of that group who was the first to walk down the path, or be in front of the others in battle. They were the most exposed. They did such so as to provide for, as well as protect the others that chose them to be of leadership. There were no hierarchical structures at all. All of the decisions of the group and society were made by Tribal Council. Each member had an even position and voice as to what was decided upon and The Creator was also always included. All Beings and Things were considered even in importance and value. The child actually was in a sense more precious than any adult, but still held as being even, in most every sense and way. The Elders were also held as being most precious and even too. In such a society, each participant operated in a manner of honor and loyalty. In the most part, no individual of such a culture and social order would do anything that might jeopardize or dishonor themselves, their relatives, or the others in any manner. In such a society, each member pursued efforts and expressions that would add to the wellbeing and lot of the whole. They certainly would not try to best or take advantage of another member in it, which is the taught and accepted practice in the current prevalent culture. Clearly, in such a fertile condition for self-expression and development, each Self was much more healthy in Self-awareness, image, and esteem. And so also was each society or group, simply because of that condition. Yet the present prevalent culture seems to operate backwards when compared to this model. And the problems that exist in it should be of no surprise to anyone, simply because of that condition in itself.

One might next ask what they might do about the conditions in such a culture, as the one that is prevalent and pretty much worldwide at the time of this writing? Certainly most, if not all of the things that have been mentioned do give cause and reason to the Why it is that one feels the way that they do, and desires what they desire in the most part. The answer to this question is simple as well. Simply choose differently! Instead of a worker bee aspiring to King or Queen bee status, choose to become complete and sufficient in oneself at any and all times. And of course as that is happening, pass it along to one's own children and the children of others, no matter what! To accomplish such a metamorphosis in oneself is no simple matter though. Yet knowing that whatever one does in oneself will ultimately redefine and impact the group Consciousness of the society as a whole, certainly makes it worth the work and effort. This is especially real and true when one considers that the very future for life experiences and expressions to continue on Mother Earth for any and all Beings and Things depends upon it as well!

In recent times, one might hear someone commenting about another Being or Thing having "Good Energy". Another expression might be that they send out "Good Vibes". There is actually something to this phenomena, although I do not like it when someone is being judgmental in such a manner. It seems to me that usually the person that is making the comment is doing such simply to place themselves above others by having the ability to notice or judge such a condition or effect. Yes, to me those comments are a prime example of secular and hierarchical thinking and behavior that I mentioned before. And what I find really funny is that in almost every case, the individual doing the judging does not have a clue as to what they are talking about! One might hear some others talking about "Auras" as well, and the same holds true in these circumstances. Unfortunately, it is mostly a case of someone getting a little knowledge so as to gain status or develop a group following in the most part. Of course, they do such with themselves as the King or Queen bee in it.

A while back, someone asked me:

White Eagle, what religion are you? Expanding, Original Spirituality. Or perhaps Expanding, Core Shamanism might be more understandable for you. *No, what religion?* I am a PohTiKahWah. *What church is that?* I am chief of the Rainbow StarLight Church, Tribe and Nation. *No, I mean, are you Christian and accept Christ as your Lord and Savior?* I know Christ, and I know Great Pop. *No, I mean do you believe in God and that Christ died on the cross to save you from your sins?* I know Christ, and I do not believe in the ideas of sin or heaven or hell as promoted to the general population. *No, I want to know what church you go to or were baptized in, or were you even baptized?* I was. I also go to synagogues as well as churches and any other places where people invite me to share in their ceremony or talk. *White Eagle, if you do not believe that Jesus died on the cross to save your sins, you are going to hell....*

Actually, I have had similar conversations and experiences many times with different people. I certainly do not take much offense at what these people are trying to do. Clearly many do such as a well-meaning expression of their care in some fashion or way. Of course they are always amazingly rude about it, and these people might appear in any color. Yep, it is obvious that they are programmed real tight as I call it. They do not want to hear anything such as is being expressed in this material, simply because someone made them afraid at some point. I have oftentimes noticed that they become something other than just themselves in such experiences as well. It seems like some overlord or authoritarian and self-justified God-like image takes over their persona.

In the experience of the Odyssey of Origins, I did get many great understandings through its many lessons and experiences, and one of them was about energy. Most of the time, when someone uses the word energy, they are talking in reference to some type of power supply or source. And in the understanding, that is in reality one type of energy. However, there are several others as well. In fact there are four more.

The previous interaction was included as an example of one way of looking at a thing. So also is the taught pattern towards energy and most other things that some call the "Supernatural" of which are all most natural to me. Most individuals are taught not to believe what they cannot touch and see, and only half of what they hear. And in the prevalent culture, this may actually be quite good advice. Yep, it is much harder to be tricked or taken advantage of, if you are not open and confident, such as would develop in a more primitive society as previously described. You see, the prevalent social order exists and operates on an energy as well, and that energy is Fear. Need mentality is no more than being afraid that one is not in constant supply. The idea of hell, such as in the previous dialogue is perpetuated so as to manipulate the masses into behaving as someone desires - who is obviously not Great Pop - through Fear.

Yet Fear is an Essence as well and therefore it can have many faces as I call them. Some of the more obvious faces of Fear are anger, worry and doubt. But others, like guilt, shame, ambition, or vanity are some of the much more subtle ones. As I learned from Great Pop in Origins though, Fear is perfect. And it is most perfect when it stimulates us into motion in some fashion. Of course that is only proper when it Walks in Balance with Harm to No One Being or Thing, including that of Oneself! Also, the neat thing about the "pseudo" Essence of Fear, as I like to call it, is that it does in reality have a time limit, always. Whatever one is afraid of has a condition to time, no matter what. And in time, that Fear will simply go away. This is real and true even about the Fear of death, which is another illusion. Examples of this condition and reality are; being afraid of being late for an appointment, fear of heights, fear of drowning or snakes, anger over loosing a game, being worried about one's appearance or performance, the need to be successful, and on, and on, and on...

No matter what, in those examples, in time one will no longer be afraid of what they saw as being of monumental importance for that moment. Fear has a time limit, as well as some mixture of the five Founding Essences, which should be relatively easy for one to recognize, but it also has a certain kind of energy as well. It is actually this energy component of Fear that makes it most useful as well as powerful, although I do not like the idea and use of that word. Yep, Great Pop made no thing that is not perfect in His intent and design, but sometimes because of Free Will, things become put to ill use. Certainly Fear is good when it keeps you out of harm's way. Yet as anger it has killed and destroyed many of a thing. There is actually a part of oneself to which Fear and the energy from it is a most familiar ally, and other parts of oneself that it has no effect upon or contact with at all.

One might wonder what type of energy is in Fear? The answer is simple. It is Kinetic energy. In fact, Kinetic energy is the type of energy that is most commonly referenced in the arena of Mother Earth and the structure of the Physical realm. In a sense, it is the glue that holds it together as well as the motivating force that propels objects apart. Just about everything that one might think of in the way of energy or a type of it is kinetic. It is the type of energy that I project with my hands or fingers in healing work, as well as what keeps the molecules of them in place and allows me to move them about. Kinetic energy is the type of energy produced in combustion, as well as the type of energy that is called gravity. Magnetic force is Kinetic energy, as is the heat from the sun. The waves of the oceans move as an expression of it, as well as the wind at the mountaintop. Birds fly with it, snakes move with it and people eat so as to get more of it. No physical thing that exists is without some condition to it at any moment in some manner or way.

One might now wonder if energy is an Essence in total, and the answer is that it is not. It is in reality a separate thing altogether. However, energy did have an Essence as its root in each individual case, as to type. The five types of energy you see are:

Primal

Life Force

Thought

Memory

Kinetic

To gain a complete and comprehensive understanding about oneself, one must have a working knowledge about each of these things. That is because not only do they make up What and Who one is, but also they are what facilitates one to be, as well as do any of a thing at all. And by the way, what the person was talking about as being "vibes" or "energy" was in reality another person's or thing's Emotional Body, which is also what some call an "aura".

Simply put, the Primal type of energy is what Great Pop uses to make stuff with. And rest assured, it is Only available to Him, thankfully. When Great Pop "Creates" something seemingly out of nothing, this is the stuff that he uses to create it with. Actually, Primal energy has always existed, as has Medicine and Essences as a part of The Law of One. It was Primal energy that was used in the real beginning by The Law of One to segment a part of itself, with that resulting in the five Founding Essences and Group Consciousness thereof. It is important to know and understand about Primal energy, even if it is not available for our use in any way.

The second type of energy is that of Life Force. Actually, most every Being and Thing is acquainted with Life Force energy at all times to some degree. Some refer to "chi" being Life Force energy. However in most circumstances they are confusing it with, you guessed it, another of the many differing appearances of kinetic. In relatively recent times scientists have been able to measure a small weight loss in some individuals as they expired and exited their bodyform. It is the change in Life Force energy that they actually got a measurement of. When a Being or Thing chooses to become outwardly expressive from the Essential Will of Great Pop, they already are, and are something. This is real and true for every stone, person, plant, wind, cat, or anything, period. In Origins, one shares in the experience of Great Pop making what I call the mega-multitude of Potential. In that event, it was like being in a whirlwind of hustle and bustle.

Once the first few Potential were made, Great Pop sat down so to speak. He then in one monumental effort and event, made, through mixing different Essences, Primal energy and Consciousness, a uniquely patterned and composed Potential of any and every thing that would ever exist. He made it all in one sitting and seemingly at the same moment. It was in this event that He converted some of the Primal energy that He used to make each individualized Potential, including those that would become ourselves, into a new type of energy called Life Force. Kinetic energy did not yet exist at that moment, so Great Pop designed Life Force energy to keep the mixture of Essences in each Potential unique, intact, and individualized. Like some scientists profess, energy cannot be destroyed. In that they are correct, by and because of Great Pop and the Law of One. Life Force energy is like that as well - once you are, you will always be. Each and every thing that will ever exist or happen is simply an outwardly expressive Potential - meaning outside of the Essential Will of Great Pop. This is real and true for events as well as people and things. It is real and true in the appearance of a storm or drought, a lightening bolt or an airplane, a house or a family, a town or a puppy.

In the process of becoming "in life" on Mother Earth, each Potential chooses to become something for an outer experience and expression. Great Pop designed things to operate this way because He desires for us to have as much as possible of what He enjoys for Himself. After making the mega-multitude of Potential, Great Pop set them about making their own free personal expressions in The Great Void. He had not come up with the idea of the Physical realm yet. Nor had He even thought of the body forms of Beings and Things that we now so oftentimes use and enjoy. But we all were, and were ourselves at that point. We were all out there in The Great Void, floating around and doing as much as we wanted to in that state. There were no "Wills" yet, especially the one that would be called our "Free" Will. Nope, these would become developed and perfected later as described in Origins. But we did have Life Force energy, and were uniquely patterned self-expressive Potential with Consciousness. And it was because of our portion of Life Force energy that we were doing our thing in The Great Void, and in that sense, were most alive.

That was pretty much how it was and all there was, for quite some period, as Great Pop still had not made time, ha, ha, ha! Great Pop then decided that all was not yet perfect. He also remembered when He realized that the five Founding Essences might tire of doing anything, which had spawned the developments to that point. He recognized that at some point again, perhaps there would be the possibility of nothing new to experience. Great Pop ultimately decided upon a fix to this predicament. The result was His proposal and "Promise". Not only was this a most important and significant event, it was Really Brilliant by any standards. He told all of the Potential both outside and inside His Essential Will that if all of those outside would return inside, He would promise to continue to create and maintain a continuum of new opportunities for them to become outwardly expressive in. The brilliant part about this was that He masterminded a way for them to have what He most wanted for each and all of them. And what He wanted was for them to have a continuum of expanding self-realization, actualization, expression, determination, and awareness. The really brilliant part of this offering was that by simply posing the choice to them, self-determination was already realized in the choice itself!

    In the short version, what then occurred was that all did choose to return inside His Essential Will. Great Pop then went back to work so to speak and developed many new things out of Essences, Operatives and Consciousness. One of those new things included the first arena and the prototype of what is called the "Personal Structure". Great Pop developed the Personal Structure, which is comprised of Essences and Operatives, for each individual Potential to use to be self-expressive with in the arenas of outer experience and expression. Also, by and because of the Law of One, when a Potential decided to go outside for a personal outer experience, it had to make a choice. At first there were not a lot of different things that a Potential could choose to be outside of the Essential Will of Great Pop. In fact, it was pretty much limited to being a Being or Thing, sort of in the way of an object to be used in play. The first bodyform that Great Pop developed for use at this point was that of being basically a lightform. The ThunderBeing was the original pattern for just about any and all that existed outside of Great Pop. Therefore, at that point being a "Being" was pretty much all that there was to choose from. And, again by and because of The Law of One, once a Potential chose to become a Being when first going outside the Essential Will of Great Pop, it was that. And once it chose to be that, it could only again be that, forever and a day, as I like to say.

Once a Potential such as yourself chose to become a Being, your choice cannot be changed at some other time to be a plant or tree for example. So, once one chooses to be a Being, one can just be a Being. Now at this point is where Great Pop again got busy, and much happened during the ensuing events and processes that have resulted into the current conditions. Two of the significant things that also were developed in those early times so to speak, were more important than any thing like physical stuff, including atoms or such. Nope, much more important was Great Pop making the other two forms of energy, being that of Thought and Memory. In Reality, these two types existed when He made the mega-multitude of Potential in the first place. So in a sense, He only refined and specialized them.

Thought energy is really something though! Actually, Life Force energy is familiar to most PohTikaWahs and is the energy that one feels when in the presence of what I call a discarnate, which most consider as being a ghost. It is also what one feels in the presence of a deceased relative, or a helper Spirit or Guardian Angel as some call them. Life Force energy is ever-present whenever there is a Spirit, be it physically incarnate or not. Now, here comes the messy part about Thought energy, and it is also something that is very familiar to most PohTikaWahs. Whenever a Being or Thing issues forth, or even processes a thought, a pattern of that Thought energy remains for a period of time resultant from that activity. Also, this type of energy can be and oftentimes is, projected. Have you ever been in a room that is empty, but still seems real busy? Go into a banquet hall or courtroom right after everyone has just left and you will see what I mean to some degree. This is the stuff that witches use, and oftentimes is what makes us sick. Have you ever thought about someone and then the telephone rings and it is them? Yep, this Thought energy is something else! Have you ever wondered about something, only to have the answer dropped right at your feet so to speak? Or have you lain awake sleepless at night simply because your mind cannot shut down? In Origins I learned how all of this works. And in so doing I learned that just like Fear, Thought energy has a time limit to it. However, unlike Fear that seems to simply evaporate, in time, Thought energy turns into Memory energy!

As a PohTikaWah, I actually spend a lot of time dealing with both Thought and Memory energy in some fashion or way. In a sense, one could say that it is a part of the job requirements, ha, ha, ha! Each and every prayer, be they of Fear or Hope, is Thought energy that is projected either to the All of Creation or is focused directly towards a single target. That is really all that one does in a sense. Yep, all that really happens in life is that some Potential receives that Thought energy and then follows it back to its source like a magnet. Think ill of someone and they will get ill from the thought as a realized Potential. That is unless of course they choose to ignore that Thought energy, which some are more prone and able to do than others. Have you ever been around a person thinking ill of you and noticed something uncomfortable? That is the 'stuff' as I call it. There is something that I call "thought forms" as well. A curse or spell is just such a source of these nasty little things. There are no real demons or hell that I have experienced. However, I have seen where thought forms and Thought energy have been used to make just such an illusionary condition and place. Thought energy misapplied can in fact kill. Some other willful ones use it for power. None of this is pretty, or Proper. At times I will neutralize thought forms, of course always asking Great Pop if I should or may do so, first. Sometimes I will have to check myself as well, so as to issue no bad thought. There also is an envelope-like area above and within Mother Earth that is crammed full of this type of stuff and type of energy. I call it the "Zones". Yep, Thought energy can be considered Very dangerous stuff, especially in the hands of someone that is Willful and cares little about what is involved in getting what they next want.

The last kind of energy to be discussed here is that of Memory energy. It is not the same as the kind of recording medium used in this writing machine, but it is very similar in many ways. In time, as mentioned, Thought energy does in fact turn into Memory energy, and in a sense it works the other way around as well. Have you been angry at someone and in time forgotten about it and then have something trigger the memory of it, only to get angry all over again? Unlike the magnetic and as you guessed it kinetic means used to record things with in this writing machine, Memory energy can cloak itself. And Memory energy can cloak itself on anything, anywhere. Just like with an Essence, Memory energy can go deep inside stuff too. In reality, one's Emotional Body is a walking billboard of one's Prayers of Desire. It is also a permanent record keeping device that goes back inside the Essential Will of Great Pop when one exits. Therefore one can safely assume that one's Emotional Body does in fact embody both Thought and Memory energy.

As a PohTikaWah I have to deal with a lot of Memory energy problems so to speak, especially when I do ceremonial and clearing work. The technique that I use to neutralize Memory energy is not for the purpose of destroying it, like some might think appropriate. Nope, the method and procedure that I use, after asking Great Pop if I should as well, simply brings it to a condition of what I call zero or balance. In this sense, what was there is sort of erased, or at least made non-problematic in a way. Have you ever been in a room where a violent struggle of sorts took place? Or perhaps a location where some type of Fear or suffering occurred and felt like it was still happening? Now do you understand why this is so? Yep, you guessed correctly, it was and is that way because of Memory energy.

So that should pretty much cover the basics at this point. Now we have an understanding of not only how everything came to be, but also what it is that it is made from. Everything that exists, anyplace at all, is fundamentally a Potential made from an Essence or is a combination and blend of Essences, period. Each type of Essence has its own specific qualities as well as Nature and that is its Medicine. Therefore any and all things that exist have Medicine or a combination of Medicines. Also, the way that anything occurs is simply the self-realization and actualization of one of the mega-multitude of Potential that Great Pop made way back when. When a Potential becomes self-expressive or actualized, it does not die. Nope, it just returns back to the Essential Will of Great Pop until it decides to venture out again for any reason. Everything that exists, is a Potential being in just such a condition of itself in some way. There is no death nor even an end to life this way, just endless new beginnings. This is what Great Pop promised. And He has and will keep that promise forever and a day.

There exist five forms of energy. It is one of these types of energy that supports not only things to happen, but even for things to stay together or move about. By and because of The Law of One, once a thing is, it cannot be destroyed, ever. This includes oneself, Great Pop, and energy. Each and every Potential has a relative measure of Life Force energy, as well as Thought and Memory energy.

Everything that exists in the Physical realm is actually a Potential that has chosen to venture outside of the Essential Will of Great Pop so as to be self-expressive, self-actualized, self-determining, self-realized, and self-aware. All Beings and Things know that they come to the Physical realm for a visit. And all know that at some point they will in reality, return to the Essential Will of Great Pop. It is the Kinetic type of energy in some form that is most commonly recognized and employed in the Physical realm. Also, Fear is a pseudo type of Kinetic energy that Great Pop made to stimulate Beings and Things to motion. He did such so that it could be used to safeguard the vehicle of the physical bodyform so that one's Spirit can still use it. Fear has a time limit in all conditions and cases. The pseudo-Essence and energy of Fear also remains with the cocoon of the physical bodyform upon the exit of one's Spirit. That is unless a choice is made not to return, but instead hang around and operate as a discarnate or what most commonly call a Ghost, for a while.

PART II

THE SELF

WHO AND WHAT AM I - REALLY?

Certainly at some time in one's life, unless one is totally unconscious in it all of the time, this particular question has posed itself. Amongst the many labels and judgments of others I have been called many things, from an enigma to a looser, stupid, and a lot worse. Right now I might be called 'sick in the belly Injun' for that matter. Have you ever eaten something that soon starts to seem like it is going to burn a hole right through your belly? It starts in a flash and takes over your every movement and thought. No matter where or how you sit or lay down, it still is a crippling cramp and hurt. Yep, that is what I have been experiencing since yesterday's meal that I ate last night and I consider that I am fortunate to have one meal each day. Actually, more than from the food, the pain probably developed as a response to what I was writing about in the last chapter. You see, I do live every word that Great Pop has me write about in these books, which are His more than mine. I take no credit, only responsibility for not only what is in them or how it is presented, but also the very way and timing of such. One by now might have wondered a little bit about the title of the first part being that of 'The Circle and Odyssey Continues.' The reason for such is that this material is pretty much an extension of the process and product that was realized in Origins. Therefore, at this point I will give another update as to the current conditions that is the life of myself.

It is now about 5 p.m. on Saturday the 15th of December, 2001. That means that I was able to complete Part One of this material in only five days, which seems to be a miracle in itself to me ha, ha, ha! Of course, most of it came from you know what? Yep, Memory energy! The rent is due again today, but being Saturday I do not actually have to have it in the landlord's office yet, which is a good thing. I say such because with this belly problem, I am not in fit condition to walk the five or so miles each way that is necessary to do that. I have to walk you see, because my driving privilege is still suspended from what occurred in one of the episodes of Origins. I will be able to re-apply for one, once the 19th of January of next year has passed, so they say. I do have enough resources to pay the pending rent as I was able to work in Southern Pines a couple of weeks ago. I worked for a whole week, meaning seven days at over ten hours a day, only to return with about 300 dollars and some cigarettes. They fed me well and gave me a place to stay though.

Also, Coyote sister who lives at Seven Lakes took care of TohNaWah and for all of it, I am most thankful. But I had really hoped to return with more resources, especially since this is the hardest time of the year for me to get work. Actually, when one thinks about it, it is all seemingly miraculous. Especially in that here I am with a car that I cannot drive and people come and get me so that I can do the things they want done and bring me back home when I am through. Yep, in most every sense and way, I am most Blessed! I have a little extra money left but I have to pay the phone and other bills soon too and I am really concerned about the electricity one. That is the one bill that really skyrockets at this time of the year and it is either pay it or freeze. Someone sent me some money for Christmas and that will help but I am concerned as to next month's rent and bills with the added expense of what it will cost to get my driving privilege and vehicle legally operating again. Of course when that happens I will have many more Potential to call upon and work with! Ha, ha, ha!

Last week it drizzled and was cold most of the time. The ceiling cracked and a leak developed in the middle bedroom. I live here in High Point, in the more dangerous part of downtown by the railroad tracks. Trains shake the house all of the time and I am sure that is part of the reason that these things with the structure have finally occurred. However, I also know that it can be because once I get my driving privilege back, I will start looking for a better place and conditions to live. This is especially necessary I feel if I am ever going to be able to let TohNaWah go outside again or have Nolayte stay with me. Nolayte's birthday has come and gone, again. And again I did not hear from him but every day I think about him and wish to be in his life somehow. Unlike my other two older children, Nolayte really has had no opportunity for the Potential of us being together to be realized, much less be a family. This is singularly due to the Prayerstick, Attitude, and Will of his mom. My older children knew exactly where I was for five years before I came to North Carolina. For all that time, they did not care to call or come by. So my status at this point is "hurting in belly Indian man," in more ways than just one.

As this material continues to develop, I will be going back to my normal mode or process, which is to periodically lay down, leave my body and join Great Pop at that wonderful table of Understanding that is described in Origins. The table, as are the chairs, are wooden. At least they look and feel like the wood called Oak. The table is round most of the time, ha, ha, ha! And the chairs are high backed, like my mom's parents used to have in their kitchen. Other than that the room is pretty empty except for some cabinets built into the wall near the table. This place is one of the rooms in the pictures contained in one of the earlier chapters, just so you know where it is that I go. Also, Great Pop likes things real neat and tidy and this room and place is a prime example of it. I believe I will lay down for a bit now, as my tummy is really hurting still.

 After talking with Great Pop and asking for His Blessing upon Nolayte, my older children, TohNaWah and myself, I was able to get some semblance of rest. I knew that I had to make the trek across town to pay the rent the next morning, so I set my subconscious to work on fixing the problem in my biology to some degree, as I slept. I did feel a little better when I awoke so I worked on the weekly update to the website named ASpiritWalker.com. Great Pop had me make and start it operating after I had completed Origins and The Medicine of Numbers at the first of this year. After making sure that I was somewhat stable and would not have to use any restroom facilities on the way, since there would be none, I told TohNaWah I would try to get him some food that he might like and set out across town. I wore a hat, coat and gloves as it was chilly and in my unstable condition I did not want to become even sicker, especially since I had no money to pay for any type of remedy.

 As I have mentioned, I do live every word in these books and what happened in this trek across town is a perfect example of such. I started out walking and watching my feet while talking with Great Pop, as is my normal manner of such. Great Pop told me to go by the bank and get some cash and check my balance so that I would have peace of mind. I received twenty dollars from the ATM machine as being Sunday this was the only way of getting such. Now remember what the title to this chapter is, being that of the question: "Who and What am I, Really?"

 There are several paths that I could take across town to the place where I have to make the rent payment. The landlord is an attorney and his office is by the local courthouse and jail, which makes sense. I make the payment through the mail slot in his office door and usually no one is there. There is a shorter path that I have found, but my going to the bank first precluded my taking that one. As one might imagine, the police station is also in close proximity to his office as well as what some call the "Projects," which are actually a lot newer and nicer than where I live. The area on the whole is pretty dark as some say, and Real dangerous by most people's standards. I do not really care about that though. And of course it is not like I have any options either, at least not for the moment. So here I am walking along and almost to a point of being a block away from the landlord's office. It is sunny but cold and about noon on Sunday here in High Point, North Carolina. I am thankful that I even have the limited resources that I do have and am glad to make this payment so as to continue to live where I do. I have just passed the project housing and I am walking down the sidewalk of a very poor neighborhood. There are a few people out but not many and I am basically not of any specific concern. I hear a car stop behind me and soon a person calls to me to stop and turn around. It is one of the local police officers and still I am not of any real concern. He then asks me, "Who am I?" and for some identification. I tell him *White Eagle* and give him an old driver's license that I keep in my wallet for such Potential need. Then He asks, "Are you Really White Eagle? Is that your Real Name, and are you an Indian?"

I said that I was. He then got on his radio and almost instantly another police car showed up. Then, even before anyone got out of it, another car showed up. The first guy then starts having a Pow Wow with the other two and tells me to have a seat - on the real nice for that neighborhood - bench seat by the sidewalk. A playwright could not have orchestrated a more perfect setting or condition. I read the minds of those officers and determined that one of them actually had heard of me. I told the first one that I had been living in High Point for about three to fours years now, and that my driving license had been suspended. I also told him that I was going to be able to get it back in January. I then thought via a message from Great Pop, to show him the envelope that I had my rent payment in. From my mind reading ability, I could tell that things were pretty much in the air as far as the Potential for me to be arrested at that point. It did not even matter whether I had done anything wrong you see, for me to be arrested. Being Native American and looking the way that I look, I have become not only aware of such possibility, by now I am pretty much almost used to it. At this point, some fifteen minutes after the first guy stopped, there were many people now out in their yards checking out the situation.

After some more chit chat and another radio call, I am sure to make certain that there were no outstanding warrants on me of which there were and are none, I could sense the tension drop a bit in the other two officers. Finally, the first officer came over to me and gave me back my license. He then told me to go ahead to the attorney's office and make my payment. As I started off, He commented that I looked like a suspect that they were seeking, except that the suspect was much younger. I thanked him and bid them all a nice day and holiday and again started walking while talking to Great Pop and watching my feet. Of course they did not respond or even say anything more to me at all. After all, to them the Who and What I am Really, is that I am White Eagle, just a poor Indian.

After pushing the payment through the mail slot in the door I started to retrace my steps. After listening to Great Pop's response to my question about such, I decided to go back a different way because I could sense that I was not welcome by the not friendly people in their yards that seemed most disappointed that I was not taken to jail previously. I had gotten the twenty dollars, (with the number twenty having the Medicine of Communion) so as to get some food for me and TohNaWah on the way home. On a previous trek of such a Nature, I had discovered a real grocery store in that vicinity. It was a very "poor man's" store, basically supporting the needs and budget of the local Black population. It also was certainly less expensive and had more to choose from than the local offerings at the two gas stations near my home. So for fifteen, (with the Medicine of Realization) dollars I left the real store while carrying two heavy bags of food for me and TohNaWah. I was thankful that the store clerk could tell that I was a "walker" as they naturally put the items for us types in more than one bag each. I believe they call it "double bagging". Anyway, as I set out I prayed to each bag and asked that they hold things intact until I got home. I did that in response to some Thought energy that came my way from some unknown source. It gave me the image of a bag breaking and then my difficulty in being able to carry all of those items the long distance home.

As I plodded home carrying the two heavy bags, I passed by one of many showroom buildings along the way. As I walked past one of them, the thought entered my mind of breaking the window and grabbing some of the stuff that was placed there against it. I would never do such a thing, but the thought was there. I recognized that it was there simply because of either Memory energy of it happening before, or the store owner's worry that it might. I realized also that the second condition of this was in fact Thought energy, operating as a Fear prayer. I then realized how inundated we all are in this "wookie" as I call it and that it really is the cause of many people's misbehavior to some degree. I asked Great Pop then if I should do something to neutralize it, and He simply told me, *"No."*

The bags held up well and as I got nearer to my home I saw a man on the sidewalk in front of me. He had some items on a little cart, like people use to carry their luggage in airports and train stations. There is a bus station that is located a block from my home. Since we were near it at that point, I suspected that he had just arrived on one. As I progressed towards him I swung the bags around indicating that I would gladly let him pass by me. Instead of doing that, this man who had Cart Medicine, just waited. When I finally reached the point where he stood, he looked at me sort of funny-like and then asked me, "What is your name?" I told him that I was White Eagle. He then asked me if there were any restaurants nearby. While I was trying to think of one that might be open on Sunday, he asked the direction to Krispy Kreme. Obviously he was somewhat familiar to the area, I then thought. I told him how to get there and about some other restaurants nearby that would be open and he went on his way towards it. How perfect I thought, as I finally reached my doorstep with the two bags that I carried. Yet, "Who and What am I, Really?"

CONSCIOUSNESS

Earlier in this material, we talked about the things that always have been and what everything that is, is made of. In the very beginning, even before The Law of One segmented off a part of itself to see what that part would do with itself, there were three things that existed. Those three things have always existed and will always exist. Those three things were and are; The Law of One, Essences and the Medicine thereof, and Consciousness. One might be now wondering as to what specifically I am talking about in this use of the word Consciousness in this English language, that I am presently trying to use to relate these things to people with. Is it simple awareness? Nope. Is it being awake? Sort of, but much broader in scope and Potential. Actually, it is vastly different than just that idea of it. Is it thought, like what happens in one's mind? Nope.

Perhaps the most specific as well as simple description of what I am trying to identify in this use of the word Consciousness, is that of an element that all Beings and Things have. This element is like a perimeter or a farthest reaching boundary of their individual perception, connectivity, awareness, sense, or influence. One might liken it to being a bubble that contains all of oneself inside of it, at all times. Wherever one goes, it goes in front of oneself and also trails behind. It is above one at all times, as well as below and to each side. And the real neat and tricky part about Consciousness is that it is in Reality, segmentable.

Unlike my physical bodyform which can only be in one place at a single moment, I can send one or more segments of my Consciousness as separate little bubbles, anywhere there is a where, at the same moment. Consciousness facilitates awareness. In fact, Consciousness facilitates everything in a way, especially with regard to seeing, sensing, feeling, or even doing anything at all. And not only is Consciousness segmentable, it is by Nature and thereby of the Medicine of, multidimensionality.

What do I mean by stating that Consciousness is multidimensional? I mean that it is not limited to single or even two or three simultaneous orientations or capacities. There are only so very many things that one can do with a single finger. Yet there is no limit to what one can do with their Consciousness. Besides, if the idea of it were not in one's Consciousness first, then the finger could do no thing, period. In this sense, Consciousness is not linear or flat, or even limited to being global and round. Consciousness exists and operates at many more levels and capacities than one can define or conjure up. Even in the process of defining or conjuring up, it is one's Mind Operative inside the envelope of one's Consciousness that is doing that. Consciousness exists and defines not only the shape and density of an object, it is also what is inside the smallest part of it, as well as with the electrons being sent out on their own by any type of decay or causative force.

You see, Consciousness can be considered as being the envelope or container that Great Pop placed the mixture of various Essences in when He made each of the mega-multitude of Potential. Consciousness was what Great Pop was the Group Consciousness of, after the Law of One segmented off a part of itself in the very beginning. The five Founding Essences and Medicines each have their own personal Consciousness. And because of the Law of One, whenever there is more than one of a thing, there automatically becomes an individual Group Consciousness formed of that collection or group. And if and when that group becomes separated or dissolved, since Consciousness cannot be destroyed, a segment of it remains with the Memory energy of that collective and the remainder becomes absorbed back into its source, which is the Potential for that group experience. And any Consciousness that is free floating, such as curiosity bubbles, returns and rejoins the sender or the Law of One in all cases. So now one can see that not only is Consciousness multidimensional, it is also multileveled in a sense, beyond that.

Does every person have a Consciousness? Of course. Does a Puppy? Certainly it does. Does a Tree? Absolutely. As does a stone, the mountain, the ocean and every other Thing that is. Some forms of existence cannot express themselves in the same manner as people, but that does not mean that they do not have the very same thing in the way of Consciousness or Medicine. One might in the simplest terms consider this use of the word Consciousness to mean the multidimensional bubble of awareness, perception and expression, and the extent of thought or influence that is ever about every single Being or Thing of Creation. It is what lets one feel as well as speak. It is what lets one sense, as well as love and care. It is the membrane about us through which we receive thoughts and feelings as well as express ourselves through. It is how we are able to perceive as well as communicate, period. Consciousness is the outermost extended portion of oneself, at any moment and at all times. It is the part of oneself that can never be really hurt or destroyed, yet is the first to sense and feel pain. It is the part of oneself that recognizes things and the same part that one tries to desensitize and ignore with drugs and alcohol. It is the part of oneself that one has to consider and manage to focus on a single task or thing. Consciousness is the part of oneself that never sleeps, as well as the part that goes inside one's Emotional Body to have the experiences of one's dreamtime. Yep, Consciousness is the outermost, most flexible and most integral at the same time, part of any and every Being or Thing. One might think in one's Mind, yet one's Mind is an Operative Element of one's Personal Structure that is ever present in the envelope and bubble of one's Consciousness. A person might think that they are something in their Mind, however they really are and always will be themselves and their real Medicine of themselves, in their Consciousness.

Mind and Consciousness are clearly not the same thing, although most of the time we might think of them that way. Consciousness does in fact perceive as well as think in a sense, much like the Mind does. Yet it also does so much more and is much more dynamic in every sense. The Mind actually just processes Memory and Thought energy and forms. The Mind does not have the capacity to feel, or process things like Care, yet all of these things and processes are going on, at the same moment, all of the time, in one's Consciousness.

Imagination is not a part of the Mind at all, it is however part of the Medicine of one's Consciousness. Imagination is actually feedback Thought energy that is passed to the Mind Operative from co-creative activity and expressions that first occur in one's Consciousness. The Mind is restricted to processing and using Memory and Thought energy, however the Consciousness as mentioned, has a subset of Primal energy that it is made from and has an everlasting supply of, all of its own.

The Mind is actually what most Beings consider as themselves, or in a way, as being. Of course, this is pretty much just taught behavior. And until now for most, there really has not been much else to consider or to choose from. So there is a lot of misconception of what the Mind really does or is. Actually, the Mind gets a lot of credit for what one does in one's Consciousness as well as with one's Wills. "Put your Mind to it and you can do it" some may say. However the real elements to be considered in such a statement are one's Wills, in a collective sense. Actually, one's Mind does little else than process, sort out, and catalogue stuff. Your Mind cannot hug a puppy or child, nor does the desire to do such come from it at all.

Yep, all Beings and Things have a Consciousness element of self, as well as embody Memory energy. Have you ever driven someone else's car or just gotten a new or used one, and it seemed strange and a little uncomfortable to you? Have you ever worn someone else's clothing, and even though it fits fine, it still feels different and strange? In this last example, one at times will even feel like or identify closely in a unique way with that person. This is the Reality of Consciousness, and is the cause of such feelings in those things and oneself. Of course to some degree, it can also be due to Feeling and Memory energy. This writing machine has a Consciousness, as well as its own unique blend of Medicine.

In my earlier years I used to program computers when that expression first became possible. I became real good at this new occupation when there were not so many computers, or so many people doing that work, as is now the case. I did not get good at it because I studied all of the working aspects of the machine, nor did I get real good at it because I remembered all of the different instructions that would result some effect from it, or not. I got real good at it and still am to some extent, simply because I learned early on of a method by which I could get into Medicine with each computer I worked with. What I mean here by "get into Medicine with" is to see and consider the machine Spirit that is a computer as being the same as myself. To get in Medicine with any of them, all that I had to do was to open my Consciousness so as to merge with the Consciousness of each individual computer, and learn a way to communicate with them. And the last part of "getting in Medicine with" is that of becoming in a union of sorts. In this I mean that I become part of them, and they become part of me. One might consider this to be a condition of resonance as well. I did this very same thing with every car that I raced or owned. I do it with every thing that I have, use, or do. And to some degree, so also does each and every Being and Thing, period.

This very material has a Consciousness already, as well as the writing machine that is helping it to become self-realized. In a sense one can say that I am the least instrumental part as to this material becoming self-realized and expressive. In reality, I am simply operating as a channel of it to oneself. Thoughts and the words used to express them have Consciousness, but symbols have Consciousness as well, such as the symbol that was shown earlier of my Beginning Medicine. The ancient peoples knew of this and that is why they used symbols to communicate with.

Actually, the Consciousness of symbols can still communicate long after one's making of them and one's exiting the Physical realm. Symbols have powerful Medicine. Their Consciousness is specific in a way, especially as relates to being open to support communication. I have a tattoo of my Beginning Medicine symbol on my back. I also have the one of Great Pop that appears on the title page and covers of these books. It is on the inside of my left arm so as to be nearest my heart, and because the left is the receiving side. On the inside of my right arm and opposite of the one of Great Pop, I have this symbol:

This is the personal symbol of myself. At any time, if one were to take a plain piece of paper, and draw upon it this symbol of myself, a significant and special thing can and most often will occur. And it can and will occur singularly because of Consciousness and the Medicine of symbols. After drawing the symbol and placing the piece of paper with the side that the drawing is on against one's forehead, one will be able to connect with me. And one will be able to connect with me that way wherever I am, forever and a day.

To do such, first one has to accept and believe such is possible. Then, once the symbol is in place, simply shut one's eyes. Next create an opening in one's Consciousness for this to be effected, meaning that one is to make room for the shared experience. To do this is much the same as thinking about going to a fair or carnival and imagine being on one of the rides. To get to the carnival, one must first make the opening and that is what I am talking about doing now. The next step is to project one's Consciousness into the symbol by expressing a Real Desire to experience such, as being the Will of oneself. This must be done with focus, commitment, openness, and passion. If a union or meeting is really desired by both you and I, then it will happen. And since I have already committed to facilitate such, the rest is up to oneself. The symbol must be drawn on a new piece of paper each time one desires to make "contact".

I find it important to add here that just like in learning to Meditate, some people will find some of these exercises to be relatively easy and others will continue to struggle or not be successful. Too often in this prevalent culture we are given to consider success in terms of winning or losing as in a competitive event. In reality, Real Success is found in the experience gained by one's endeavor, not in the outcome. The message to be given in regards to any sense of failure is that if one has attempted at all, there is no failure to be considered, only a temporary lack of personal success in doing such a thing at the time. If one is persistent in their self-determination, success in some measure will eventually be realized.

Great Pop said to put this offering in here, so there it is. Whether I am alive on Mother Earth or long after the passing of my current life expression and experience, this will work for anyone that opens their Consciousness and merges a part of their Consciousness into the symbol. This does not mean that I will be a discarnate to be able to do such either. Some may only feel my presence, others will see and or hear me as well. I will give my support and care to that which Walks in Balance with Harm to No One Being or Thing of Creation. Actually, this technique using symbols is just a spin off so to speak, of the very means and method that Great Pop gave for me to use in my way of Meditation as well as to teach others. This process and capability of Consciousness is how I can see and be with Him, or anything else for that matter. Also, such is the power and Potential of the Consciousness and Medicine of symbols.

Here is another symbol that will also work in a similar fashion:

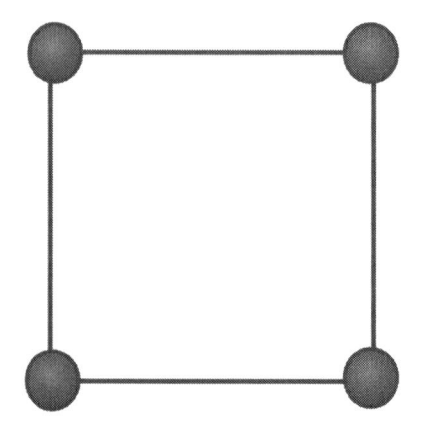

Yes, these things are real and therefore, possible. And the Why is of course because of Great Pop, Medicine, The Law of One, and Consciousness! Speaking of Great Pop and Consciousness, it is in my Consciousness that I hear and communicate with Him, not in my Mind. I have to interpret in my Mind what I hear from Him in my personal language, but I also have to use my Consciousness to do that too. I have been unconscious before, and like the word conscious, that is not what is being described by this use of the word of Consciousness. My biology kept working during those times when I was unconscious not because of any idea of wakefulness or even because of one's Mind. Nope, it did and does such, simply and always because of one's personal Consciousness.

At this point, I am being given to warn against opening one's Consciousness to too many things that one is not specifically aware of. In this I mean that one must take responsibility for one's use and methods of using one's Consciousness at all times and in all conditions of oneself. In the exercise using the symbols, there is protection against invasion or takeover, unlike what can occur with the use of drugs and especially hallucinogens. Alcohol can be problematic in this regard for some individuals as well. This is really what the condition that they call the "DT's" are all about - lack of maintaining responsibility and the integrity of one's Consciousness. Know well sure, the exercises are in Reality, safe from any such possibility and Potential. However, also know well and sure that no other Being or Thing can ever invade or take over your Consciousness, Mind or body unless you do not care, or welcome them to it. The experience of the material on Possession taught me all about such Potential, as well as provided remedy to any such occurrence.

In my earlier years I learned that because of its expansive and open Nature, our Consciousness can at times become easily attached to by Thought Energy, be it our own or from other Beings and Things. I also found that because of my personal "Sucking Medicine" which comes from having an overload of empathy, I get what I call an overload of Thought Forms, or what can be considered as associations. And where this becomes really evident as well as problematic was when I would try to Meditate and go to see and talk with Great Pop. In a condition of "overload" I found that I struggled when I tried to clear my Mind as all of those "alien" thoughts would keep becoming processed instead. Once I had finally struggled past that, Great Pop gave me the following "Tree Clearing Ceremony" method to use and it has become a standard for me to use since that point and event. The method and ceremony is as follows:

*****

The first thing to do before anything else is to give the tree of choice a gift of a pebble or tobacco. This is done for several reasons, not the least of which is that one must always give something before one can receive anything more than what one already has. Also it is a way to honor and help the tree, which will be converting your Thought Form "Wookie" into food, thus making good use of it and letting it serve a good purpose that way. Once that is done then:

To Go Into the tree, one stands against it while holding it with one's hands at heart height with one's feet at its base. With one's belly and forehead pressed against it, take a deep breath and while exhaling, allow or project one's consciousness through the bark and into the heart of the tree. This is done until one can see the rings of the tree around oneself and then one can go anywhere, as one is now in True Spirit Form. One will often see light forms floating around oneself and can see the Spirit of the tree or even The Creator (Great Pop) easily in this condition of oneself.

In the Medicine Way of clearing oneself of Thought Forms and associations, at this point one should ask the tree Spirit to strip all Bark of tree (Ego) and associations from oneself so as to be of clarity. Also in this particular practice, when exiting the tree, one is to thank it and ask it to provide new, thin, and slippery Bark on tree (Ego) for one to use in the next and future expressions of oneself.

*****

Clearly, Consciousness is one of, if not the most important part and aspect of any Being or Thing. It is not the What and Who we Really are though, at least not in total. Clearly it is the most dynamic and flexible component that we have to use to sense things or be self-expressive with. It is quite special by any standard, and obviously quite powerful as well. This makes me wonder why we would do anything to keep it from being in the best of condition or function at all times. Perhaps it is the power and ability of one's Consciousness that we become most afraid of. Because of taught behavior, most people do not want to believe in things that change or challenge their ideas of what is right and wrong, and especially about what is real. One person who recently looked at ASpiritWalker website commented that the things discussed in it were against their upbringing, and thereby they had to quit looking at it. Certainly this is an example of what I call deep programming and thereby, taught behavior. Yet all Beings and Things clearly do know what is Proper and Real, at the deeper levels of their Consciousness. Clearly at this point, an outwardly expressive Potential and Consciousness that embodies a certain mixture of the five Founding Essences is a part of the Who and What I Really am, but that is not all of it.

DESIRE PRAYERS AND FEELINGS

At this point it is clear that I can be considered to be my Consciousness as well as the unique blend of Essences and Medicines that it envelops which makes up the Potential of myself, and is held together somehow by Life Force energy. Certainly this is some of the answer as to the What it is that I Really am. However, it seemingly falls way short of answering the Who. What makes me unique and different? Obviously by definition, the unique blend of Essences and Medicines within the envelope of my Consciousness might be part of the answer to that question. Maybe. But what is my Real Self? What is it that makes me, me?

In experiencing the material on Possession and Origins, I learned that pretty much all that we or any other type of outwardly expressive Potential do is to choose and issue forth 'Prayers of Desire'. Prayers of Desire are expressed from us and operate pretty much like a fishing pole, line, and hook, with the Prayer of Desire being a magnetic kind of bait. Also, Prayers of Desire are patterned in a way so as to be a mirror image of that which is sought. In this design by Great Pop, only the Potential that is prayed for, versus any of the multitude that are floating about in the Sea of Creation, will end up attached to one's hook of Hope or Fear, which is tied onto the line of Belief, with the knot of Trust. Therefore, for one to have any desire of any nature fulfilled, one must in fact issue forth a Prayer of Desire for it to be realized. Also, one has to use some semblance of the other expressions thereafter, no matter what. If one does not believe that they can or will get what they desire, then it simply is not possible for them. And usually what happens in such cases is that everybody around that person keeps getting the things that they are issuing forth Desire Prayers for themselves to receive. On top of that, if one is afraid of something happening, it is the same as a Desire Prayer for that to occur. Therefore, all Prayers of Desire can be considered as being either of Fear or Hope.

In both Origins and Possession, it was shown that all Beings and Things have their own personal value system from which they operate. Also in some capacity or sense, all of one's Prayers of Desire are conditioned to this personal value system. In the remedy to a Possession scenario, the process does include the identification of just such things for a person. The whole purpose of such a discovery process is to provide an identifiable pattern of themselves in a condition of balance and completeness. By having this pattern defined and available, one then knows what is proper to choose to become next in oneself. This personal image and pattern is self-determined and defined. Each and every Being or Thing brings one of these patterns with them when they incarnate, and this personal pattern is modifiable as one progresses through a life experience. All Beings and Things are in some condition of or to it, at any and all times. Clearly this value system seems to be a part of what makes me, me. At least it certainly influences some of my choices, if not all of them in some way. But is this value system the source of the Who I Am? Or simply a result of it in some manner or way?

Here is another fun little project that some people might like to try for themselves. Imagine being in what is called True Spirit form. To do so, consider oneself to be sitting on a cloud and all that there is, is oneself, Great Pop, and whatever it is that one is sitting on. In this state and condition of being, there is no physical thing, period. One has no body and therefore no hands to touch or move things with, and there are no things to touch or move anyway. Yet one still is, and is oneself. One can move about, but there is really no reason to move at all because everywhere is all pretty much the same as where one is. In this state of being, one is neither hot nor cold, and all is at peace and perfectly comfortable. And by the way, this is pretty much what it is like after you take your last breath and are going through the Tunnel of Transition that takes one back into the Essential Will of Great Pop. Of course in that case there is nothing else except for the tunnel and one's guides that are ever present. Once that idea of being and existence is clearly established, write down eight things that you value about yourself in that condition and framework. List eight things that make you, you. An example of some of the things that make me, me, are my Passion, my Loyalty, my Desire to please and serve Great Pop, and my Courage.

When you have it narrowed down to eight things which are honestly qualities that you now possess and that you would not want to be without, you have identified the major players in your own personal value system. Obviously, how important this information is depends upon the use that one makes of it, which can be most beneficial in many ways. Also, there is no good or bad here. And do not include things that sound good, like loyalty or honesty, if these are not always things that are most important and often chosen over any other behavior or expression. My loyalty can be even considered to be a fault, or the reason that I get betrayed and taken advantage of at times, yet I would never want to not be of it even so. Again, it is most important to list those characteristics of oneself that are honestly aspects of oneself, not things that one might want to be or that might simply look good on paper. Also, some of what one might consider as being a less attractive characteristic at times can actually lead one to a positive value. For instance, if one does not like how they behave when they loose their temper, then consider not having the depth or Nature of one's Passion or Care. You see, one can value their Passion or Care, even if they are currently experiencing conditions whereby it may not be such a positive experience or expression in some senses.

I value my courage even at times when it is really hard to be that way, and there are times when I was not courageous. I value it not because I am perfect in it all of the time, but there have been more times that I was of the courage that I value in myself than when I was not. I clearly would like not to have to choose to use it, or have any experience or condition that would make such a quality and expression necessary. And again I have not always passed the many tests of such, especially those tests caused by the behavior and desires of others in this culture. Yet I still value that condition of courage about myself and would not want to be without it, even if it was never to be used again at all. Also, my courage is a part of me that still exists and is actively available even when all that exists is Great Pop, myself, and the cloud upon which I am sitting while developing this list. Obviously, I do have to continually draw upon courage just to live the way I have had to live, because of the prevalent culture. Of course I value my courage most of all, when I continue to trust in Great Pop and that He will keep providing that which is necessary for me to continue. I do not value my courage as might be considered or seen by others, you see. No, I only value the courage that I have expressed and will continue to express, to and within myself as necessary. Remember, there are no other Beings or Things on that cloud, only oneself, it, and Great Pop. If one is really honest in this exercise, then eight real and unique qualities will be pretty much all that one can come up with. Many qualities that I find people place in their list usually end up being either different words of the same quality such as Honesty and Integrity, or things that require some other person or thing. Examples of this are: being a parent, an artist, mother, friend, able to create or fix things and so forth, which do not exist in the condition that was defined earlier.

Once one's list is completed, the resulting value system may in reality be a part of the Who each one of us is, but is it really a source and thereby cause, or a result? We started out with Essences and everything that exists is made up of them as well as has Consciousness and Life Force energy. And whether it is distorted or not, every Being has a value system as well. Also, when I further consider the eight qualities in my personal value system, I am not too surprised to find that each and every single one of them is made up of a blend of the five Founding Essences in some manner. Yep, Loyalty, Courage, Passion, and obviously the Desire to serve and please the Will of Great Pop, all have as their core, some portion of the Essence of Desire, as well as Onement, Feeling, Balance, and Change. And the Essence that seems to be of the most significance as well as frequency is in fact Desire. When I mentioned in an earlier chapter that all that we do is issue forth Prayers of Desire in order to attract specific Potential to us so as to be self-realized, I was not incorrect or just kidding as that is really the way of it. However, do we possess the values because of the desires, or the desires because of the values?

Certainly I am something. That something might be a Consciousness bubble or envelope that is full of Essences and perhaps many other things. Certainly one of those other things most likely is a value system. And this value system is uniquely managed, chosen, applied, and defined by myself, and myself alone. But maybe I am not so much specifically the value system, as the Prayers of Desires that makes it, manages it, and orchestrates my use of it in some way. In the final analysis, it now appears that I am in a sense my Prayers of Desire first and foremost, because they are what brought forth the Potential that is represented within my value system, as well as the value system itself within me. At times I choose to honor or apply it and its contents. In that condition of myself, I become self-determining as well. Like any and all Beings and Things, I personally choose the content of my Prayers of Desire. Likewise, I also choose the when it is that I express them, as well as the manner and way of such. But that just describes what I do. It does not describe the Who and What I Really am, except maybe a choice maker and issuer forth of Prayers of Desire, ha, ha, ha! Certainly my value system is an integral part of myself, but not quite as important as being a chooser and issuer forth of Prayers of Desire. Maybe at this point it is safe to say that in a way I am basically a "choice making praying machine".

Clearly it is pretty easy to see and understand where my desires come from and how that operates in a sense. One might even consider that I am my desires in a way. After all, they are an Essence that exists as a core part of myself, and everything else for that matter. If that is the case, then am I not also my feelings as well? Feeling is also one of the five Founding Essences that is found in every Being and Thing that exists. Therefore, one can say that Feeling is also an equally important part of myself.

Feelings are one of the really wonderful things in the All of Great Pop's creation. Yet some individuals seem to not embrace or express them as whole-heartedly as others. Part of the reason for this is taught behavior I am sure. Have you ever heard a person define and comment to another that they were being "too sensitive"? I certainly have. I have had it said about myself, especially in my youth. Actually, the prevalent culture promotes insensitivity in fact. Part of this is due to the promotion of "need" mentality that is Fear-based so as to keep the worker bees working under the rule and control of the King or Queen bees. Drug and alcohol abuse happens as a direct result of such a distorted value system and ideology. Why I say such is that in each and every instance of such abuse, the individual or culture of them is trying to numb or desensitize themselves. "Out of sight is out of Mind" some people say. But this does not in reality work for feelings. This is real and true because it is not one's Mind that processes one's feelings at all. Nope, it is the Operative of one's Heart, the Essence of one's Emotional Body, and of course, one's Consciousness that do such. Another saying that I much prefer more than the last one is that of, "If it feels good, then do it". Of course that is only as long as it Walks in Balance and with Harm to No One Being or Thing, including that of Oneself.

Clearly, my feelings are definitely a part of what makes me, me. Feelings also operate quite differently from that of Desire, and in the experience of Origins one easily learns why that is. One actually can have a Feeling about a condition or thing without having any type of Desire associated to it. One can certainly abhor abuse without desiring it upon oneself or any other Being or Thing. Yet the opposite condition of Desire and Feeling is always true for any case or circumstance. In this I mean that a person cannot really Desire anything at all, without there automatically having some type of Feeling that is associated with it right from the start. This is why we feel very hurt, angry, or disappointed when we fail to get what we want. It is also why we begin to feel hopeful or express any other type of the Essence of Feeling in the way of anticipation, expectation, or even worry over an outcome when we "risk" an expression of Desire.

This unique condition of Feeling and Desire is resultant from the original expression of the Group Consciousness of Medicine in the event that resulted in the making of the first Operative. In that event, when the Essence of Feeling offered a part of itself to be used with that of Desire so as to make that first Operative, this condition and relationship became everlasting. Simply put, from that point forward, all desires have an associated feeling, while feelings are always independent of desires.

And feelings are really powerful stuff! This is especially true when they are mismanaged or become in the control and use of one's Bark on Tree which is my name for ego. Oftentimes people confuse Feelings with Care, or use these two words interchangeably. Of course one's Real Care is actually a different thing altogether. And at times one might have a certain feeling associated with one's expression of care, or not. Of course that is mostly when one's expression of care has no desire associated with it. An example of this is when one strips one's Bark on Tree about the outcome of an expression being made by some other Being or Thing, such as in wonderment. For instance, one observes a clam burrowing under the sand and while one might care that it is doing that, there is no personal investment in feeling any particular way about what happens later to it in the most part. Of course that is unless one does in fact express some desire about such at some point in the experience.

You see, one's Care is really an Essence-Operative and as such it is a separate part of the Personal Structure of oneself. As such it can issue forth Essences, such as Feeling and Desire and it can do such in a limitless number of ways and forms, at the same time. This capacity is the essential part of the Essence-Operative of one's Care, but it still is basically a conduit of Essences and thereby an Operative. This condition of one's Care is why it is that one can care many different ways about a single thing at the same time, such as to love and be mad at someone in the same moment. I like to consider one's Care Essence-Operative to be much like a faucet that has many hoses. I choose to whom or what I associate each of the limitless number of hoses that I have, at any moment or not. I also choose what I then give forth or receive from that person or thing through the hose of my Care, or not. And I do such through each one of them, and all of them collectively, each moment, all of the time. So, if it "feels good" I will naturally continue to give forth more, most of the time. Therefore at this point, it now seems safe to say that perhaps I am an outwardly expressive Potential and Consciousness embodying a certain mixture of the five Founding Essences, my Desires and value system in a way, as well as my Feelings and Care.

THE PERSONAL STRUCTURE

 A part of the problem it seems in knowing Who and What I Really am, has to do with outside influences as regards our idea of self and what some term as our self-image. This comes to mind at this point of course from Great Pop, but also by the fact that in the previous chapter we started considering self-expression in consideration as to what we Really are. In this I mean to say, "Am I Really what I do?" Many people seem to consider just that idea of themselves and others in the prevalent society. When Jack befriended me as described in Origins, I was a person already. I was starting to learn about computers at a place where he also worked. Our job situation was the beginning commonality between us. And even though he was older and more experienced in many ways, Jack saw and treated me as his equal in most senses. Actually, if one were to ask Jack about me, he would have said that I was much smarter than he was.

 Yet it was not my "brains" as some call it, that was what he really liked about me. Nope, it was my openness and heart. Also, we shared a lot of common values such as integrity, loyalty, and in many ways innocence and trust. Yep, Jack in many ways was another Sandy in my life at that point. And in others, he was nothing like Sandy to me at all. The difference, you see, was that Jack was not so much my hero as he was a brother that I never had before. Jack grew up as a pretty much rebellious, yet quite privileged, white person in a white western prevalent culture. I obviously did not. However, even so, Jack did not think he was better than anybody else. In fact, even with certain advantages he pretty much thought less of himself than others in most senses. And in a way, we both did have that in common as well.

 Jack was a very passionate person, and so was I. He had a ranch he did not live on, or even use much. Jack had a lot of things in fact. He even had the sole custody of his son. Yet, Jack had some older lady take care of him most of the time. While he had the ranch, Jack still chose to live in a less affluent little house with his mom while his dad lived in a mansion with a much younger second wife. Jack went into the Navy before he even finished high school. He owned a part of the company that we both worked at. Jack took me hunting, which was something that I had always wanted to experience when I was growing up. He took me surfing and to nightclubs. He even took me as his partner when we played pool in some of the little bars and lounges that we both liked to go to, even though I was just learning how to play.

When I was in that time and experience with Jack, being a good pool player had a certain merit. It was valuable not so much in making money, which could and did happen. It had to do with having increased value and esteem in the eyes of the patrons and thereby mini-culture so to speak. If you were a good pool player, not only did everyone want to be your partner, you almost had a hero-like privilege and status to some. Early on, I pretty much wanted to be a Great computer person and programmer when I first started working with Jack. I recognize now that I did have such a Prayer of Desire as it would give me a certain sense of personal esteem and value, which I could employ to feel better about myself with. After being with Jack for a little while, I found that I also aspired to be a Great pool player as well.

What is really funny is that after Jack had exited, I moved down to where NASA was located in South Texas in taking a new job there. One day during lunchtime, I was standing in line at the local bank. I was there to make my weekly payroll deposit when another fellow came in and called out to me in a loud voice, "Hey, Pool Shark!" Boy, did I want to get Real small and hide when he said that! You see, in the bank were all of the people that I wanted to know me as being a Great and successful computer person. I definitely did not want them to know that I frequented bars. And I certainly did not want them to think of me as being a pool hustler, of which by that point I had become pretty much accomplished at as well.

But All prayers are answered you see! Of course sometimes we do not want everyone to know about it or even like the outcome, ha, ha, ha! Yep, at that time I pretty much led a double life or perhaps even triple one or more. During the day I was a successful computer person and at night I was a relatively successful pool player. Both of these expressions seemed to make me have a certain status in two vastly different subcultures. Actually, for quite a while I made more money playing pool and gambling at night than I did in working all week or sometimes even all month at my "day job". It was during this time that might be called my "hell raising years" that I found myself wearing many different hats or faces so to speak. In this I mean to say that I had several if not many images of self, that were presented or seen by others of me. At the core of all of this was obviously my effort to be accepted and seen as being even in a way. And in reflection, a part of such perhaps was an effort and way for me to deal with the loss of Jack as well. In the final analysis though, I did have a certain self-image "problem" or condition long before I met Jack, and we both had that in common to some degree.

While it is obviously a response to taught behavior, this looking at oneself through the eyes of others can be very problematic if not even most dangerous. I say this because in such a dilemma or condition as regards one's self-image, many people have compromised their True Value System just to be accepted, or even worse. Of note is the fact that simply because of my having won while playing pool, I have been beaten to death twice, as well as have been now stabbed twice. I guess that one can say that it is obvious that some people just Really do not like to lose, ha, ha, ha! With such potential in mind, one can perhaps more clearly now recognize the value and potential of understanding the Who and What one Really is, if only with regard to personal safety.

Jack was a doer, and of course having the resources and privilege of his circumstances allowed him to do many things. Jack was the first person to ever skydive in Texas, and his picture was even on the cover of a local newspaper for doing just that. He had a friend that was a championship water skier and that friend had a very powerful race boat that he used in competition. One weekend Jack got all of us together on the San Jacinto River with that boat. You see, Jack wanted to try to do what they now call parasailing. And this was long before anyone else had thought of doing it and had the process perfected. We tied one of Jack's many parachutes to the back of that powerful boat and then took turns trying to take off on skis with the parachute trailing behind. In our attempts to do such, one person would drive the boat. Another would be holding the chute open and running along behind with it as the third person, while strapped in it and wearing skis, was quickly launched off from the edge of the river by that Really powerful boat.

It was a beautiful July afternoon that day, and there was no problem from any wind gusts but there certainly was a problem in getting aloft in that manner. All of us were okay with being able to ski and stay up on them and we each in turn left the bank in relatively good shape. Yet time and time again, each of us would have our armpits stretched and lengthened by the harness before letting go.

This was because each time the open chute would begin to lift up, it would twirl around and subsequently dig into the water. And when that chute grabbed the water -Wowie, suddenly the harness pulled on your armpits real hard. Of course the instant braking drag of the chute as it caught the water would snatch your arms loose from the towline, seemingly at once. A couple of times we were sucked right out of the skis and flipped over in our efforts to hang on and stay up. And on occasion we did get off the water and into the air for a brief moment that way. Yep, it was really a something to watch and in most instances it was quite hilarious. Of course in hindsight, if we had made the right cuts in the parachute then we would have been the first that day to ever parasail. To me though, it was still a great day and one of the many such days and events that I cherish experiencing with Jack.

Jack had told me about a couple of times that he tried to exit this life before meeting me. Most often it seemed that his suicide attempts had to do with his failed marriages. One time he decided that he would go, doing the thing that he most loved doing, so after he jumped out of the plane he did not pull the ripcord of his parachute. However when he was only a hundred feet or so from the ground, he decided to change his mind about it all, ha, ha, ha! What resulted was that the parachute opened up a second or so before impact. From that attempt, Jack went to the hospital all broken up. He had to stay there for months, instead of ending up dead as he had intended that day. Another time that Jack told me about was when he decided to drive off an overpass. The part of South Texas where we both lived was real flat, as were most of the structures in that area, but there were freeway overpasses, and one that was just about the tallest thing in that vicinity. It was a curved section which went over the edge of a large cattle ranch that just so happened to belong to a friend of Jack and his dad. So Jack got his car going real fast so as to break through the side railing at the turn of the overpass, thinking that should do it, in another airborne attempt. As planned, when his car hit the railing at speed, Jack went right on through it and thus started his decent. But instead of some kind of nosedive into the ground below like he envisioned, the car sailed like a glider, ha, ha, ha!

Yep, when Jack's car landed it came right down on the barbed wire fence below. Actually, it became impaled on two fence poles that went right through the floorboard! In that attempt, he was hardly hurt at all except for perhaps the embarrassment of it all. And when Jack was finally killed in a car accident that occurred later, he was not consciously trying to exit at that time and in that way at all. I say such, as I am certain that he would have told me if that were the case. Yet, at a deeper level of Consciousness, I am sure that it was in fact in his plan and prayerstick.

Yep, there is great humor in these stories, when one looks at them in the Proper perspective. My first wife was pregnant with our second child at the time of Jack's exit. We were all down at the beach with our one-year old son and waiting for Jack's return when the fatal accident occurred only two blocks away. I named my soon to be born daughter after Jack. Ironically, and for some unknown reason to me, she seems to dislike me as much as Jack disliked his own father.

Getting back to the What and Who it is that I Really am, in consideration to what I do, I could not really do much any of a thing at all in the Real beginning. Nor could any other Potential when the All of us were floating about in The Great Void. At that point, Great Pop had yet to become His persona as such. Yet, He still was The Creator in every sense and way. And one of His most brilliant creations is what is called the "Personal Structure". When one considers all that one is able to do, this particular brilliance of design becomes even more awesome to me. Remember, in the beginning all that Great Pop had to work with were Essences, Consciousness, a couple of forms of energy, and The Law of One. Perhaps the single most important development that occurred and facilitates just about any thing that one does, is the creation of Operatives and Essence-Operatives and the collection of such with Essences that is one's Personal Structure. Just the idea of making something to allow for the direction and flow of an Essence is phenomenally brilliant to me. Consider how things were then, whereby nothing much could be done except to just be. Then with so little to work with, Great Pop in His brilliance came up with a means whereby any and all Potential could be self-expressive as well as self-determining and so forth.

The first Potential was a result of the first Operative being formed in the real beginning. In accordance with His Promise to the Potential when they all returned inside His Essential Will, Great Pop made things. He made Operatives so that we could express Essences through them, just like He Promised. He then made more Operatives, and Operatives that worked inside other Operatives, and on, and on, and on...

And He kept making Operatives and discovering what would happen if He tried using this component with that stuff there so to speak. And Great Pop kept doing this until He had something that not only would work, but also would work perfectly. As one will discover in Origins, at this point Great Pop's first and foremost goal so to speak, was to make a solid acting semi-solid. He wanted to develop such a thing because He needed it for something, and that something was a bodyform! He wanted a bodyform not only for Himself and The ThunderBeing to use so as to be better equipped and able to make more things with, but also one for all of the Potential to use in outer personal expressions in order to do things for themselves with as well.

You see, Great Pop recognized early on that if He could make a bodyform for each Potential to use, He could then make all kinds of wonderful things and places for them to use it in and to experience with it. At this point, just being an amorphous bubble or lightform was not enough for the Potential, but even that was a lot more than what existed before. And not only did Great Pop have to design and develop stuff for the Potential to play with, He had to develop the means by which one could feel and touch and sense and thereby play. Just being was not enough for the Potential in Great Pop's idea and plan you see. And it is because of that reality, that is why we can do what we do.

The first arena of outer personal expression as described in Origins is what I call the Orange Place, and in it one does in fact operate as a lightform in most every sense and way. Yet, one is much more than just a glimmer or glow in this first place of outer experience and expression. And when one considers such, for one to be even able to do or control that lightform took a lot of design brilliance and work. And this design work started with Great Pop beginning with a semi-solid bodyform to which He developed and added a prototype Personal Structure. The net result was that after some trial and error and much refinement, Great Pop finally did perfect a Personal Structure for outer personal expression from His Essential Will that looks like this:

True Spirit Form
Of A Being Or Thing

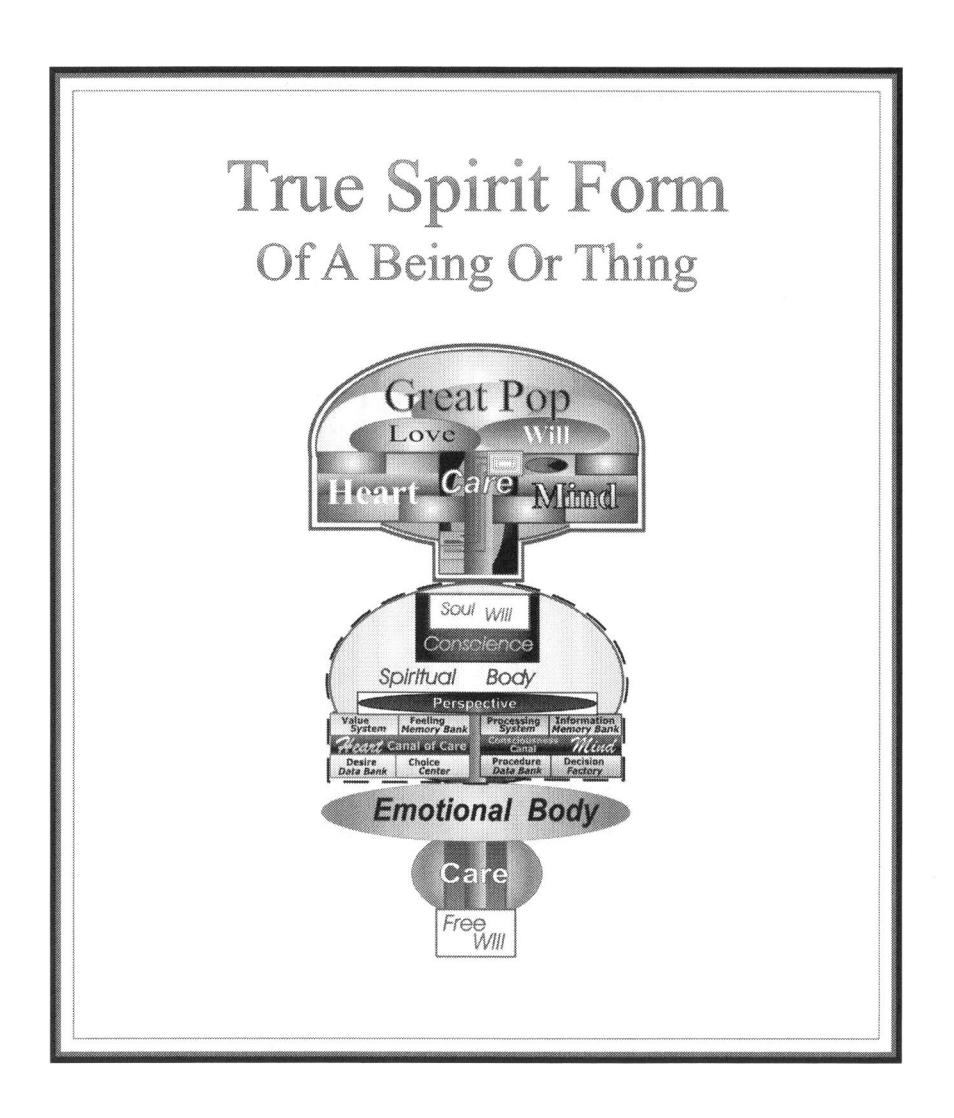

Yep, this is what you could consider to be the inner workings of oneself, or anything at all for that matter. The above Personal Structure is what is added or perhaps better stated applied, to any Potential when it chooses to venture outside the Essential Will of Great Pop. And once that happens, it is also what they take back with them when they return inside it. When this Personal Structure becomes applied to a Potential, from that point on it can be said to be a Spirit and it then remains a Spirit, forever and a day.

Those Potential that never choose to have an outer expression are still Potential, it is just that they cannot be classified as being Spirits also. When a Spirit chooses to incarnate into the Physical realm something else happens to it though, and that something looks like this:

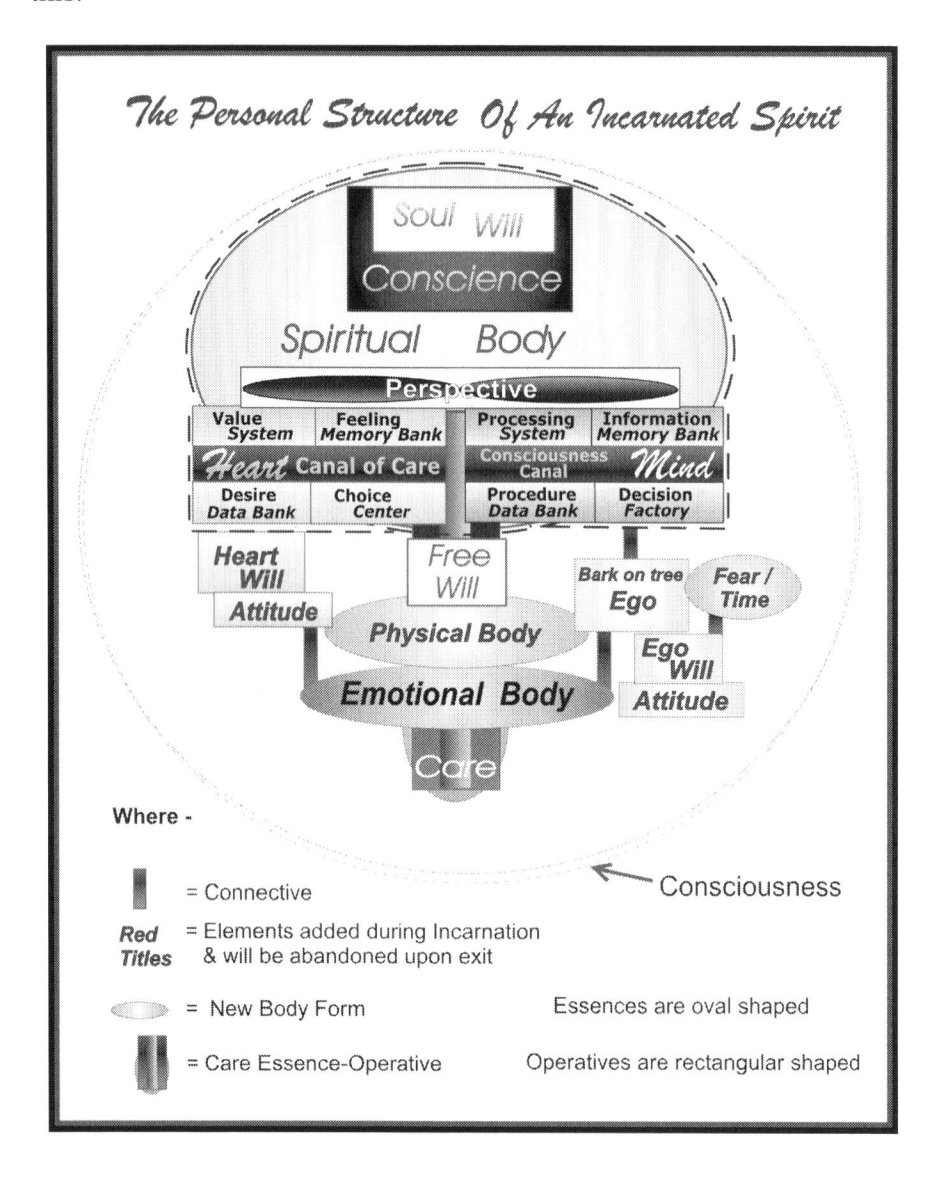

The Personal Structure Of An Incarnated Spirit

- Soul Will
- Conscience
- Spiritual Body
- Perspective
- Value System | Feeling Memory Bank | Processing System | Information Memory Bank
- Heart Canal of Care | Consciousness Canal | Mind
- Desire Data Bank | Choice Center | Procedure Data Bank | Decision Factory
- Heart Will | Free Will | Bark on tree Ego | Fear / Time
- Attitude | Physical Body | Ego Will
- Emotional Body | Attitude
- Care

Where -

▮ = Connective

Red Titles = Elements added during Incarnation & will be abandoned upon exit

⬭ = New Body Form

▮ = Care Essence-Operative

← Consciousness

Essences are oval shaped

Operatives are rectangular shaped

It is important to note the differences between the True Spirit form and that of the physically incarnated Personal Structure. I am not going into an in-depth detailed description as to the workings of these inner components of each self and the reason is that it does not fall within the scope and purpose of this material. A precise description of each of these elements is given in the material of Possession, as well as Origins. What I will explain at this point is that when one

Selves – Vol. 1

incarnates, the Ego-Operative and extra Wills and Attitudes are applied, as is the pseudo-Essence of Fear. When one exits, basically these elements are left behind and remain for Renewall with the matter of the physical bodyform during the process of Transition back to the Essential Will of Great Pop. It is during the process of Transition that the elements are sloughed off and one then becomes of the True Spirit form again, as first depicted. In this I mean that one starts as a True Spirit upon one's first outer expression, and that structure is modified upon Transition to the Physical realm. Once one's visit there is completed then one's Personal Structure is changed back to True Spirit form during one's return to the Essential Will of Great Pop. If one subsequently chooses to incarnate into the Physical realm again at some later time, then new elements are added and so forth. Also as shown, one's Free Will manifests the development, maintenance, and growth of one's physical bodyform. Therefore, one's Free Will is basically the single element that is most responsible for its condition at all times. Perhaps now one can better understand as to how it is that each Being and Thing operates, and how we are actually able to do what we do.

Yet even as important as one's Personal Structure is, it does not seem to really have any influence upon the What and Who we Really are, at least not to me, at this point anyway. Of course one's Personal Structure is what is also within one's bubble of Consciousness with one's own unique blend of Essences and value system at the present moment. And it is all of these things, and especially my Personal Structure, that is how I can make these fingers move across the keyboard of this wonderful writing machine.

THE FOUR WILLS

Before starting this chapter, I was given to make repairs on my telephone. You see TohNaWah has great Chomping Medicine and he likes to chomp on everything, especially me. I know that he does it at different times for lots of reasons. Dogs do it a lot too I know, but not too many feline types do it as much and as ardently as does TohNaWah. I know that a lot of times he does it as a means of play as well as to assert dominance, which is in Medicine with Cat Nature. TohNaWah has chewed off the lacings of my moccasins as well as those of my boots. He did that partly because he did not want me to use those things so that I would not leave him alone as much. TohNaWah is real smart that way, as well as perceptive in the way that some call psychic. All I have to do is to simply think about TohNaWah and he will show up. And with that statement, TohNaWah just came over and climbed into my lap. We are that connected in our Consciousnesses you see, and that is the How as well as Why of it. I also believe that TohNaWah likes to chew up cords and cables because he gets a little charge from them. Literally. Knowing that Lightening and Thunder are a part of his Medicine and Nature makes this behavior make sense to me too.

For me to be able to fix the telephone this time I had to get another soldering gun and some solder. During one of my longer walkabouts the other day I went to several drug and grocery stores. Previously I had noticed that some of them do carry such "Fixing" Medicine items. I did find some replacement Christmas light bulbs, but no soldering iron. Great Pop wanted the lights taken care of anyway so I got some of them. He then told me to go to the auto parts store behind where I now live, the next day, which would be yesterday. So yesterday morning I went to that store and at the bottom of the cheap tool bin that they had items for sale in, there a soldering iron was, just like Great Pop had told me it would be. Of course for all of this to happen in this way, as was earlier mentioned I had to believe that it would be there. Also, I found myself having to choose to continue to believe that such was possible and would occur as I went through the process of going there and searching for it.

Over the years I just happen to have saved several phone cables, so that made the project less expensive. As I was soldering one of them to the telephone, I reflected upon the fact that some people would not be able to do what I was then doing. Fixing the telephone was as easy to me as unsoldering two wires and re-soldering two others in their place. Certainly this was a simple task for myself to accomplish I then thought. Next I was given to reflect upon the fact that in the past I had learned how to solder things from several different sources. Actually circuit board soldering is a much more delicate operation than some of these other soldering projects and I deftly handled this one with ease. Also I am sure that a part of the ease in which this project was accomplished is that I "get in Medicine with" all of the elements involved, before, during, and after the repair. Yep, it seems clear to me that at least my desire if not also ability to "fix" things is a part of the Medicine of myself in a way.

    I then began to consider the fact that I do share another Medicine with TohNaWah, in that I too am quite Curious. Actually, I am quite curious about a lot of different things. My curiosity is clearly evident in that I like to figure things out. My favorite games are puzzles. It is not so much that I am smart or anything like that. Nope, it is because like TohNaWah I am simply quite curious about a lot of things. As I was "operating" on the telephone, I was given to consider another thing as well. I noticed that the cord that I was replacing was old and cracked anyway. I was then given to consider that perhaps it could have been that the Spirit of the telephone had something to do with TohNaWah's action because of that condition of its cord. Clearly, TohNaWah's behavior could be considered most Willful by any definition. Yet, was not my very repair of it now, my behaving like-in-kind to some degree? Obviously TohNaWah had Willed it to be chewed in half, while I had Willed it to not be that way, ha, ha, ha!

    For several years now I have known about the four different Wills that we have, which we use to experience and express ourselves during an incarnated experience on Mother Earth. Most of the time we consider them in the collective sense, with the singularly most often referenced one being that of one's Free Will. "Put your Mind to it and you can do it" some say, while really meaning one's Will. But really, which Will are they talking about? In Origins one realizes that any and all choices are the result of Free Will expressions. Also learned is that one can and often does make certain decisions in the Operative of one's Mind and that while a decision is similar to a choice, it is not a real choice. An example of this difference is for me to decide to look for a soldering iron. Once made, that decision in itself is complete. In a sense decisions are much like sorting mail because once it is done no letters have been read by anyone as of yet. Therefore any decision that is made will effect no result other than to do that in itself. Making a decision is to put a Prayer of Desire together and keep it on the back burner so to speak. I often have desired a lot of different things, with no direct response or fulfillment. I am most certain that the reason for this condition is that I have not followed through with making a complete choice and thereby Will expression, about any of the decisions resulting in those desires, period.

Decisions occur in the Mind and Heart Operatives all of the time you see. However, Choices are much different than that. Decisions essentially prioritize thoughts and feelings which are internal. Choices are outward expressions of Prayers of Desire through one or more of one's Wills, which solicit Change and thereby Action. Nolayte's mom decided that she wanted to be married to me and be a family. I decided and expressed a choice and Prayer of Desire to do that as well. We both decided to pray for Nolayte to be born so as to be a part of the family that we had both chosen to commit to. Clearly, the decision to do such in itself did not effect Nolayte's coming. Yet, the Prayers of Desire followed by the choice expressions of Will from the two of us and Nolayte, did. Obviously any behavior is an action of oneself, and all actions are Will expressions that are resultant from some earlier decision being made. However unlike changing one's Mind about an earlier decision, which is internal, one cannot change the effects of any Real choice or Will expression once it is made, because these are always external.

One can decide that one would like to have a new automobile. In itself that decision will effect no result at all. Many new automobiles may suddenly then appear in one's life and most likely will. Yet none of them will become the property of oneself. A new automobile will become the property of oneself if and only if, one follows through with the issuing forth of a Prayer of Desire for that new automobile after the decision is made to desire one. And to do such requires that a choice must always be made internally to express such through one or more of one's Wills externally. In Origins one learns that any and all choices are a function of one's Free Will-Operative. A Prayer of Desire can actually be issued from one's Heart Will-Operative, Ego Will-Operative, Soul Will-Operative, or Care Essence-Operative as well as from one's Free Will. Yet, even the choice of which Will to express the Prayer of Desire through and from is in Reality a function of one's Free Will, no matter what. For any Being or Thing to experience or express anything at all outside of oneself, requires both internal and external action for it to do so, with ultimately one or more of one's Wills becoming involved, no matter what. Clearly this example of how all Beings and Things operate shows the very reason as to why it is that Great Pop made the Personal Structure. Of course, it also illustrates just how brilliantly designed and perfect it is.

Another example of the difference between decisions and choices is the case whereby one is sitting at a table in a restaurant. Of course for one to be there, one already must have decided to go out to eat as well as which restaurant to go to, otherwise one would not be there at that particular one. You see, one can only be at that location as the realization of an outward Potential that was drawn forth to oneself because of the Free Will expression of choice of oneself, period. This is Real and true even though that choice expression was based upon some decision that first took place. Likewise there were many subsequent Free Will expressions of choice that also had to occur during the process of each step along the way. In Reality it is singularly because of those choices and this process that one has arrived at that location and condition of oneself, or can do anything at all for that matter. Even when walking, this process takes place as we continuously have to decide to continue to move and then make continuous Free Will choice expressions as to the direction and timing of each single step. One might seem not conscious of this process that we do over and over again, but it happens and happens just that way. And as one can now realize, it is in fact not our decisions that get us there at all. Nope, it is always one or more of our Wills. Period.

So there we sit and peruse the menu of available substances to ingest. Once that process is complete we then make another decision as to what to order. However, unless we inform someone of that decision or take the action of making a subsequent expression in some manner of one or more of our Wills, we will go hungry for the rest of our life. To our benefit, the waiter then chooses to come by our table as their own Free Will expression of self. And if we are real fortunate they likewise then choose to ask us what we would like to eat. Thereafter, based upon the previous decision regarding the options from the menu we then make another Free Will expression of choice, to tell them, hopefully in a language that they can understand, what it is that we have decided upon to choose to eat. And of course sometimes the waiter then decides and next chooses to tell us that they just ran out of that particular thing. In such a case, one then gets to begin again this very process that we all go through in each and every moment of our daily lives, ha, ha, ha!

You see, life is not really all that complicated at all! Life is simply a continuum of decisions followed by Free Will choices upon those decisions, which ultimately effect the issuance of Prayers of Desire which then call forth and become self-realized Potential, or not.

Have you ever been walking along and somehow trip over something, or step into a hole? I call this experience and expression a perfect example of not praying to the ground beneath one's feet. To experience such a Potential, a Prayer of Desire was issued earlier to go along the path and it was answered when one took one's first step. However, for one to trip or have any such discomfort in the process can only result from omission, or what some call a lack of follow through. In reality we are each individually responsible for any and every thing that we do, or might happen to us, no matter what. Why I say such is because of the reality as well as Nature of our two Wills when we are in True Spirit form, or four Wills when we are physically incarnated. Of course this is due to and in testimony of, the perfection of Great Pop's design of the Personal Structure.

As shown in the first illustration, unless we are incarnated into an arena of the Physical realm we only have two Wills to manage so to speak. Life gets a lot more complicated when we choose as an expression of our Free Will, to incarnate. Actually there are more arenas than the single arena of Mother Earth of which we can choose to go to. Each of the arenas have many "rides" so to speak, of experiences that are available for one to experience or express being themselves in. Also, each incarnating Being and Thing knows about all of the Potential rides that are or will become present in each arena before choosing to incarnate there. Therefore, when a Being or Thing incarnates, we all know what is going to happen because of our prayerstick and plan, which are simply Prayers of Desire. Of course these too are determined by ourselves and expressed as Free Will choices. If anything at all happens to us that is not from these two sources then it can and does only occur because in some manner or way we chose to include the Prayers of Desire of another Being or Thing into our plan and prayerstick for whatever reason. This does in Reality happen all of the time and especially when one becomes involved in a relationship with another Being or Thing. Also, the awareness of all of these things and processes does in fact remain at a certain level of Consciousness in all Beings and Things at all times. So not only do all Spirits possess a Personal Structure, they also possess the awareness and processes of operating such, as was just described. Therefore it can be said that these mechanisms and processes are a part of each individual Spirit that chooses to experience something in a physical sojourn and thereby life expression.

To incarnate anywhere is always a Free Will choice. Most oftentimes that choice is realized as an expression of a Soul Will desire. Therefore one can see how there can be expressions of Prayers of Desire which become simultaneous expressions of multiple Wills. Also, any and all outer expressions, be they of an individual Will or a collective of such, are released to the All, outside the Consciousness bubble of oneself via the vehicle of one's Care Essence-Operative. In the previous diagrams of one's Personal Structure, the supporting elements to the means and processes by which we express ourselves or do anything at all is shown. Obviously, while one is in True Spirit form one is not encumbered by the competitive Nature of one's Ego, Ego Will, or its Attitude, which become attached in the process of incarnating. Nor are we of need of a Heart Will and its associated Attitude, which balance the effects of one's Ego upon one's Mind and other parts of self. In True Spirit form, the Essence-Operative of our perspective is round or circular, thus making it easy for us to have undistorted clarity in the condition of what is called the many faceted lens of it, as well as perceive things globally. When we incarnate our Perspective Essence-Operative becomes twisted in a sense, so as to have one part of it serve one's Ego Operative and the other part serve one's Heart Operative. Naturally this incarnated condition of one's Personal Structure becomes more work for, you guessed it - one's Free Will. It is much easier to see the perfection or many differing aspects of things in True Spirit because of this difference in the condition of the Personal Structure of oneself, which always happens when we incarnate.

Most likely we have all heard someone say that some Being or Thing has a "bad attitude" or even a "good" one at times. Attitudes are important in as much as they are like a billboard - a means in which to express Prayers of Desire and attract "like in kind" Potential to oneself. As mentioned earlier, all outer expressions including that of the "bait" of one's Prayers of Desire, exit one's Personal Structure and bodyform to the All of Creation through one's Care Essence-Operative. Also in any outer personal expression, one's fishing pole of Faith becomes resident in one's Attitudes with a mirror image of one's Desire being illuminated so as to attract like in kind. Because of this condition of these elements and the pivotal role that they play in receivership, one can see how important one's attitudes can be.

However, the Wills that they are attached to are much more Potentially powerful than their associated Attitudes either singularly or collectively. In Reality one's Attitudes be they considered singularly or collectively, is the easiest thing for one to change at any moment or in any manner. As was also learned in the Odyssey of Origins, the easiest method to effect such a change in one's Attitude is from the application of Perspective, such as in choosing to be thankful for something. This is Real and true because our Consciousness knows what is going on all of the time and we at times focus a certain part of it with our Mind towards some aspect of ourselves or that of another Being or Thing. When we do this, we oftentimes refer to it as focusing or being in focus on something. To regulate or change one's Attitude is simply to de-prioritize one's portion of Consciousness that is associated to a disappointment or Fear, and shift or realign it to focus instead so as to see through one's Perspective Essence-Operative. Of course for one to do such is possible as being simply another Free Will expression of choice! Actually there are many "good" things about these additional components to the Personal Structure when a Being or Thing incarnates. This is because they are what facilitates any and all "physical" expressions, period. Actually, I cannot make the fingers of my hands even press the keys on this keyboard as I write these words without any and all of them.

Also illustrated in the diagrams, one will notice that we have our Emotional Body in both the incarnated and True Spirit forms of self. Just like the Essence-Operative of one's Perspective, when one is incarnated, one's Emotional Body has a lot more work to do. In the experience of Origins, we learned that Great Pop made the Emotional Body to serve as a protective bumper for our Spirit and the elements of our Personal Structure, much like is found on an automobile. Actually one's Emotional Body has several other uses, but protection of those elements is the primary one. The theater place of our dreamtime is within one's Emotional Body in support of this purpose, as our dreams occur so that we do not have to bear the effects of our Fears and so forth in the Physical realm.

Just considering how this all works certainly impresses the puzzle person in me. Even more impressive is how Great Pop made it all work so well, with seemingly so little to work with at the time. Most assuredly the idea of "hanging out the magnets" of our Prayers of Desire on two well illuminated "billboards" of our Attitudes that are affixed to our Emotional Body for any and all to see is simply brilliant by any standard. In this manner any and all can see what one desires and is up to, in a sense. Also, they can then use their Free Will to choose to support and participate in the realization of such Potential, or not. Have you ever passed a person on a sidewalk and just "known" that they are in pain or anger? That is just one example of how well one's Emotional Body and Attitudes work. Clearly, this design of Great Pop's does work and it works perfectly!

In His brilliant and perfect design we have a Heart Will and Attitude that supports the True Desire Prayers from our Heart, which is separate from that of our Ego. In this design of the operation of our Personal Structure, He made it so that the Prayers of Desire from one's Heart can and do appear on the billboard of the Attitude of one's Ego as well as the Attitude of one's Heart. Yet in all cases and conditions, only one's Prayers of Real Hope Desires can ever appear upon the Attitude of one's Heart. Of course one can easily guess what the effect of this "Double Billing" of one's Hope Prayers of Desire from the Heart can have over the Fear Prayers of one's Ego in this manner.

This is how any and all Beings and Things are able to do or receive anything here on Mother Earth. Obviously one's Free Will is a most significant and instrumental part of the design of it all, as are the other components that were just described. Certainly at this point we can now see and understand the How of it all, and How it all works and happens. But even so, I still find myself wondering as to just Who and What it is that I Really am?

BARK ON TREE

In the normal process of such, as I start each chapter, Great Pop will most oftentimes have me begin by first making the illustrations that they are to contain, and as my life is dynamically linked to the content of this material, I was not too surprised to find this chapter to be no exception. You see, once I started this chapter I soon found myself to be in another dilemma as concerns what I call my Bark on Tree. For several months now I have known that the main disk drive of this computer needs to be replaced. This is due to the fact that not only am I now using most of the available space on it, but also because it is now getting bad sector problems more frequently. When a bad sector problem occurs, there is a program that this Machine

Spirit can use to scan the surface of the disk and try to fix the bad parts of itself. The way that this feature works is that the program shifts the location of the readable information of the bad parts of the surface to any available spare good parts of the surface of the disk. So what is happening with this writing machine is that the disk drive is becoming of a condition whereby the surface of the disk is "going soft" as some say. So, as I impatiently watched the program scan the disk drive time and again, I did know exactly what was going on inside the device. Yep, I knew each of the actual events and processes that were happening when it failed and when it tried to fix the problem. In reflection, I realized that it was when I started working with Jack that I started getting interested in these things about the inner workings of computers. Of course my Curiosity Medicine is the reason for my interest in the way that things work, which is something that TohNaWah and I both have in common.

Actually, the following explanation about this Writing Machine Spirit's recording methodology and technique has something in common with how we "operate" as well. The simplified version of what was going on with the disk drive of this writing machine is the same process for any magnetic recording device and material, such as a cassette or CD recorder. First of all there is a surface coating on the tape or disk that is specialized in a sense. The nature of this basically iron oxide type of powdery coating is that very small portions of it can be magnetically energized. And what is special about it is that because of its Medicine and composition, the adjoining portions will remain unaffected. Therefore one might liken this condition to the surface being made up of a whole bunch of little boxes. Each of these boxes has little windows that are aligned in several adjoining straight lines that we will call a matrix. In this matrix, each window is separated at a fixed distance from the next window.

Next is what some call the read / write head, which is present on any magnetic type of recording device, and each of these has several electromagnetic segments. This means that they have little electro-magnets as separate segments, which can be individually energized or charged or not, with electricity. When one of these segments becomes charged with electricity, it will in fact cause a similar sized portion of the surface of the coating that is exposed to it, such as the surface of the disk in my writing machine, to become charged as well. The specialized coating will continue to hold a charge on those little portions of itself pretty much indefinitely.

Selves – Vol. 1

The read / write head that does this has the segments of itself situated so that they also are of the same spacing and pattern as the windows in the boxes as described about the recording medium. Of course this is due to the fact that it is the segments of a read / write head that establish such on the tape to begin with, ha, ha, ha! In the process of recording something the read / write head magnetically energizes only that portion of the surface that is inside the window of certain boxes. The result is much the same as turning a little light on in those windows. Also, there is what they call an erase head that passes by in front of the write head in this procedure. And you guessed it, its job is: "Lights Out Everybody!!" Yep, the erase head essentially turns all of the lights off before they get to the write head which then selectively turns some of them on in the process of making a recording.

Later, when the read head of a similar device follows along the same path it looks to see which lights are on and which are off. Yep, basically that is how it all works. There is more to the process both before and after what was explained, such as in the manner of encoding patterns so that certain windows with lights on or off in a certain matrix of such will mean a certain thing. However, in a nutshell this is the means by which magnetic recordings are made. Even the memory that they refer to as being "Core" or "Ram" memory in computing devices, operate in pretty much this same fashion. While things certainly have become smaller over the years, meaning many more smaller windows with lights on or off so to speak, it is still the same process. And for those that want to know, "going soft" means that the surface of the disk or tape is no longer able to continually hold a charge to a certain level. This means that it would be like having a light come on that is flickering or real dim in certain windows and places on the recording surface. While there is not really a little light in a window, the difference in detectable Magnetic energy patterns is pretty much the same as that.

Yep, that is How this writing machine remembers and thinks. Actually it is not all that different than the way that we remember and think as well. Have you ever wondered what really happens when you think or remember things? How about what really is going on in the decision process? And what I am talking about here is not some type of electro-magnetic / chemical reactionary process of stimuli / response scenarios, like what is talked about in a biological laboratory. Yet, if they have one, the way that such processes work in the brains of Beings and Things is pretty much the same as that which was just described.

When I drowned at four years of age I could have been described as being physically unconscious as well as physically dead. Yet in that condition and time I still was, and I was very conscious in fact! Actually, I had not lost real Consciousness from the moment of my last breath and my exit of my bodyform, which I then saw was laying at the bottom of the pool. My Consciousness and Spirit was next to it, but no longer inside of it at first. I floated around it and then finally above it as I have often seen Spirits do. I did such so as to make certain that no part of me was left inside of it and then I simply floated above it and out of the water. At that time and in that condition, I was most conscious of everything, as well as in a sense, even all knowing! Most certainly I was thinking, too! It was as if I was still in my human bodyform, yet without the limits of it. One of my first thoughts was in fact that of, "Gee, why are my parents that I can see below me not even caring that I have drowned and am now dead?" I was a decision maker too in that condition of myself, and I did decide to follow the advice of my Guides, by then choosing to start the return journey of Transition.

So guess what folks? If all of the thought and mental processes are isolated to being a function of one's anatomical structure and brain, then can you explain just how I was still aware, conscious, thinking, and making decisions and choices after I had left my body? Have you heard some person use the term of being "brain dead?" I say that about myself a lot now, ha, ha, ha! Of course I know that death is an illusion, and not just because I now have had many such experiences personally. Besides, what about one's feelings? Just how do they Really work? I was certainly still feeling, and pretty poorly about myself as well as my parents in that condition and those moments that are now so many years ago.

Great Pop explained to me in the material of Origins and Possession that the Real thought, decision making, and feeling processes occur in the two Operatives of one's Mind and Heart in the most part. He also explained to me that one can sense things and have certain feelings and choices arise in the Operative of one's Ego as well. Great Pop further explained that these particular Operative elements of one's Personal structure are pretty much configured as follows:

Heart Operative

True Value System	True Feeling Memory Bank
Spiritual Care Canal	
Canal of Passion	
Spiritual Desire Canal	

True Desire Data Bank	Choice Center	Care Center

In → / Out →

Mind Operative

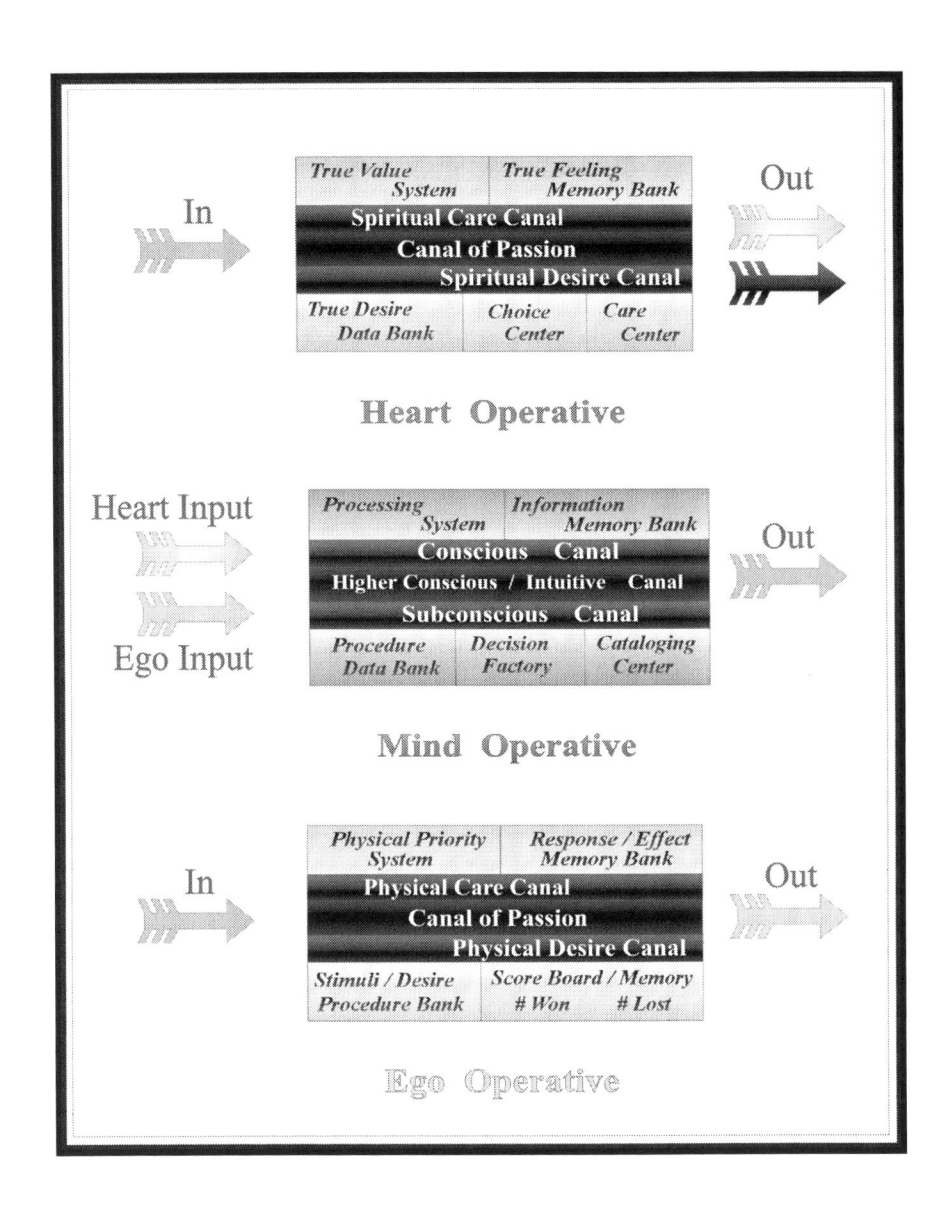

Heart Input →
Ego Input →

Processing System	Information Memory Bank
Conscious Canal	
Higher Conscious / Intuitive Canal	
Subconscious Canal	

Procedure Data Bank	Decision Factory	Cataloging Center

Out →

Ego Operative

Physical Priority System	Response / Effect Memory Bank
Physical Care Canal	
Canal of Passion	
Physical Desire Canal	

Stimuli / Desire Procedure Bank	Score Board / Memory # Won # Lost

In → / Out →

   In His explanation of such, Great Pop told me that it all began when He first started "compartmentalizing" things. In this development, which occurred long before He had made the first physical thing, Great Pop started making Operatives within Operatives such as the rectangular sections illustrated in the diagram. As shown in the Heart Operative, there is an Operative within it that is one's True Value System. It is important to remember here, that even though Great Pop at this point did not have some type of specialized magnetic powder to use, He did have other things. At this point,

101 *Selves – Vol. 1*

Thought energy and the patterning of such was already a happening thing, as was Memory energy and the patterning of it too. If the current ability of micro-miniaturization of computer technology can be considered to be something special, consider what Great Pop can develop with the limitless capacity and Nature of Essences!

As is illustrated, there are several canals that pass through each of these Operatives. These canals pass along "messages" and all kinds of Thought energy from various sources through one's Mind Operative, just like the tape in a recording machine. And of course these canals do such in the same manner with "Feelings" through the Heart. The compartmentalized Processing System Operative then becomes like the read / write head and processor of this writing machine. If it likes or finds something interesting or desirable come by on the "conveyer belts" of the canals of the Mind, it does not in fact take it off as some might first suspect. Nope, instead it makes an abbreviated "micro-miniaturized" copy of anything that is of importance. One's Mind Operative will next catalogue the copy with a sort of reference code in that compartmentalized Operative, and if applicable, a priority is assigned to it as well. It will then pass that copy along to the storage area of the memory compartment or sub-Operative of one's Mind, which is at all times dynamically linked to one's Emotional Body. You see, the Real Thought or Memory patterns all end up being recorded forever and a day in the mega-memory bank of one's Emotional Body!

Yep, this is the why of "selective Memory". Selective Memory is actually the Real process by which patterns are recorded as was just described. One only chooses and stores copies of parts of experiences, thoughts, or feelings inside these Operatives for immediate short-term access, just like the cache memory of this writing machine. The people that made this writing machine just copied this Real process of these Operatives and design that was originated by Great Pop. This is why at a certain level of Consciousness people can remember parts of some experience, but not all of it. Also, it is because of the reality of this process and condition that hypnosis works the way that it does. You see, in the real conditions and experiences of someone being hypnotized, it is pretty much like being dead, as I described earlier. In this I mean that in the process of real hypnosis, one's Consciousness is associated to one's Emotional Body and the totality of information that is recorded and available there! Also, in the assignment of priority in the processing of thoughts and feelings, as well as memory pattern copies, it is much like having a light on in a window again. And based

Selves – Vol. 1   *102*

upon whatever criteria is involved, to give a priority to some encoded pattern "copy," the "light" in a sense, is given a different color as well as brightness.

So you see, the way that these Operatives function is really pretty much the same as how this writing machine works. Yep, it is just little windows with lights on or off, of different colors and brightness, and this describes each and every Being and Thing's way of thought, memory, and feeling. Any decision is simply the act and process of applying a specific and encoded energy influence to a pattern of thought, feeling, or memory energy. And this is like turning a little light of a specific color and brightness on or off in the window of a box, that contains the referenced thought, feeling, desire, or care. Naturally, the Heart Operative works the same way for desires and feelings. Little lights are turned on or off in windows of little boxes is Really all that happens, and such is the very how that one thinks, what they think, like what they like, do not like what they do not like, feel what they feel, and on, and on, and on....

Yep, little lights in windows and Operatives within Operatives! This is the prime ingredient to life as we know it, because it is the foundation that enables all processes in general. Now we have that part covered, have you ever heard of someone being described as having a great big, or a lot of, Ego? I certainly have. For many years it seems I have wondered with the cat curiosity that I share with TohNaWah, just what people were really talking about or referring to in such comments about what they call one's Ego. It has been many years now that I did finally break down and asked Great Pop what they were talking about in this Ego idea. In doing so, I asked Him to help me understand what one's Ego is Really all about and might be used for. This actually occurred about the time that I was just starting to consider doing any of this writing at all. Actually, it was about the time of the beginning of the material that would develop into the work named The Medicine Way.

Great Pop's first response to me at that time was something like: *"Well, Little One, it is actually your Ego that is causing your hesitancy in doing that which I asked of you in writing a book, Ho, Ho, Ho!"* He went on to explain that my reluctance to begin such was that I did not feel secure in my capacity to accomplish the task in a manner that would be acceptable to Him. He then told me that any insecurity is simply one of the many faces of Fear that one's Ego uses to stimulate us to motion and action, or not. In this I mean to say that one's Ego can cause us to do something as well as cause us to not do something.

Also, it usually uses the Essence of Fear that is associated to itself to make such occur. Great Pop then showed me the following illustration to further explain this part of ourselves to me at that time:

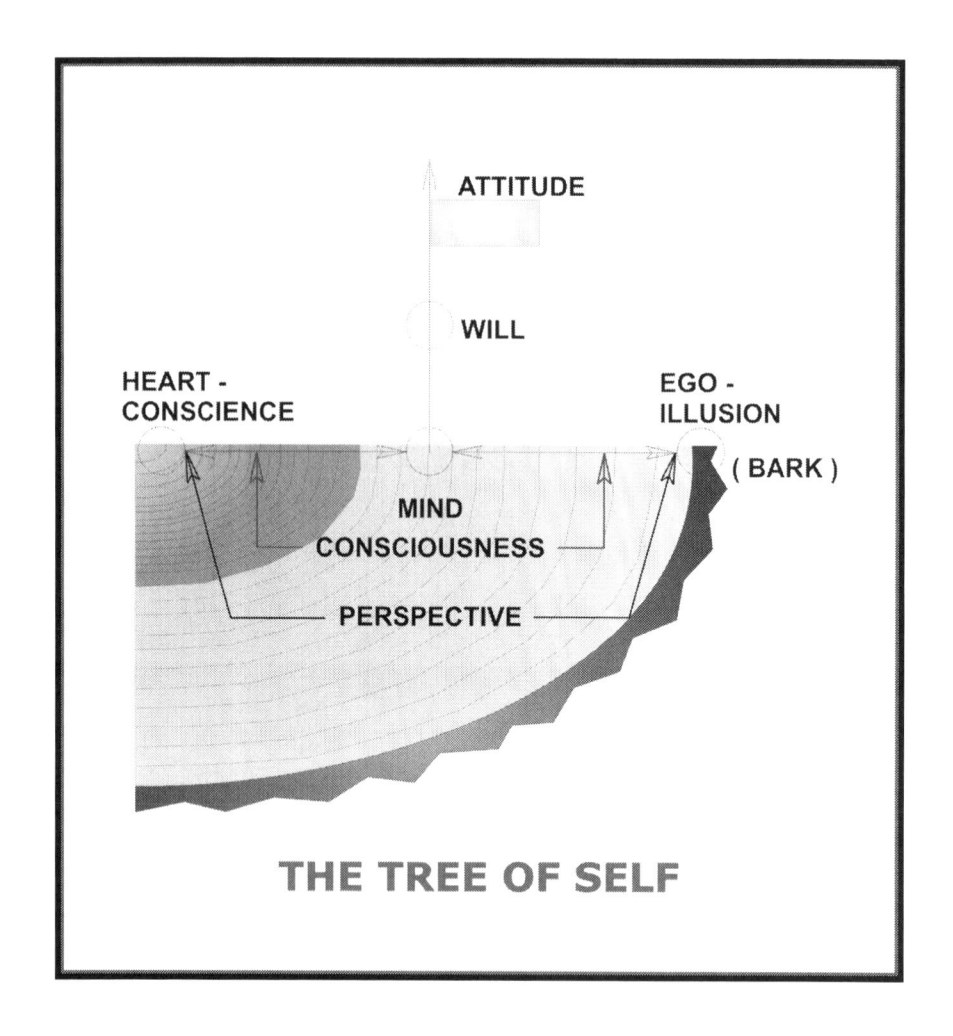

ATTITUDE

WILL

HEART - CONSCIENCE

EGO - ILLUSION

(BARK)

MIND
CONSCIOUSNESS
PERSPECTIVE

THE TREE OF SELF

Great Pop then went on to say, "Remember Little One, when you asked me how to grow, and I told you to grow like the tree and thereby from the inside out?" And when I replied that I did, the short version of what He told me then was that like the Heart of the tree which goes deep in the ground through its roots, so also is the Heart of oneself. In the same manner as the Heart of the tree and its roots are connected to Mother Earth, one's Spirit is ever connected to Him, via the "umbilical cord" of one's conscience, basically. He then showed me the rings and stated that these are like the rings of the Mind, and that we are continually expanding the numbers of these as we choose to experience things. He then showed me how there was a thin fabric-like layer between the rings of one's Mind and one's Heart, which is called one's "conscience". Next He showed me how there was another fabric-like layer on the other side of one's Mind that is called "illusion". He told me that when incarnated, the lens of one's perspective is, in a sense, always looking at things through these two layers and it is one's Consciousness that enables the flow between it all. He also stated that the Mind can and often will pass along some of one's Prayers of Desire through one or more of one's Wills and these prayers are then outwardly exhibited and expressed as being one's "Attitude" so to speak.

Great Pop then asked if I saw the outer most portion of the tree, and I replied that I did. He said that the outermost portion of the tree was like the Operative of one's Ego. He made it that way so that like the Bark on the tree protects the bodyform of the tree, so also does one's Bark on Tree of Ego serve to protect the physical body of oneself. He made the pseudo-Essence of Fear, as well as the fabric of illusion just next to it, for the Ego to be able to use for just that purpose. He stated that at times one's Ego will use the fabric of illusion with the Essence of Fear so as to be able to gain control of the Mind and thus stay in charge. One's Ego does that at times, because it is one's Bark on Tree and its associated pseudo-Essence of Fear that is part of what one does eventually leave behind when one exits. From that last statement, one can see that it is one's Bark on Tree of Ego that will ultimately no longer be of capacity and therefore, "die".

In Reality one can trace any one of the multitude of expressions that I call "faces of Fear" to being an issuance and thereby expression of one's Bark on Tree in some manner. Hence, if it is of Fear, then it is of Ego. Period. Also, because of the connectivity of one's Bark on Tree with the associated fabric of illusion, one's Bark on Tree can and often does disguise Fear in many ways and fashions. Obvious examples of such, is the case of bravado, lust, ambition, jealousy, envy, greed, vanity, insecurity, impatience, competitiveness, depression, and on, and on, and on...

It was in the process of the development of the material titled Possession, which occurred long after my first introduction to this Bark on Tree concept, that Great Pop gave me the design of the internals of the Ego Operative, as shown in the following diagram:

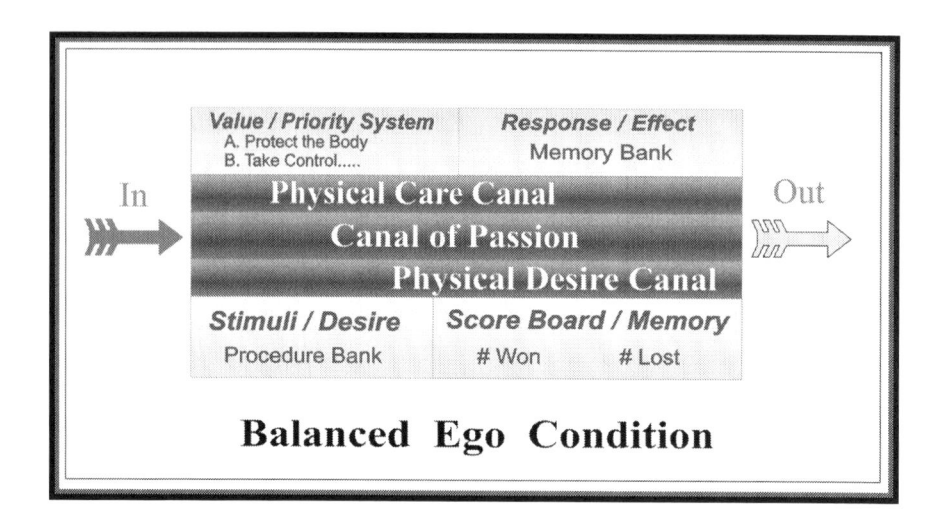

```
                Value / Priority System        Response / Effect
                A. Protect the Body            Memory Bank
                B. Take Control.....
    In                Physical Care Canal                        Out
  ▶▶▶               Canal of Passion                           ▶▶▶
                       Physical Desire Canal
                Stimuli / Desire       Score Board / Memory
                Procedure Bank         # Won         # Lost
```

Balanced Ego Condition

Obviously in this depiction of one's Ego, when one is in a balanced condition of being, there really is not all that much difference in the internal structure of the Ego Operative than those of the Mind or Heart of self. One's Ego Operative does have a memory compartment that gets a lot of activity, which I liken to being some type of a "Score Board". This compartmentalized section is one part that I personally have difficulty with at times. Also, this Operative compartment has what I call a "false feeling" generating aspect of its operation, which I sometimes have trouble with too. It obviously is a combined influence of this compartment with the associated pseudo-Essence of Fear that makes one feel good when they beat someone else in an experience and expression of competition. Even so, all in all, one's Bark on Tree is really perfect and another "brilliant" design by Great Pop.

Yep, most of my troubles being in life on Mother Earth are primarily due to some condition of my Bark on Tree, or so it seems. My Bark on Tree is what made me want to become good at working with computers as well as playing any game, like shooting pool. My Bark on Tree is what makes me have trouble sleeping at times from wondering about how I will be able to continue to live. My Bark on Tree is what makes me afraid of anything at all. It is what makes me doubt that I can or will be in Nolayte's life at all, or will again see my other two children. My Bark on Tree tells me that I am now getting hungry and that I need to eat to continue to live. My Bark on Tree then tells me that I cannot really afford to spend the little money that I do still have on food right now, and on, and on, and on....

Certainly I have a lot of Bark that I have to keep stripping off the tree of me just to get through each day and sometimes even the next moment. It is most obvious to me now, that my Bark on Tree clearly has a lot to do with my condition and circumstances in life. Even so, in the big picture of such, am I Really just my Bark on Tree in some fashion or way? Clearly my Bark on Tree does have a lot of influence upon my very existence in life, yet we do not have such a thing when we exit. So that again makes me wonder just Who and What am I, Really?

PART III

THE SELVES

ONEMENT

Phew! It sure is good to be through with that last chapter and beginning this one. As I live every word of this material as it is being written, as one might imagine, lately I have been having quite a time in dealing with my Bark on Tree, ha, ha, ha!

It is now January 3, 2002. When I finished the last chapter, Coyote sister from Seven Lakes came and took me there for Christmas and to do some work. She arrived on Christmas Eve and brought me home again on New Year's Eve. It was in the low forties in this place when I arrived home and it is still that cold inside, even with the little heaters going. Actually, I have to keep warming up my hands to even type these words, so that is just some more Bark on Tree stuff you see. TohNaWah went with me to Coyote sister's place. He had a good time there as usual, but I can tell that he is now very glad to be home too. It snowed about six inches here last night and I really love snow. Snow makes everything look white and beautiful and white is the color of Spirit.

Two days ago I had to walk across town in the bitterly cold wind to pay the light bill. Of course that task was just more Bark on Tree building stuff too. Since I grew up in South Texas, I never had too much time in the cold. I figure that is why I am still not really comfortable in it like some people seem to be. I do not mind being real hot, but I do mind being cold. Well, with that trek to pay the bill being accomplished, at least now I will have electricity for these little heaters to use, and in that I am most thankful. Coyote sister gave me a lot of food and enough money for the next months rent, and I certainly do appreciate that.

When I got home again this time I naturally first started doing the update to the website. That task took a couple of days this time because I had to also update the month and the year parts of it. Also, the disk in this writing machine developed some more problems, so now I know that it is not long before it will have to be replaced. Of course for me to do such will require more money and because of that situation, I have to do more personal Bark on Tree management. On New Year's Day I did my normal beginning of the year's Prayer Ceremony. This caused me to have to deal with more Bark on Tree stuff about Nolayte, my older children and my life conditions in general. On the plus side so to speak, these things did serve to help me realize that all of my issues at this point are in relationship to Flow in some manner. I began to become aware of this issue about Flow in my life when I had more trouble with my Bark on Tree in the work that I did for Coyote sister.

The main project that she wanted me to do was to install a water filter system that would filter all of the water coming into the house. Well, that sounded simple enough to me, but as is found in the experience of the Odyssey of Origins, simple things are "Not Always So Easy!" This project happened while I was in the process of the development of the material in the chapter on Bark on Tree.

To accomplish this objective required my crawling on my belly in the dust and dirt under her house. I had to inch my way through very tight spaces, the whole length of her large place in order to find out where the water line first came inside. Naturally, I finally found that it was all the way to the other side of her house from where one could first go beneath it. This whole situation required that I had to deal with Bark on Tree issues about being in cramped small spaces and so forth. I was already aware that any physical activity or expression always has one's Bark on Tree involved in the process of such. Therefore in the quiet aloneness of that very cold, dirty, dark, cramped space where I had to frequently squeeze face down in the dirt while inching my body under the many large beams that supported the floor and structure of her very large home, one could not help but consider one's condition of being and life, as well as one's Bark on Tree. To accomplish the project, I had to crawl back and forth under her house at least six times, with each pass taking about twenty minutes. On the plus side was the fact that at least it was not as cold under there as it was outside, and for that I was thankful.

I should have taken notice of Potential difficulty or a resistance to support in this project, in the fact that it took us two whole days just to find out where the water meter shut off was located to begin with. Even this simple but most important step was only accomplished by our finally going to the water department and having them come out and showing it to us! After that location was established, in order to install this new, whole house filter device, I realized that I first had to find the source of the Flow of water to it, underneath. It took me two round trips of crawling on my belly around the whole perimeter of her home to finally locate the point of entry. Once that was located, I had to determine a convenient, yet hidden place in the house above where I could locate the filter. A cabinet beneath one of the many bathroom sinks on the side of the house above the water line entry point, while cramped, seemed like the appropriate place. Of course all through the process of this project, I asked the filter, the house, and Great Pop what to do, in the normal Medicine Way of such.

So at this point, after all of the previous effort, I was pretty much ready to begin the installation. I began by drilling a hole through the floor of the cabinet and the house. This was quite a feat in itself, even though I just happened to have brought a long enough drill bit to accomplish it. Once that was done, of course I had to go back underneath the house so as to determine and measure how much of what size hose and fittings were required to cut and splice into the existing water line as it entered the house. And remember, each time that I went underneath meant crawling on my belly in the dirt and dust, face down at times, beneath timbers and air conditioning ducting, some of which I first even had to dig under just to be able to barely squeeze beneath them. And I had to do this from one side of a very large and long house to the very opposite corner, not just to that point, but back to the entry point as well!

At that point we finally knew what we needed to get in the way of materials, yet even that was "not always so easy" either because there was a special type of waterline that we needed. After finding no success in trying several of the normal places, we finally went back to the water department, which finally directed us to the right supply place. Once we bought the hose, filter and connections, we went back to her home and after turning off the water at the meter, my next step was - you guessed it - to go back underneath her house again. This time I had to make several passes back and forth underneath so as to move all of the materials and tools and such in order to splice the new feed line into place. At least all of the materials that we had procured fit the first time. After I enlarged the first hole that I had made through the floor, I was able to get the two ends of the splice hoses through the floor and into the cabinet. My next step was to give a tobacco blessing and prayer to that which was now connected below. With that accomplished, after crawling on belly again, I was finally topside and starting to connect the filter to the two hoses from below.

As it was getting dark and even colder outside my next step was to put all of the pieces together for connecting the filter to the water lines. I connected it to the new lines that I had fed up into a little space in a cabinet from below. I turned off the valve that was one of the parts that I had assembled, and then went the two hundred yard distance outside and across the property, to where the water meter was located and gave a tobacco gift and prayer that there would be no leak under the house. I turned on the water and went the distance back inside. I turned on the new valve to the filter system and guess what? Yep, there was no leak downstairs but all of the new fittings were now leaking inside! Of course my Bark on Tree danced with that development.

Of course, that also meant that I had to go back outside and turn the water off again. Naturally I did go underneath again and checked that part out for leakage a couple of times before once again ferrying all of the tools and materials that I had taken there back outside. Then after returning, I had to struggle with removing the filter system so as to refit everything and try to make it tighter. Of course in the many times of doing this, I would fix the leak on one side, only to have a new one develop on the other side. This went on for a couple of days in fact. I even ran out of the sealing material and had to wait for one of the stores to open up to get some more. Again and again, I would take it all apart, put it all together, go outside and turn the water on, go back and turn it off, remove all that I had put inside the cabinet, and then take it all apart again. I reassembled the filter components over and over again until finally everything became in Medicine with each other, which is what I was trying to accomplish. As a side note, I also did some electrical work and installed some lights. All of the things that I tried to accomplish that were not dealing with water, went well and easy for me but even the drainpipes under the sinks started leaking when I touched them! Naturally, I ended up having to replace all of them as well. Yep, if it had to do with Flow, then I had a hard time with it, ha, ha, ha!

The status of my life at this point is that I have enough food for a while and I still have enough resources to pay another month's rent. I am cold, but I am not sick yet. I have no idea as to how I am going to be able to continue or be able to get more resources for living at this point, much less to be able to drive again. I do not know where Nolayte is now living, or how I will ever be able to be a part of his life in the way that I would like to be. The disk drive in this writing machine is going to have to be replaced soon, and since my drawing program quit working a while back, I need additional resources for both of them now. It is snowing and therefore I presently am most thankful and happy with what I do have, and those that have helped me, including of course, Great Pop!

Actually, the recent plumbing project does have something to do with this chapter too in a way. I say such because that project was a condition whereby Onement was also an issue, or required. At this point we have pretty much figured out How we "operate" such as to think, make decisions, express choices, and so forth. This understanding is important because if we are not familiar with all of the parts of the project or puzzle, then we can not get it to work like we desire of it, such as was the case of that water filter installation. Obviously there seems to be some leaks as regards "Flow" in my being in life at this point also. It seems that whatever I do or no matter how hard I try, it is just not enough, or something unexpected happens that keeps any success or fulfillment from being realized. Certainly this is the case with many of my efforts, like my experience with Nolayte's mom, my trying to get these books published, or my even having a normal condition of life and employment. Certainly if I can find the answer as to the Who and What I Really am, I will be better empowered in a way, so as to realize some of those objectives, maybe. Perhaps Onement is a clue to the problem. Most certainly Onement is another one of the pieces of the puzzle that needs to be considered!

At this point, some people might be wondering as to what I mean in this use of the word of "Onement". As one might recall, within the five Founding Essences that started all of this happening so to speak, Onement was in fact one of them. Onement and Balance are two of the Founding Essences that are embodied in any and all things that exist. Onement at times might be confused with Balance, because both share some of the same "Nature" and thereby Medicine. Perhaps the simplest distinguishing aspect between these two Founding Medicines and Essences is that one can be considered as being inclusive and the other as exclusive. Balance can be considered as exclusive even though it is always to be considered in relationship to the All of everything in Creation. An even better idea of this idea and use of the word of Balance might be the word "completeness". If something is in Balance or complete, then it is stable within its very Being and self. This means that whatever walks in Balance does not walk in the Consciousness of Need. Instead of walking in Need, it only walks in the Consciousness of Have. Also, whatever walks in Balance and thereby Have, needs no support from any other Being or Thing to do such, or anything at all for that matter. Yep, Have mentality and Consciousness and thereby completeness and sufficiency in oneself, clearly, that is Real Balance. Therefore, Real Balance can only be realized singularly and is therefore exclusive of the All else of creation.

Onement on the other hand is more like the word and idea of Resonance, and hence could be considered to be inclusive. This is real and true because for a condition of Real Onement to exist, there has to be more than a single, or "One" element to be considered in it. One can consider Onement to be the same as the Group Consciousness of several elements or things, and to some degree it is just that, in itself.

If one were to see four policemen standing on a corner, then the group of them would be considered, as well as each of the individuals. If someone were to ask as to where the Police were, then one would describe the corner to them as being a correct response. However, the real Onement of the condition of Police would not be the Where they were at all. Nope, the Real Onement would be the What they were, in both personification and representation. Each of the four individual policemen on the corner would be considered to be in a condition of Onement not because of their job title, their uniforms, or occupation. Of course these elements would certainly be evidence of that of which they were in Real Onement of. Actually the four individuals on the corner would be considered to be in Onement primarily because of their shared value system in the most part, as well as choices of personal expression and commitment.

In the process that I sometimes describe as my "getting in Medicine with" something, it is really Onement that I am referring to in most senses. Actually, for me to get in Medicine with any of a thing requires a joining of sorts. When I get in Medicine with something, in a sense I become part of it and it becomes a part of me. In such a condition, we both become part of the other and the union of the two of us is an expression that is not unlike that of a marriage. Resonance might be considered an aspect of Onement, however it really is a separate thing all together. To become in Onement with any of a thing, one must first become openly embracing as well as resonant. Of course resonance can be of several conditions, such as being in harmony and accord, or in discord or conflict with something else. Resonance can even be considered as being neutral at times as well. However, resonance only can be extant if there is more than one single thing or element to be considered. This is real and true about resonance even if that which is to be considered is embodied within a single Element, Being, or Thing. An example of this is that I can be resonant to the Fear of death that is constantly being promoted by my Ego Operative, or the reality of everlastingness that is ever present in my Conscience and Heart Operatives.

To be in Onement, one must embrace another Being or Thing in openness and then establish a resonance of harmony for it to occur at all, which describes the very means and method of one's "getting in

Medicine with" anything at all. Clearly, one can regard balance in respect to the elements that are within or outside of oneself. However in this use of the word of Onement, one considers it as being the things that one is a part of, as well as is a part of oneself. You see, to be in Real Onement, one must cede over a portion of oneself so as to make room to accept something that is either within, or outside of oneself and that something can be anything from oneself or another Being or Thing. Obviously a Proper marriage is just such a condition of Onement, as well as is the definition of a tribe or family in the Proper way.

As with the other four Founding Essences and Medicines, no matter what exists or happens, there is and always will be a condition of Onement. This is actually real and true whether one chooses to participate or not in anything, because there exists a condition of Onement in those that do not choose to participate, just as with those that do. As mentioned, Onement is one of the five Founding Essences that are a part of any and everything that exists. And therefore like all Essences, it too has many different and at times multiple ways of being realized, expressed, or experienced. Of course this condition makes Onement a little "tricky" to recognize or understand in some aspects.

When I assist others to go into a tree for clearing, or even do such for myself, Onement is a condition of the process as well as a goal in a sense, that is to be achieved. Before I begin such a process I am in a condition of Onement. If I am associated to thought forms or the ill intent of others, it can only be because I am in a condition of Onement with them. So to Change - which is another of the five Founding Essences - my condition of attachment and thereby Onement with these things, I have to consider Onement as being a part of the process as well as goal to be realized from it. In the Medicine and Proper Way as guided to me by Great Pop and my personal Guides, I have to not so much slough these attachments off, like so much litter that one finds now strewn about everywhere it seems on Mother Earth. Nope, I have to find another place to put them or associate them in Onement with, and preferably in a manner and place that Walks in Balance and with Harm to No One Being or Thing. Obviously to do such is to be Responsible, and to do other than that is simply not. In fact there are many ways of doing a thing such as this type of clearing activity and process. There are many practitioners of different methods that I know of who smudge and so forth in ways that they feel is beneficial. But to do such without having a target that is desirable to become in

Onement with that which one desires to release from oneself or others, makes the stuff that is released in such a manner to become free floating in a sense. And as such, it probably will associate itself right back to oneself or others in the near proximity of such endeavor.

It is actually the Medicine of Onement in water that makes it willing to join with the dirt on one's body. And it is the same nature of Onement or the lack of it, in oil, which keeps it separated from water and in Onement to itself. In the practice of clearing oneself or others with a tree, I always ask the Spirit of the tree if in fact it desires to participate in the process, and some trees do not. Those Plant Spirits that do offer their support, use that which is associated and removed for food in a way, and that certainly Walks in Balance and with Harm to No One Being or Thing. Remember, what we are trying to get rid of are patterns of Thought and Memory energy and as such, these things cannot ever be destroyed. Yet they can be changed or brought to a condition of Onement and thereby made to become neutral. Therefore, what is really involved in this type of clearing process is that what was in Onement with my Consciousness and Being, becomes separated from it by associating it to a willing partner - the tree - that then becomes in Onement with it.

Clearly, every single thing that exists is in some relationship or condition of Onement with everything else, as well as itself. This condition of Onement can sometimes make it difficult to recognize what the Real stuff is that makes oneself, versus other things than that which are really of Oneself in a sense. Certainly one's attitude is like that. Hang around angry people or bully types and one will most likely start thinking and acting in the same way to some degree as well. This very condition or possibility is simply another example of Onement. If one desires to be in Onement and thereby acceptance with those individuals, one has to cede over the portion of oneself that is different. And unfortunately, one's Bark on Tree tries to make just such happen pretty regularly in the current prevalent society. My behavioral change from being around Sandy that was earlier mentioned is a perfect example of this condition and potential. In that time and experience, the requirement for me to be accepted was for me to change, by choosing to operate and in a sense become like-in-kind and thereby in Onement with Sandy and his behavior to some degree.

Yep, this Onement can seem to be really tricky when one thinks about it. Onement is a condition that is ever present in and about everything. Not only that, it also in a sense can be construed as being causative to some degree as well as being a direct effect, result, or at times objective. My personal method and practice of Meditation is to leave my body and the Physical realm. Of course the reason for me to do such is so that I can go to and be with Great Pop. Also in my practice and way of Meditation, I go there not just to see and be with Him, but also talk with, not just to Him. Clearly, Onement is an operative tool as well as goal in that condition and ideal. At this point, it is obvious that the Real me has all sorts of conditions and aspects that are resultant from this Essence of Onement. It certainly might be what makes it so hard to define what the Reality of myself is at any single moment. However, I am at this point quite positive that I am of it in some or many ways, but what does that Really mean or matter? Also, how can I distinguish the core of myself from all of the associations that have developed simply because of my choices to be in Onement with some other Elements or Things? One can now perhaps better understand as regards the Who and What I Really am, that to some degree Onement must be considered as one of the key elements or ingredients.

THE FOUR SELVES

It seems that at this point I have pretty much exhausted all of the Potential that I have in finding out the answer to the question of just Who and What I Really am by myself. Recognizing my limits of self, I now choose to go to the source. Following my normal method of doing such, I laid down, left my body, and zoomed back to where Great Pop is located. Soon thereafter, I was once again sitting across from the smiling face of Great Pop at that wonderful table of Understanding. In so doing, Great Pop again told me that He was glad to see me and welcomed me by asking if I would like some treats. I replied that I would, and so with a snap of His fingers a golden platter then appeared before us. It contained all sorts of little cakes and goodies that I do so like when I am in the Physical realm, as well as here with Him. It seemed like only a moment or so later that with a flourish and wave of his hand He also manifested two golden goblets of that wonderful elixir for us to drink as well. This elixir tasted sort of like a mixture of honey, cinnamon, apple, and something else that is kind of almond tasting. I then noticed Great Pop pause as if He were reflecting on something. Then after a gleam and twinkle appeared in His left eye, a lemon meringue pie also appeared before us on that table, with golden plates and forks to eat it with. Great Pop then completed the setting by causing a large white candle that was already aflame to magically appear in the center of the table before us.

As I have oftentimes been here like this with Great Pop, I am pretty much accustomed to the way He manifests these wonderful things before us. Even so, this time I was still a little apprehensive for some reason that I could not quite understand or explain. I began the conversation by mentioning that I had tried to go as far in this material as I could on my own, like He had asked of me when I started it. Then I told Him that now it seemed that I had finally come to the point that I really needed His help with it. In response, Great Pop just laughed in His all-knowing way and said, *"Well Little One, actually you have done quite well. Perhaps you would first like to know why I decided to add this pie before us?"* I replied that I did and He continued, *"Well, I know that it is one of your favorites, and also it will help in the explanation that I am now going to provide. To begin with, I will explain the Why it is that I am having this material presented through you. I know that you thought when you finished Origins that you would be starting the material on Tribes next. But until the Medicine of Selves is Understood, Tribes will have to wait. I am very aware that you desire to serve My Will first and foremost. You have prayed for a better condition in being in life on Mother Earth and also a means by which to somehow share in Nolayte's upbringing and life, amongst many other things. I have not dismissed your desires over that of Mine for you. Yet all of this is necessary for the fulfillment of My Plan and in the bigger picture, your individual Plan as well. So you can now perhaps realize why certain things have developed and happened the way that they have in your life to this point."*

I thought for a moment about what He had just said as He had a slice of the pie magically present itself before me on the plate. Many times lately I have considered just what He was describing. In this I mean to say that I have tried to consider the greater picture of my life in a way. While I do not have the same conditions of others or what some would call "normalcy" so to speak in my life, I do have so very much more in many ways. I do not have Nolayte and family, nor do I have the security of a job or steady employment. Actually, my sheer existence is relatively tenuous if not downright scary at times. Yet, I do have this project that will hopefully help others as well as myself. I do have this wonderful writing machine and the things that are necessary to do this "work" for Great Pop and in this, I am most appreciative and even wealthy. This is especially true when one considers that I have the time as well as privacy in a way, to be able to focus on it. Also, I am sure this will continue for the time necessary to realize its development. Yep, in so very many ways I am most blessed!

Having come to that realization, Great Pop then continued with, *"Well Little One, consider the pie that is before you and the piece that is now on your plate. What is it that you see there?"*

My first reaction was to respond with the single word "pie", but I checked myself in that one. I then looked at it not as something to eat or the like, but instead in terms of what had just been discussed in this material. And as if on cue with that thought Great Pop began again.

"Yes Little One, as you just realized this is a perfect example of Onement! I chose this particular example for several reasons, not the least of which is that I know that this pie is one of your favorites. Another reason is that it exemplifies through its separate layers of crust, lemon filling, and meringue coating on top, a perfect example of Onement. Actually this pie perfectly exemplifies Onement in a perspective that we can use in furthering the Understanding of the Medicine of Selves. You see, Little One, obviously the filling, crust and topping are parts, or pieces of the "puzzle" of the Self of the pie. However the pie is not any single one of these things. No, the pie is only the Onement of them, and so are you in a way. Actually, before we start talking about the Who and What it is that you Really Are, lets talk about the What and Who I Really am.

Certainly, there exist many differing stories and ideas about Me. And as you know Me, these stories may or may not be Real or factual. I am not the idea of Beings, as you are well aware. Yet in a sense, I can be considered to be the originator of the idea of everything to begin with. I am a unique persona just like you, or any animal, plant, or stone. Some individuals presently like to consider Me collectively, and I find no great problem with that. But as you know, I am Myself, and in total I am just that. Some individuals might consider Me to be the "All that Is" of which I am certainly a part of, if not even primarily the source. However, just as one might consider the pie to be just the filling, there is not fault in such an idea, only a misrepresentation. As you know, I do think, care, and feel, just like you do Little One. And perhaps the most significant difference between Me and you or anything else for that matter is not just that I have no Bark on Tree or the like. No, it is that I am solely of the ability to Create. Many individuals consider me to be primarily that which I can do, or have done, which is a commonplace practice in the prevalent culture. As you experienced in the development of the material of Origins Little One, in the very beginning I was, and I was the Group Consciousness of all that was. In a sense I still am that. Yet even in that condition of Myself, I was and still am an individual and unique persona and Consciousness as well. Hence in that sense, I can only be considered to be the pie, not just one layer, piece, or part of it. Therefore the reality of the What and Who of Me, can only be considered in the totality of Myself and so also you, you see?"

    With that last statement, I took a bite of that wonderful pie. As I sipped upon the magical elixir, I soon found myself again spiraling backwards in time, or so it seemed. It was just as I had so many times experienced doing in Origins. This time, I found myself back in a room in the Home of The Future that is depicted at the beginning of this material. The room was all white and one wall was missing. Where the wall should have been, there was an opening to The Great Void. It was the same room in which I had previously experienced my Spiritual Birdform being made by Great Pop. This time I watched again as He stood there, lovingly fashioning each of the white feathers of the early Spiritual bodyform He was making for my Spirit to be self-expressive with. I was then given to think about Onement again and how the feathers of a bird's wing must be of Onement for it to be able to fly on Mother Earth. Next I remembered my first expression when Great Pop gave me the ability to make one. It was to make a great squawk-like, "Hey!" I did such at that time in hopes of pleasing Him. I remembered that it had, as when I did such, Great Pop had reeled back in laughter and joy. My success in that first expression made me want to do it much more often, and in many more ways. Hummm, I then thought, as I reviewed this experience of the past. Certainly wanting to please Great Pop is clearly another part of the puzzle of the Who and What I Really am.

    With that realization, I found myself back from that earlier time and again sitting at the table in front of Great Pop. Great Pop was just taking another bite of one of the many treats on that golden platter before us on this wonderful table of Understanding. As I reflected more upon that experience, I watched as Great Pop finished His treat. I then recalled that my desire to serve and please Great Pop is in fact one of the eight things that I most value about being, and being myself. I also remembered that this desire was also described as a part of my Value System that was defined in the exercise that was presented earlier in this material. I then remembered how in the past Great Pop had me use that same exercise in making a Resource Wheel for myself, and at times some others. I found that exercise and Resource Wheel to be an invaluable asset in resolving issues of imbalance. The end product of the exercise and Wheel becomes a description of the pattern of oneself that one can always choose to Renewall to, in a sense. In developing such a Resource Wheel one will regain not only one's balance, but also Proper perspective and self-image. I then recalled that to begin the development of such a tool and asset, one must first identify the eight things that one most values about oneself that was described in the earlier exercise.

    I reflected upon the fact that a while back Great Pop had given me the ability to see and define the Medicine of the four Wills of anyone. I then saw how this becomes even more valuable in a sense, yet is not necessary at all in another, ha, ha, ha!

    As one might suspect, each of these Values and Will definitions do have a specific placement in the diagram of one's Resource Wheel. An example of mine is as follows:

My Resource Wheel

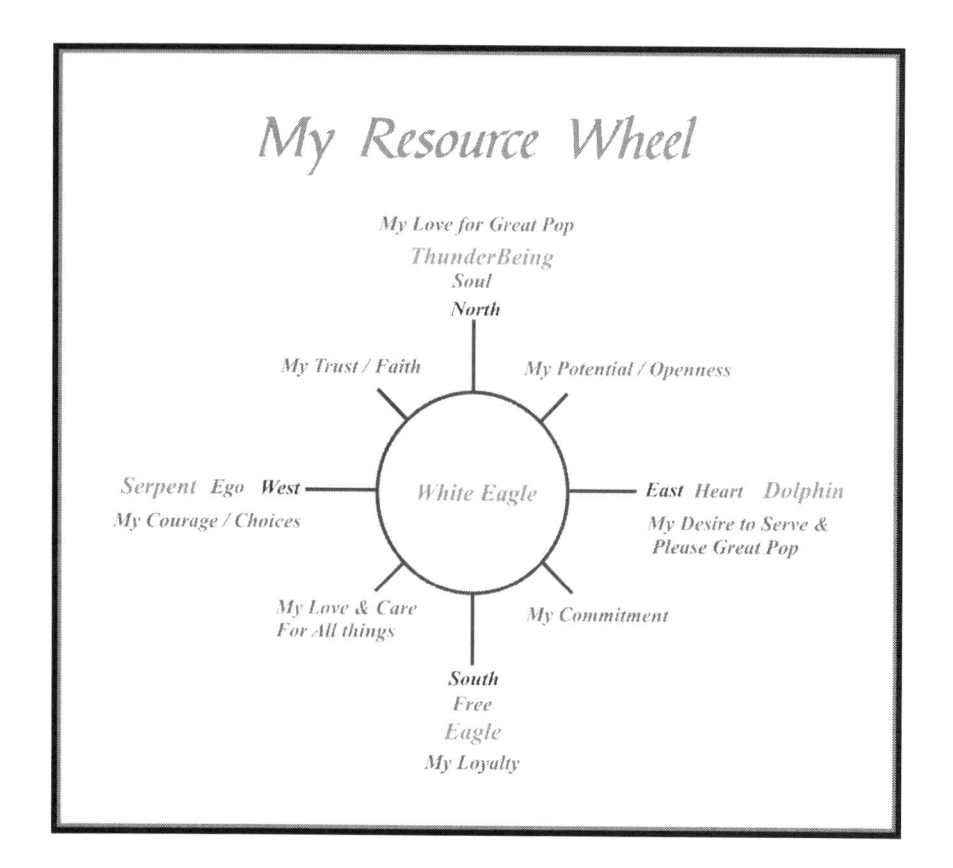

```
                My Love for Great Pop
                   ThunderBeing
                       Soul
                      North

      My Trust / Faith        My Potential / Openness

  Serpent  Ego  West ─── White Eagle ─── East  Heart  Dolphin
  My Courage / Choices                   My Desire to Serve &
                                          Please Great Pop

       My Love & Care         My Commitment
        For All things
                      South
                      Free
                      Eagle
                    My Loyalty
```

The way that this Wheel works is that everything above the East / West axis is Spiritual, and all that is below it is Physical. Everything to the left of the North / South axis is about direction and growth, and that to the right of it is about enlightenment and understanding. Also, there are numbers that are associated with each of my values, and I will explain that part after a while, maybe, ha, ha, ha! The Medicine of my Free Will is that of the Eagle. Therefore what some call Way Finding and Honor, are extremely important considerations in everything that I do that is physical. As one can see, that condition certainly coincides with the Loyalty element of my Value System that is present there as well. As one will now notice in the diagram, my Bark on Tree or Ego in the West is that of the Serpent. This means that I naturally react to issues about danger, direction and growth and such, pretty much the same as a Serpent would. My other two Wills should be pretty much understandable from that explanation as well. Therefore, when I am about any personal expressions, things, or issues regarding my Love and Care for all things, then it is actually a means

Selves – Vol. 1

by which I experience and express physical direction and growth. And when I do such, it is always as a combined expression of both my Free Will in the South and my Ego Will in the West. It also means that I use both Eagle Medicine and Serpent Medicine whenever I am about those kinds of personal expressions. So, one can see that the rest of my expressions, when I am incarnated, operate in a similar fashion as regards these placements of my Value System elements and my Wills.

Needless to say I have found this personal Resource Wheel to be a great asset, not only in understanding the why it is that I might be interested in or might desire certain things over others, but also why certain behaviors in others would at times become problematic to me. It certainly does provide me with a pattern to use to consider myself as being in a sense, where before no such thing was available. Just having and knowing such about myself has made my being in life easier for me in a sense. It also has helped me with regard to self-esteem and acceptance to some degree. That is at least until I walk out the door and into the Need mentality, Fear, willfulness, and wantonness of the prevalent culture. I clearly have no difficulty at all with being and being myself, except for being in the Physical realm, or so it seems, ha, ha, ha! Yep, it seems that most everybody has an idea of Great Pop that is different than the Reality of Him. And oftentimes so also do many people have such different ideas about me, or what they want me to be, including myself. Yet even with this great asset, at this point I am still puzzled with the question of just Who and What am I, Really? It seems to me that if I can find that out then I may be able to resolve many of the issues of being in life on Mother Earth in the present term, I then thought.

Thankfully Great Pop again saved me from myself like He so oftentimes does, by starting again. *"Well Little One, which Self are you considering? Did you know that when you are incarnated, you have four of them to operate with?"*

Well let me tell you, that little bombshell of information sent me spinning. But this time, I did not go anywhere, like back in time or anything. Four Selves? No wonder I am having trouble with this stuff, and myself for that matter, I then thought! Naturally Great Pop heard those thoughts and just sat back in His chair and laughed. He then went on saying, *"Take it easy Little One, it is relatively simple. Actually, you can regard each of the four Selves that one has when incarnated to being a projection or aspect to each of one's Wills in some senses."*

I thought about that for a second and then asked, "Then Great Pop, do we just have two when in True Spirit form, like we do with our Wills?" With that, I got a "Triple Bingo!" in response from Him, which signals that I am correct. Great Pop then continued His explanation. "*Yes Little One, each Being and Thing operates with four Selves when incarnated into the Physical realm and with only two when not. And as you are now wondering, these four Selves might be considered as being the Real Self, a Projected Self, an Imagined Self, and a Cosmic / Communal Self. Of course the somewhat tricky part is that except for that of the Real Self, one can and often does have multiple as well as combined expressions of these.*

Yep Little One, as you are now surmising, the Real Self is always associated to the Soul Will. Also, like the Soul Will, the Real Self is in a sense superlative over the other Selves in every sense and way. Of course the Real Self is the easiest part of the pie of Selves to identify that one considers collectively as being oneself. However, it also becomes the one that becomes the hardest to distinguish from the others when one is incarnated. The Real Self is the core of Self, as one might think of these elements, and all of the other Selves might be considered as being extensions or in association to it in a way. The Real Self is that which one considers as their Being and persona when one is in True Spirit form. It is the Self that returns with and is an integral part of one's Spirit in all cases and conditions. Yes Little One, this is Real and true even when possession occurs, as you are now wondering. You see Little One, in a possession scenario it is not the Real Self that is the part of oneself that is taken over. Nope, possession can only be effected through one or more of the other types of Selves. Of course, as you are now surmising, this restriction is a safeguard that I designed early on and means that possession can only be at best, a temporary condition that is resultant from mutual choice and agreement. As you are now wondering Little One, one's True Value System is held as a sub-Operative component in the inner workings of one's Heart Operative, which is actually a perpetually resident part of one's Real Self as well. And as you are now wondering, one's Consciousness is equally ever present and associated to one's Real Self in the same manner.

Also, just as one has a Free Will as to whether one is incarnated into the Physical realm or not, so also do all Beings and Things have at least one Cosmic / Communal Self. Yep, as you are now thinking, Little One, this type of Self is directly associated to one's Free Will. Thereby all Choice expressions become an aspect of a Cosmic /

Communal Self-expression and experience, including the choice to incarnate or ever leave My Essential Will. It is the Cosmic / Communal Self Little One, which is actually the Self that one makes most of one's personal expressions with and through. And by My design, one actually can have as many of these types of Selves as is desired. Also, a Cosmic / Communal Self can be an outward expression of any of the other three Selves, as well as of the singular Real Self. This means that one can have a Cosmic / Communal Self that is associated directly with one's Real Self, and many that are not."

With that statement Great Pop could tell that I was now getting a little lost. So He took a pause and then asked me to think of the Selves as being different colored balloons. When I finally replied that I had the idea of it pretty much down that way, with a flourish of His hand He produced the following diagram:

The Selves

Consciousness

- Cosmic/Communal Self
- Imagined Self
- Projected Self
- **Real Self**
- Imagined Self
- Projected Self
- Cosmic/Communal Self
- Projected Self
- Cosmic/Communal Self
- Imagined Self
- Projected Self
- Cosmic/Communal Self
- Imagined Self

I took a little while to study this wonderful example of how we are, that Great Pop has provided. The first thing I noticed was that they all looked like different colored balloons, with the Real Self being central to all of the others. I then recognized that one can have a Cosmic / Communal Self that is a direct extension in a way, from the Real Self, as well as more of them that are outward extensions from any other types of Selves too. Then I realized that this capability was the same for the Projected Selves as well as the Imagined Selves. I also was quick to recognize that in Reality all of this is happening inside the greater envelope or bubble that is one's Consciousness, and that it is most definitely a separate element than the Selves. I then was given the idea by you know who, that perhaps this could be correlated to a tree in some way. Great Pop has always told me to be and grow like the tree, and that trees exemplify the Proper "what to be" and "how to grow" in life. As if on cue, with that thought Great Pop then had the previous diagram turn into this:

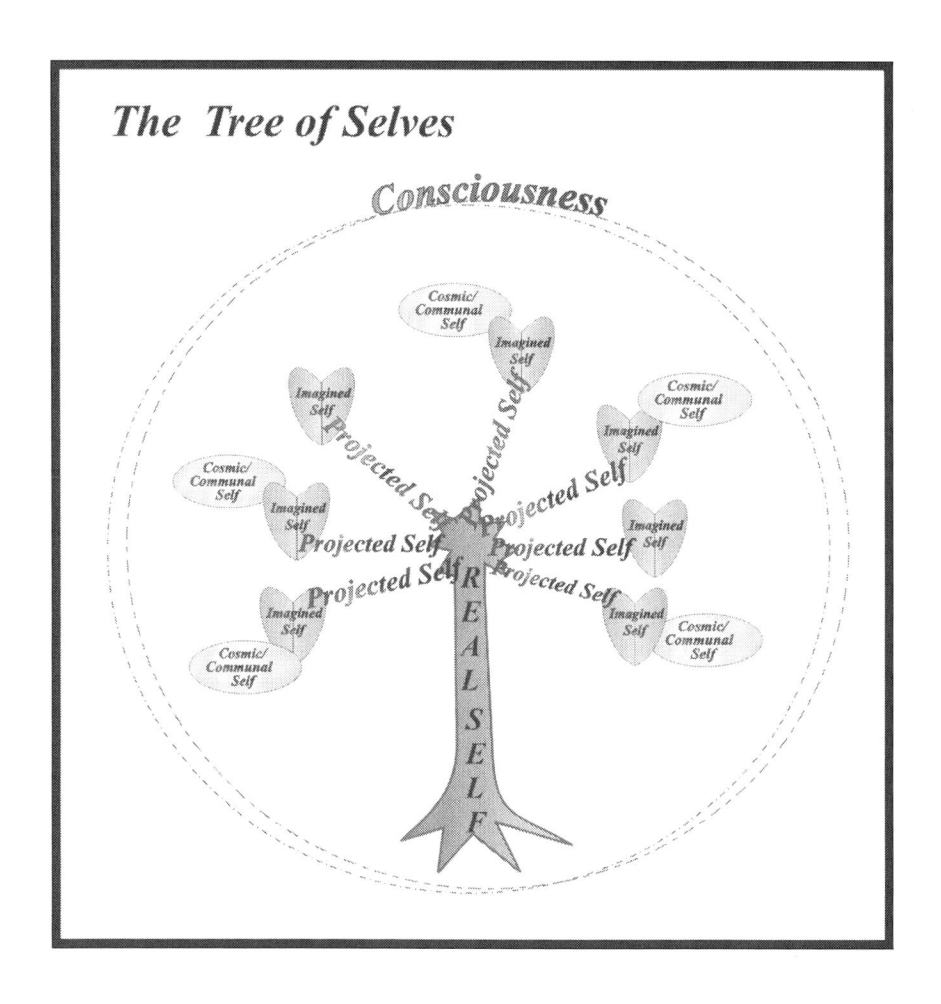

The Tree of Selves

Consciousness

(diagram: a tree labeled REAL SELF as the trunk, with Projected Self branches, Imagined Self leaves, and Cosmic/Communal Self surrounding, all within a Consciousness circle)

He then continued His explanation of the four Selves saying, *"Very good Little One. Triple Bingo on that correlation! Yep, one can in fact consider the Selves as being the parts of a Tree of Self. In such an example the Real Self becomes the trunk of the tree and the Projected Selves become its limbs, or branches. The Imagined Selves in reality are pretty much like the leaves of a tree in that they too provide the necessary ingredients and processes of one's outer personal expressions. Thereby it is one's Imagined Selves that serve to support one's Potential of growth or expression in that manner. And like the falling and Renewall of the leaves of the tree with the seasons of life, so also do all Beings and Things release and replace their Imagined*

Selves from time to time. One may also replace Projected Selves or discard some of them at any time too, just like the tree with its branches. And of course, the Cosmic / Communal Selves then become like the flowers and fruit of the tree. While it is not depicted, there can be and often is the condition of the fruit of a Cosmic / Communal Self that becomes directly expressed from the trunk of the Real Self of the tree. Also Little One, it is in the Cosmic / Communal Selves that all relationships with other Beings and Things occur. Just like I designed the fruit of the tree so as to contain seeds of new beginnings, the Cosmic / Communal Selves bring forth the same Potential to oneself and others."

THE REAL SELF

As I sat there before Great Pop at the beautiful table of Understanding and took another bite of that wonderful pie, I started considering how fortunate that I have been in so very many ways. Before me now was what seemed to be the parts of the puzzle that I had been missing, or at least in some way, was looking for. Perhaps once I understand the inner workings and dynamics of what Great Pop was now sharing with me, at least all of the "What it is" that I am will become clear to me. Great Pop then saved me from myself once more by beginning again.

"Well, Little One, perhaps the easiest place to start is with a more complete explanation and understanding of the Real Self. And as you are now wondering, these four aspects as they might be considered of oneself, are in Reality simply specialized Essence-Operatives. While they appear like Essences in the balloon shapes of the diagrams, they are in fact Essence-Operatives in most senses, like that of one's Perspective. Now that we have that clear let us consider first the condition of being in True Spirit form, as that will be much simpler to start with.

Inside of My Essential Will as you know and have experienced, all of the Potential that are resident there do have a certain kind of form. That is actually where I got the inspiration to make these aspects or elements that you can consider as being parts of oneself from. As you recall from your experience of it in Origins, the Potential at one time were all free-floating about so to speak in The Great Void. They *could move about in their containers of Consciousness and actually maneuver about from point to point within The Great Void. Other than just doing that or spinning about and bumping into each other, there was not much more that they could do at that time and in that condition. Of course that was quite a lot, when one considers the limits of what existed at that point.*

As you know, at that point I knew that it was not perfect yet. So I considered, even before making the offer that resulted in the choice for them to come inside My Essential Will, that I needed to provide a better means by which any Potential could be self-expressive, realized, and aware. And this was whether they were inside or outside of My Essential Will. As you recall, now there are all sorts of forms that Potential can use to be self-expressive with inside My Essential Will and this is the When, as well as method of the Origin of such. You see Little One, early on I knew that not all of the Potential would ever choose to go outside. I was in fact certain that some would remain inside it forever and a day, as you say. And as you also are aware, each and all of the Potential are ever even, in my esteem, Love, and care. So, I felt early on that I had to facilitate a means by which those Potential that were inside of it could have as much ability at making personal expressions and realize certain experiences as those that went outside. That is the reason that the idea of Selves became put on the drawing board so to speak. And as you are now surmising, yes this all happened well before I ever made a single physical thing."

With that statement, Great Pop got up and went into another room while I digested not just the last bite of my piece of pie but also all of that which He had just given for me to Understand. While I sipped on some elixir, I came to the realization of how very much Great Pop had given me in the Understanding of Origins and even before with Possession and the many other "books" that He has had me prepare this way. Yet it seemed that there was so much more that I still had not yet been made aware of to some degree. Certainly this last explanation seems important enough to have been given in the material of Origins, I then thought. I then considered that He probably had already decided that this material would be written subsequent to Origins, and it then all made perfect sense. Upon that conclusion, Great Pop returned carrying Spirit. Spirit is a big white kitty cat that shared a big part of my current sojourn and exited right before Nolayte was born. Knowing that I have missed Spirit so much, Great Pop gave him to me to hold for a while. Tears of joy and Love then streamed down both of our faces, and Spirit cuddled up in my lap as Great Pop continued.

"You see Little One, the idea of Selves actually precluded in a way, My making of the Personal Structure, which did happen pretty much not long after it. That is Why there is a certain amount of commonality or overlapping of these two enabling devices, as they might be considered. I did have part of the Personal Structure design on the drawing board so to speak, when I developed the Selves, and I amended portions of it as the Selves were perfected. This is because I knew that they must share and support each other for optimum effect. Yep, as you are now realizing Little One, that is Why one's Value System is resident in both types of elements as well as several other aspects of Self. Remember here, it is all about supporting personal expression and experiences in some fashion. Each of the Potential inside My Essential Will have two Selves by which to operate, being that of their Real Self and that of a Cosmic / Communal Self. As you are now wondering Little One, these were added, or better stated, applied, all at once. And yes, it was not too long after they all returned inside that this occurred. So even before there was any outside offerings of experience and expression, every Potential inside had a personal makeup that included a Real Self and a Cosmic / Communal Self Essence-Operative by which to experience and express itself with.

The Real Self is what one could consider in a way to be the core or individual persona of a Potential, and thereby of any Being or Thing. Little One, your Real Self is the "You" that is wondering about all of this stuff, ho, ho, ho! You might also consider one's Real Self to be the place that one's Personal Structure is actually resident in. One's Real Self can also be considered as being the seat of one's Consciousness. Also, even though one's Consciousness can be expanded or segmented way outside of the bubble of one's Real Self, it is always connected to it or seated in it, no matter what! One's Real Self Essence-Operative bubble, might be considered to be located in the middle of any and all of one's other Selves as well. And no Little One, one's Real Self can Really not be hurt in any fashion or form. As you are now surmising Little One, one's Real Self bubble has one's Soul Will and Conscience Operatives contained within it at all times. One's Real Self Essence-Operative also maintains linkages to all of one's other Selves at all times. This is especially significant whenever it lets the other Selves range throughout the varying configurations of placements of the other types of Selves. There is no exclusivity to the

Free Will in these matters and it is oftentimes associated to any and all of the Selves that are extant.

As you are wondering Little One, while one always has a Cosmic / Communal Self that is directly associated to one's Free Will, it can be changed or different from time to time, even for a Potential that never ventures outside! And as you are aware, one's Free Will with a selected Cosmic / Communal Self is the only other Will that returns upon exit from an incarnated experience, as does one's Real Self and one's Soul Will. As you are now surmising - Triple Bingo Little One! Each of these elements is in Reality, simply dedicated self-expressive Potential in themselves*

And as you are now wondering Little One, what some call, one's "inner child" is a little different than one's Real Self, which is older and broader in a sense. One's inner child is Really the sense of completeness that is always the condition of one's Real Self. As you are now wondering Little One, one's Real Self is always complete in itself and thereby could be considered as being happy, as well as innocent in most considerations of that word. However, one does at times feel incomplete in a way in it, especially at times whenever one tries to do things or operate outside of the bubble of the Real Self. An example of this might be when you drowned, Little One. Did you not feel complete at that moment after you left your body?"*

After reflecting and remembering that experience again, I replied that I felt extremely complete in every way and sense. Great Pop then responded with, *"That is because in that condition of oneself, you were operating in True Spirit form and thereby pretty much singularly in and as one's Real Self."*

I took another slice of pie upon my plate then, and while considering what Great Pop had just explained to me, I was given to think about another experience that I had quite a long time ago. In a way, it seemed important so I am going to mention it here. The time and event was when I had been working at a new computer company after I had just spent seven years working at NASA. I had joined the new company with the understanding that I would be given the opportunity to function in a marketing capacity as well as being in a position of customer support. This meant that I could be able to increase my income if I were to be able to sell their products as well as operate in service to them. Clearly this was a new idea of myself than what I had been doing before in my computer career and I was anxious to be successful in it. Yet all of my efforts in selling their products through my many associations at NASA were ultimately thwarted by the "King Bee" that was in charge of our division of that little company. Needless to say, I became somewhat disenchanted after a while. Then about that time a new person joined the service department of that group, and we will call him CB. This person had moved down to Texas from Chicago with his wife and did not even try to fit in with the others. He was very arrogant and none of the other people would have anything to do with him. I had known and worked with people from the "North" when at NASA and I just understood that such was the behavioral pattern that was common to their "mini-culture". So I befriended this CB individual to some degree, when no one else would.

By the time I finally left that organization many things had happened. The little company got bought up and merged with another small company, by a larger company. At that point all of the things that I joined the little company for were pretty much lost to me. Also, I had been living together in a deeply committed relationship with a wonderful girl for the five or six years that it took all of that to occur. After finally leaving the now large organization, I did keep in touch with the other people that I had worked with there. Also, from time to time some of them would come down to the Clear Lake area of Texas where I had lived throughout that time and we would meet. I had discovered during some of these meetings that CB had divorced his wife. I also found that he had easily found a job in sales and unlike myself, he was now relatively successful in it. Of course that in itself made my Bark on Tree grow somewhat especially since he now had a boat and other things that I desired but could never afford. Yet the real straw that broke the camel's back came when CB and another friend invited my girlfriend and I to visit them in their room at one of the hotels at NASA. This particular hotel had small swimming pools in some of the rooms and they were in one of those. So, when we went there and walked in as invited, we were both surprised to see that CB and the other fellow were in the pool. The surprise was not so much that they were in there, but that they were naked with two of their "girls". The real affront came when they invited us to join them simply because they wanted my girl as well as their own, with no respect or regard to how we felt about that or each other. Yet, in this prevalent culture, these two individuals were obviously rewarded time and again for just such selfish callousness, wantonness, and Bark on Tree. Needless to say, we both declined their offer and that was the last time that I have had anything to do with CB and the other fellow. The funny thing was that I was not so much angry as I was hurt and insulted over the whole experience, and to some degree I still am.

The reason for the inclusion of this little event in the odyssey of my life is that it does in fact resonate to some degree with what Great Pop had just shared in a way. It seems like all of my experiences in trying to co-operate in this prevalent society or play a part in the "Bee-Hive Game" have resulted in only a lack of respect and failure. I have from time to time wondered how it happens that way and I have even pretty much abandoned the idea of any further participation of myself in it in the most part. Clearly my Real Self is different than those two individuals and most certainly my Value System is. I was then given to consider some of the differences between myself and some of the other people in my life including my Earth Father. Unlike these individuals that seem to covet the things that others have, I never have. I did not want to be with CB's girl, I desired only that of my own. I did not want my Earth Father's money that he coveted so, I only desired to make and have my own, and still do. Certainly such a difference in my Value System did play a major role in my having "gotten rid of" all of the money that was my share of my Earth Father's estate so quickly after he exited.

After a little more reflection on this condition of myself, I then recognized that perhaps a part of my "problem" in operating in the current prevalent society might not be actually some disorder or flaw in myself at all. Perhaps instead it is simply that my Value System, versus that of other more "successful" individuals in the prevalent culture puts me in a somewhat disadvantaged condition in it in some way. Yes, this Real Self stuff that Great Pop is now helping me Understand might be a great help. Actually, it seems to have helped to some degree already. But of course at this point, I am still not totally sure of the Who and What it is that I Really am.

THE PROJECTED SELF

Having come to that realization about my past, Great Pop began His explanation of the Selves again. *"Yes Little One, you are now starting to get the picture. The BIG Picture. As regards the development of the Essence-Operatives of Selves, I had to do some unusual things for the time. First of all, I already had perfected the idea of an Essence-Operative. I had in fact fashioned just such a device so to speak, for Myself earlier, which We will call My Care Essence-Operative. As you remember from your experience of Origins, the first Operative and Potential in a sense, was that of My Care. In its original form, it was just an Operative that The ThunderBeing had fashioned for Me from the Essences of Feeling and Desire to express Essences through to the outside, which He also made happen in that event. Basically, it was a tube or hose in its configuration, or Nature and it was not all that unlike a megaphone when one thinks about it. So, what I then set out to accomplish was to give it and thereby Myself, more flexibility in its use and Potential. What I finally perfected was a device that was in most senses Essential in Nature, but still very much an Operative that would support expressions and thereby direct the Flow of things.*

Actually, one can consider this quality to be the same for one's Real Self as well. In this I mean to say, that in a sense the Essence-Operative of one's Real Self is not all that different than one's Spiritual Body or Emotional Body. Yet one has much more capacity to make outward expressions with it in every sense and way. And of course when I had that little "gem" perfected, I saw how easily it would support a Personal Structure of Operatives and Essences when I set about making them as well. So you see Little One, before I made things, in a sense I first had to make a place to put them, ho, ho, ho.

Also it is important to remember Little One, that when one is in True Spirit form, whether inside My Essential Will or in transit from or to any outer arena of experience, one always has a Cosmic / Communal Self that I will describe in detail a little later. And unlike you are now thinking, the Cosmic / Communal Self was not the second type of Self to be developed. Nope, it was in fact the very last. Actually, all of the things that a Cosmic / Communal Self, as well as any other type can do, was accomplished by the Essence-Operative of the Real Self in the beginning. Yes Little One, the second Self to be developed, as you are now thinking, was indeed that of the Projected

Self. This *Self* was actually developed after I had perfected all of the parts of the *Personal Structure* as described in *Origins*. As you remember, I had done a lot of things in the process of my experimenting around and trying to make the perfect semi-solid for use in bodyforms. Actually, it was the expansion of elements and processes that resulted from that effort which made Me start to consider having more than one *Self Essence-Operative* to operate with, so to speak. As you are now thinking, I had at that point already compartmentalized *Operatives* and saw how much more dynamic such configurations were in any application. So, naturally I decided to see what I could do to develop a more perfect support system for any *Potential* to be self-realized and expressive with.

At that point I had no idea as to the number of *Self Essence-Operatives* that would ultimately be most perfect. However I was certain that there would be definite advantages in having more than one, at least some of the time. As you recall Little One, the first experiment and experience of the original outer "*Physical Arena*" was in a room here that you call the "*Orange Place.*" It was the initial and to some degree physical place and setting for *Potential*, as *Spirits*, to go outside of *My Essential Will* and be self-expressive in. And as you remember, in *Our* first effort at such, things did not at all go well, or at least not as planned."

As I sat there stroking *Spirit*, I took a bite of my new piece of pie and began to reflect upon my experience of that event in *Origins*. The short version of it was that *Great Pop* had made several simple semi-solid objects and such. In appearance they resembled foam-like balls, triangles, stars, and other shapes that could be seen and handled to some degree, or at least, felt. *Great Pop* had placed them in a container of sorts, not unlike a room. He had made the objects out of a semi-solid material that He had perfected at this point. I remembered that He made them for those *Potential* that would choose to go outside of His *Essential Will* and into this place and setting to "play" with. I also remembered that the *Potential* that would first venture outside of His *Essential Will* would become known as the "*Founding Beings*" and in this very first experience they were basically in the appearance of what I call "*Lightforms*". Regardless of their appearance, they were *Beings* none-the-less, because at that point that was the only pattern available for a *Potential* to choose to be outwardly expressive as. I remembered vividly the experience and *The ThunderBeing* was in there in support to all involved, as He so oftentimes is. He was standing in the center of the "room" and

137   *Selves – Vol. 1*

patiently waited for the others to arrive. I then remembered that what happened next was what became the first of what Great Pop calls an "Oops" event.

When the Founding Beings finally did come into the place, which was all orange in color, basically "all hell" broke loose. Instead of playing with the objects and interacting with each other and The ThunderBeing, all were combative and behaving like aggressive bullies and such, in great expressions of Bark on Tree. Each tried to outdo the others in massive expressions of light, which was about all that they had to work with at the time. Fireballs of light were being projected at each other and in all directions. Of course none of them could really be hurt by any of these things, but it was still very unsettling if not downright uncomfortable to say the least! Even so, The ThunderBeing patiently stood His ground in it all and calmly exemplified another behavioral model. Sadly though, none of the others would choose to emulate His example for themselves. By most all standards, it was a complete disaster of sorts. Finally, when they seemed like they had enough, Great Pop called them and they all returned back inside His Essential Will, whereupon He subsequently made the Original "fix" to the problem.

Great Pop then went on with His explanation. *"Yes Little One, that was the way of it in that first endeavor to provide an outer experience for the Potential. In fact, it was because of the review of that first Oops experience that I saw a great advantage in having multiple Self Essence-Operatives when Potential operate outside of My Essential Will. I recognized that there would be a clear advantage to having such a configuration of support, especially when "operating" in what would become the Physical realm. This was spawned by the Oops experience in the sense that I recognized that each of the Founding Beings had chosen a singular Self-expression in that first attempt at such. It was then obvious to Me that having the capacity to manifest more than one Projected Self, in addition to the Real Self, would provide what I was looking for in the way of having more optional expressive means. Hence, in the second attempt of having the Founding Beings go outside again into the arena of the Orange Place, not only was the fix manifested as described in Origins, but also it included the capacity of any and all incarnated Spirits to be able to manifest Projected Selves from the bubble of their Real Self as well. And no Little One, I had not come up with the other two types of Selves yet. At that point a limited version of their capability was pretty much still a function of the Real Self.*

As you remember Little One, the fix had to do with establishing an umbilical-like connective, linking My Heart Will to the Conscience-Operative of any incarnated Spirit when it left My Essential Will. In facilitating the manifestation of Projected Selves, I saw a great advantage in having them all associated to the Heart Will of the Personal Structure of incarnated Potential in all cases. The reason for this particular design and technique is as you are now surmising Little One. Yes, in that design, the Projected Selves would always, in a sense, reflect or be associated to the Value System of any individual Being or Thing in all cases and conditions. And as you are now wondering Little One, the type of energy involved in this design and configuration is that the Real Self embodies a sub-set of Primal Energy with Life Force Energy, and the Projected Self is maintained and actualized by a combination of Life Force and Kinetic Energy."

With that statement, Great Pop took another break in His explanation of Selves while I digested more of what He had just given for me to understand. I felt Spirit now wanting to move, so I handed him lovingly back to Great Pop. Great Pop then took him into another room or something like that, as He soon reappeared without him again. As He sat down again in front of me, I felt compelled to clarify my understanding about this part of the development of Selves.

"So Great Pop, when the first Oops happened, the Founding Beings were operating through their Personal Structures embedded in their Real Self Essence-Operative. And am I correct in assuming that in that condition of themselves, all of the functions that would later become parts of the other Selves, were contained and manifested through that one?" Great Pop then smiled and told me that I was correct. So I started our "Fishing Game" again asking, "Then, am I now correct in assuming that even now, with these other Selves, the Real Self can still do all of those functions and expressions as well?" And with that one, I got another *"Triple Bingo Little One, it is exactly that way,"* from Great Pop. My first thought at His response was that such being the case, one could easily understand the Why it is that the Real Self could be considered superlative over the others, simply because of that condition of it alone. Being successful in catching that "fish", I then tried for another with, "Then Great Pop, in the second attempt of their outer experience of the Orange Place, did each of the Founding Beings actually manifest their presence there as being simply an expression of a Projected Self from their Real Self, in order to do such?"

With that I got another great big smile from Great Pop that confirmed my suspicion, and another "fish" was landed by me. Great Pop then responded with, *"Quite correct indeed Little One, great fishing for you that time. Yes, from that point forward, all Potential have been enabled with just such a device and capacity in the mechanism of being able to manifest Projected Selves so as to enable them to have the experience of something. And, the Projected Self is not limited to just such an activity, or purpose, either. A Projected Self can be manifested by the Heart Will contained within the Real Self not only to experience things, but also to express them. However, in most senses the Projected Selves can only effect and affect oneself singularly. And what I mean to infer here, is that a Projected Self can only effect and affect, oneself to oneself. When you desired, and that is a key to Projected Selves, to become good with computers, the first thing that you had to do to accomplish such, was for you to manifest a "computer person Projected Self" from your Real Self, by which to experience and express oneself as being that. And the same is true for any of the multitude of personal expressions that you make, such as being a Father to Nolayte and so forth. So as you can now see, it is this wonderful idea of Mine in the way of Projected Selves that facilitates a Being or Thing to be of multiple capacities of experience and expression at the same time. That capability was the very reason as well as perfection of its design."*

Again Great Pop paused so that I might more fully comprehend what He had just given me to understand. As I took another bite of my second piece of pie, I considered all of what Great Pop had done. It certainly was brilliant, especially considering what He had to work with! Remembering that first and foremost in His intent, is to provide to any and all Potential that desire such for themselves, as much as possible what He enjoys in and of Himself, it all became clearer to me. His goal if there could be said to be one, was for any and all Potential to be able to flourish as it were, in being self-expressive, self-aware, self-determining and so forth. This is His agenda so it seems, at all times, and in all circumstances. That is Why He has worked so hard at developing all of the multitude of things that He has created. In a sense, His Passion to do such was not driven so as to be of that purpose in and for Himself. No, it was so that we, meaning the All of the Potential, could have the capabilities that we do now enjoy and seemingly so often take for granted.

Just consider the very ability to be more than one thing at a time, much less do multiple expressions in them as well. I am a father, albeit in most senses estranged to my children. At the same time, I could be considered to be a writer as well as a PohTikaWah and so many other "identities" that might be considered about myself, depending upon one's own perspective. Yep, this Projected Self is truly a great device and design.

When I came to that realization, Great Pop then continued with, *"Yes Little One, you are now starting to understand the How and Why, as well as the When of the development of the Projected Selves Essence-Operatives. It is the Projected Self that allows for an incarnated Being or Thing to have multiple images or expressions at any single moment. And as I see that you are beginning to now better understand, these Essence-Operatives are outward projections of the Real Self, much like the example of being limbs on a tree. The Real Self can do anything that a Projected Self can do, as well as any of the other two types. However, it can only do them singularly, meaning one at a time. Therefore, the advantage provided by having Projected Selves is being able to be of many capacities and expressions simultaneously at times. As you are now wondering Little One, it is the Personal Structure in the Real Self that actually is used to make the decisions and choices to manifest one or more Projected Selves. Also, when no longer of use, such as in the process of transition back to My Essential Will, these Projected Selves are basically absorbed back into the Real Self in a sense. Of course there may be many of these Projected Selves manifested and then withdrawn so to speak, during any single day or incarnated experience. Also, the Projected Selves can in fact express Care, motives, Desire Prayers, and any other types of expressions from any or all four Wills as well."*

After a short pause, Great Pop continued saying, *"And as you are now surmising, yes, Little One. These Projected Selves and the Real Self are associated to, as well as enveloped within, the protective display case so to speak, of the Emotional Body of an incarnated Being or Thing. Also, the Projected Selves are always outward expressions of the Real Self, meaning that when incarnated, such as depicted in the two illustrations, Projected Selves can have other Selves associated or expressed from them. However a Projected Self cannot be expressed from any other type of Self other than the Real Self. Also as a part of My design and intent, any and all expressions or what some might call responses, that are generated through a Projected Self, can only be realized back to the Real Self that it is attached to.*

This means that while a Projected Self can issue forth Prayers of Desire and so forth, spinning off into the Sea of Creation, they are not interactive by any means. Therefore, any Projected Self is only felt by and can be only affected and effected by oneself, and not someone else. Also, one can and does operate within them in the way of having one's Consciousness focused to act as being inside one of these Projected Selves from time to time and can do such in the singular or collective sense. When this happens one is still singularly involved, or what might be considered as being alone in it. As we discussed earlier Little One, all Projected Selves are directly associated to the Heart Operative within the Real Self bubble. Thereby all Projected Selves are always and in all ways reflective and expressive of the Value System of an incarnated Being or Thing."

THE IMAGINED SELF

Seemingly satisfied that I now had a relatively complete understanding of the Projected Self, Great Pop sat back again after placing another piece of pie on my now clean plate. It was at this point that I realized perhaps more fully the great significance in what Great Pop was sharing. This is because I do now feel that this information will ultimately help me and any others to be better equipped in an Earthwalk experience. Certainly this understanding will not only help me be able to more easily and quickly regain my balance in tenuous situations, it can perhaps keep me from getting into some of them altogether! Clearly, it will help me be better able to function in the prevalent society, even if I choose to remain somewhat detached from many of those in it. Also, it definitely helps me understand what has happened to me in my current sojourn to a large extent, and has taken many of the barriers and question marks out of my Potential in most every sense and way. At this point I started to consider my current self-image when Great Pop began again.

"Yes Little One, the whole purpose of presenting this understanding is to help you and others to become better able to enjoy a sojourn outside of My Essential Will. Also, I see that you are now quite complete in your understanding of the functional aspects of the Real and Projected Selves. Yes, when I made the fix that included the ability of using Projected Self Essence-Operatives and the Founding

Beings went back into the Orange Place for a second try, all went extremely well as you recall. At that point, each of the Founding Beings was enabled with this new Self, and it did not take long for all to become quite masterful in its many capacities and uses. Actually, with only a few minor amendments it has remained relatively the same as it was at that time and event. As you recall, there were not very many things to do outside of My Essential Will at that point. As you also remember, at that time I had already made many successful Spiritual Arenas that were even more sophisticated than this "primitive" first physical one. As you experienced in Origins, the additional Selves were not necessary at all for complete fulfillment in these earlier "inner" places and opportunities. With the success that was quickly realized in the Projected Self in the first "outer" arena of the Orange Place, I began to consider the advantage of having more types like it for use in certain instances, in some of the more complex arenas yet to come. You see Little One, I realized that the more that I could enable any Potential, especially in an outer experience, the more things I could make for them to experience and do."

With that statement, Great Pop then paused for a moment as He took another one of the little cakes for Himself and began eating it. While He ate His treat, I was given to remember one of my experiences in one of the many Spiritual Arenas that Great Pop had fashioned that is described in Origins. These Spiritual Arenas were the first theme parks as it were, that He made for Potential to experience being outside of His Essential Will, and while there is substance in them, it is not totally physical. I might mention that all of these Spiritual Arenas have unique themes that help Potential develop in a way. In this I mean to say that each of the early arenas that one goes into so as to have an outer experience, is developed in such a way so as to prepare oneself to then be able to function in the next more sophisticated ones. In this particular Spiritual Arena, one feels like a complete self and the theme has to do with being a part of or joining. The environment or setting of this arena is something like a sky over a pool or ocean of water. The Water Place as I like to call it, is really neat.

One starts out in this arena being like some moisture in the atmosphere and one gets a sense of, and develops resonance with the Consciousness of that. In a sense one is amorphous in form, and now through understanding more about the Selves I am certain that one is in fact operating as one's Real Self, with an amendable semi-solid-like Spiritual bodyform. When one chooses to take the next step in the experience of this arena, one then experiences what it is like to merge or condense into a single droplet of water. Certainly it is pretty easy to recognize the exemplification and experience of Onement in this state and condition. Anyway, one is now a droplet of moisture hanging out in the atmosphere until one decides to take the next step, which is to then fall like rain into the pool of water below. Throughout the processes or steps of each of these arenas one does in fact realize many different things, such as how to develop more resonance and capacity, in the sense of being able to resonate with Rain and so forth. Of course I was still a Being in the reality of my Real Self, but in that condition I got to experience what it was like to be Rain also. By design, the offering of experiences in any single arena continues as far as one chooses to go in them, such as the event of the impact of the droplet of self and the surface of the pool, and on, and on, and on....

Just as I recognized that what I had just described was also another example of "getting in Medicine with" something, Great Pop again interrupted my thoughts, saying, "*Yes Little One, it was the success of the different experiences that were presently available in the Spiritual Arenas that inspired and orientated My next development, which was another Self Essence-Operative. I really liked the resulting capacity of multiplicity that the Projected Self provided to the Real Self. From the success of the Projected Self, I decided to expand that type of capacity even further in a way. I knew that to do such would not only make any singular experience more dynamic, but also it would facilitate the development of more complex arenas in which to expand one's capacities and Potential in. And as you are now wondering, this development occurred even before I had made the Structure of the Physical realm, which is also described in Origins, ho, ho, ho.*"

As I then had another great realization come over me, Great Pop smiled warmly at me. "Wowie," I then thought, as I remembered what the Structure of the Physical realm looked like. The vanes that divide the arenas of the Structure of the Physical realm are wedge shaped dividers that are arranged about the perimeter of a tube-like core. My great revelation was that this configuration and design was almost identical to the limbs of a tree, just like the illustration of the Projected Selves on the Tree of Self depicts! At the point that Great Pop made the Structure of the Physical realm, He had already made the mega-multitude of bodyforms that were to be used in it. This meant that in one sitting, Great Pop had made a prototype pattern of any and every thing that could ever be fashioned out of semi-solid material, including the things that can be considered to be solid acting, such as the stuff in the Physical realm.

With my realization, Great Pop again continued His explanation. "*Actually Little One, in the time line of these developments I had the design of Selves on the drawing board or partially developed, even before I made the mega-multitude of bodyforms. It was the expanded capacity of utility and expression that I saw could be realized in these new elements of Selves that also expanded what I could consider in the making of each of them. As you remember, I pretty much acted out the Potential experience of each one as I fashioned them. Of course it was the design that I had already pretty much perfected in the Essence-Operatives of Selves that allowed for Me to do such in that manner and way. Also, when I made the bodyforms for The ThunderBeing and I, My design of Selves was already complete in the most part. As you are now surmising Little One, The ThunderBeing was the test model for each and all of them and He still uses them at times, just as you do! Of course, I have no personal need of them at all.*

So when the success of the Projected Self was realized, My next move was to make another Self for incarnated Beings and Things to use with it, which We will call the Imagined Self Essence-Operative. Unlike the Projected Self, I saw greater Potential in making this type of Essence-Operative to be "free floating," as it were. In this I mean to say that only the Real Self can make a Projected Self, and basically it is an extruded bubble that is projected from the core of itself. I saw that a greater function and multiplicity could be realized if I made this next Self to be capable of being projected from a Projected Self as well as one's Real Self. I then expanded that concept so that perhaps it could even be projected from parts of another Being or Thing. I quickly recognized that by making this new element operate in that capacity, certainly the dynamics of effects of such would be exponential. And of course the Potential increases even more dramatically when one allows for the manifestation of limitless numbers of these new Self Essence-Operatives from any one source. So at that point, all I had to do was decide which Will I would have it associated to.

Remember here Little One, the primary purpose and function in having these elements is to support outer personal expressions in a way, and thereby facilitate the Flow of something. In a sense, what I was striving for here was a manner or way to facilitate Beings and Things to play or experience any other type of self-expression, where without them all they could do is watch. Yes Little One, as you are now surmising, it is this new Essence-Operative in the way of the Imagined Self that allows for any Being or Thing to be co-creative to some extent. In the incarnated condition the Imagined Self is what facilitates the capability for any Being or Thing to be a "doer" so to speak. Of course that specific intent in its design and function automatically aligned it to operate with and through one's Ego Will."

I took another bite of pie and considered what Great Pop had just shared with me. My first reaction was to try not to be overwhelmed by it all. Naturally, I also had to try to re-think some of the notions that I have had about my Bark on Tree. Here it was again it seemed, that wily rascal that I have so much difficulty with at times on Mother Earth. Some of the time I even wish that Great Pop had never made it, as it oftentimes gives me so much difficulty.

Yep, my Bark on Tree! Because of its Nature and its pseudo-Essence of Fear, it alone is what makes me worry about any and everything. It is also what makes me want to compete. And in this I do not mean to play, but to "have or need to" win. It is what motivates me into conditions and circumstances and then it takes over my Emotional Body and does all it can to make me loose Perspective. My Bark on Tree is also what makes me angry or upset, and that makes me mad just to think about it, ha, ha, ha! It seems that my Bark on Tree always tries to take control over the very life and Essence of my Being. It seems to like to do this at all times, and really becomes problematic when I get tired. Of course, then it can keep me from sleep. If there is nothing else about myself that I am certain of at this point, one thing for sure is that I Really hate my Bark on Tree. Of course because of it, then I hate myself for hating it!

Great Pop just laughed on that last thought. *"Come on Little One, it is not all that bad! Actually, your Bark on Tree is what facilitates you to do the many things that you like to do as well. And as you know, by My design it is involved in each and every physical expression that you make, no matter what. I designed that part of the Personal Structure so as to protect the physical form. And in most instances, it is perfect in that. Of course when you get out of balance to it, it can cause difficulty at times. Yet, that is perfect in its design too. It is because of My design of it that one's capacity of self-determination and self-awareness is enhanced dynamically. Certainly you would not Really want to miss out of every aspect of its Potential and function. An important part of its job so to speak, is to cause self-awareness.*

Selves – Vol. 1

And as you know, no other element does it as well and perhaps as often as that one, ho, ho, ho."

It did not take long for Great Pop's message and intent to sink in. After a short pause, He continued. *"Yes Little One, the Imagined Self idea was a great excitement to me. In a way it opened many doors to other possibilities in an almost limitless fashion. As you are now realizing, it is actually an Imagined Self that does the opening or closing as well as any movement at all, of any and every single thing in one's outer expression and experience in the Physical realm. It is an Imagined Self that speaks, walks, moves things around, or does any of the things in a sojourn that one would describe as physical activity. From this condition, you now can see Why and How the association to one's Ego Will is most perfect for it. One's Imagined Selves might well be considered as being the active Self in a sense. That is because all physical activity is realized as an expression of one or more of these in some way. This includes the growing of hair, the healing of wounds, the throwing of a ball, or even the eating of food.*

In your earlier time when you were of the desire to be a computer person, you had to issue forth a Projected Self so as to become that. One could, in a sense, consider yourself complete when you manifested that Projected Self. In this I mean that at that point you were in part, a computer orientated or interested Projected Self of your Real PohTikaWah Self. In that condition of Self you could be called a computer person, however you could not do any of a thing at all with a computer! To be able to do anything with a computer, you had to subsequently express from either your Real Self or that computer person Projected Self, one or more Imagined Selves to accomplish such action with. Nope, without one or more of these new Selves with which to do such, no buttons could be pushed or code could become written on paper at all.

As most of what happens in the Physical realm is done with respect to, or the use of Kinetic Energy, I designed this new Operative-Essence so as to be fashioned and expressed from either a Real Self or Projected Self as a pattern made from Thought and Kinetic Energy. In the same manner as with a Projected Self, these Imagined Self extensions of the Real Self or Projected Selves, are absorbed into their point of origin when deemed to be no longer of use. It is also of my design that any Being or Thing can manifest Imagined Selves about other Beings or Things. Of course just because one is manifested by another Being or Thing about oneself, one does not have to accept or use it. I made such possible to stimulate as well as facilitate interaction if chosen, between multiple incarnated Beings and Things. I realized that by doing such, within a single incarnation all would have many more possibilities of experience and expression than just those manifested by the singular desires of one individual. And no, this does not compromise any individual's self-determination and thereby Free Will, in fact it dynamically enhances it in each and every way."

THE COSMIC / COMMUNAL SELF

I could tell that Great Pop was again taking a break at this point so as to see what my response would be. So I paused for a moment and took another sip of that wonderful aromatic elixir. Finally, I decided to take my turn in the discussion at this point with, "Great Pop, your explanation has sure cleared up many things for me. However, with this latest addition of the Imagined Self being associated to the Ego Will and expressed from Projected Selves or one's Real Self, at least from where I sit it certainly seems like it could get real complicated. Am I correct in stating that any Being or Thing can issue forth an Imagined Self that is primarily about another Being or Thing, such as their idea, expectation, or desire of them? And if so, can that Imagined Self then become attached to and operative by that other Being or Thing, even though it was not its own idea or manifestation to begin with?"

And so to begin playing our "Fishing Game" again, Great Pop just gave me a smile and simply answered, *"Yep."*

Sensing that the game was on again, I threw out another "bait". "So then Great Pop, if I saw a pretty girl walking down the street in front of me, I could in Reality make up an Imagined Self about her including even what it might be like for me to be with her in a relationship of sorts?" Once again, I got a simple "Yep" response from Great Pop. I then cast out another bait saying, "Then if I were to go up and begin talking with her, that Imagined Self bubble so to speak, that I had manifested from either one of my Projected Selves, such as being a Don Juan or the like, or one from my Real Self, could in Reality and fact become totally transferred to her and no longer be a part of myself?" Again, Great Pop gave me a simple positive response and added that it could, only if it was of her Free Will choice to have that occur. "Wowie," I thought, "that Really could become a problem in Self-management at times!"

I then paused for a bit and considered just how many times in my current sojourn that I personally have projected an Imagined Self on another Being or Thing, or have had another person do it to me. I realized that my parents had done it to me many times and in many ways, as had several other people that I either trusted or desired to be in some condition of relationship with. I was then given to think about my childhood. When I entered school, my mother and my dad oftentimes told me how smart they thought I was and thereby obviously manifested one of these transference types of Imagined Self patterns about me. In hindsight I guess that I accepted one of their Imagined Self patterns as a Free Will choice, as Great Pop said could occur. However hard I tried to live up to the expectations of that Imagined Self from my parents, I never was a good student. Actually, I never brought home more than two "A's" on any report card no matter how hard I tried. And of course my Bark on Tree used to beat me up a lot over just that issue by making me feel like a failure, or less valuable and so forth. Now I clearly understand how my life and Self-image has been deeply effected simply because of this transferred Imagined Self pattern that my mom and dad fostered, and I accepted and tried to live up to, or realize, in some way. In fact I do now believe that it is most likely the reason that I did not finish college, simply because that was the Self that I continued to use to go to school with!

At that realization, I was given to think about Jack again. I realized immediately that one of the most positive things about our relationship was that such a condition of transference of an Imagined Self was not the case between us at all. Then I again considered how one's Bark on Tree could Really play havoc in its use of such a device and opportunity.

With that realization, I began fishing again with, "Great Pop please let me see if I am now correct in my understanding about this new Imagined Self. Are they sort of like the fingers of my hand whereby to use them, I must first do something in my arm? And, are they always retracted into a Projected Self before it is also retracted, so to speak?"

Proudly, I received a *"Triple Bingo Little One, a perfect analogy,"* from Great Pop. He then continued His explanation of His masterful design of Selves saying, *"Of course, that is excepting the condition that the Imagined Self was issued from one's Real Self, which in that* case, it is retracted into the Real Self when no longer desired or of use. Also in the condition of the transference of an Imagined Self between Beings or Things, the recipient in all cases manifests a Projected Self from their Real Self that the transferred Imagined Self becomes associated with and operative through. Also, at the point of transference, meaning acceptance by the recipient, the transfer is complete and thus the Imagined Self no longer has any attachment to its originator. Of course, when no longer desired, the transferred Imagined Self is essentially absorbed within the Projected Self that was manifested to facilitate its use. And subsequently that Projected Self is optionally then also absorbed into the Real Self of the recipient when the experience is complete. And yes Little One, any transferred Imagined Self can be the enabling mechanism that is sometimes misused in the way of Witchcraft or Possession. Ah, now I see that you fully Understand the remedial techniques and processes that I have provided you for dealing with both. Good for you, Little One.

Remember here, Little One, Imagined and Projected Selves are only applicable when incarnated into the Physical realm. Also it is an Imagined Self by which any physical thing is accomplished at all, and they are comprised of Thought and Kinetic Energy in the most part. Therefore, when an individual makes their exit from any arena in the Physical realm, the Thought and Kinetic portion and pattern of these Essence-Operatives, be they previously absorbed from an earlier expression or remaining from the last one, is left behind with the cocoon of the physical body. And of course this is very easily accomplished simply because they are associated to those parts of the Personal Structure that are sloughed off. Yep, the Projected Selves are absorbed in Transition, and the Imagined Selves are sloughed off during that process. Real neat and tidy wouldn't you say, Little One?"

Brilliant was the only word that came to mind as I reflected upon what Great Pop had just shared with me. Sensing that I now had a relatively complete picture as it were of the Imagined Selves, Great Pop then started expanding that Understanding again with, *"Yes Little One, the Imagined Self was really a great and perfect addition and development. And as you now understand, it enabled all kinds of personal expressions for any and all of the outwardly expressive Potential. However, I soon realized that something seemed to be missing and it was not too long before I realized exactly what it was. As you recall, all of the earlier Spiritual Arenas were pretty much orientated towards singular or personal development and expressions. Naturally, I had desired and envisioned many more places where more interaction could take place. I also knew that great personal and collective expansion and growth could be realized if I were to provide such. At this point, the three Selves were in operation and they operated perfectly. Yet one could not do anything except by and for oneself in them, even with the transference feature and capability of the Imagined Self.*

Yes, at this point any individual Being or Thing that chose to go into any of the Spiritual Arenas or the arenas that were the earlier offering of the Physical realm, could do such and enjoy personal experiences and expressions in them. However, they were in a sense always alone in them. Actually, all of these things worked well, extremely well in fact. But I wanted more, much, much more. I had successfully developed both the places and means by which any Potential could be outwardly expressive of My Essential Will with as much of the capability that I enjoy, as possible. I could continue to implement new theme parks in both the Spiritual and Physical realms that would continue to satisfy new individual adventures, experiences, and expressions. Now I wanted to do the same for any and all Potential, both individually and collectively.

It was at this juncture so to speak that I considered the addition of one more Self. This new Self would enable and support much more interaction between individual Beings and Things, and it was basically as simple of a motive as that. In the Imagined Self design, I had realized much in the way of increasing the potential of multiplicity of experiences and expressions. Therefore, I naturally deemed this expansiveness or multiplicity, to be one of the necessary qualities of this new Self as well. Also, I recognized early on that the only means by which these Self Essence-Operatives were of any use at all was to have them associated to one or more of one's Wills in the design of the Personal Structure. This is because the whole purpose of having any of the Self elements was for any Potential to be able to express something back and forth through them to that which was outside of themselves. Actually, I could have associated one or more of the Selves to one's Care Essence-Operative. However through attempting such, I found early on that this type of joining of Essence-Operatives was not such a good configuration. Actually I learned early on that Essence-Operatives function better when associated to an Operative than any other type of element. In this I mean to say that if you think that you have difficulty managing this relatively simplified version of Selves and one's Wills at times, consider having a potentially continually expanding condition of Essence-Operatives. The potential condition and effect of such a design and configuration would be much like trying to manage multiple snowballs, that continue to make even more snowballs while rolling down several steep and long hills, and trying to keep them from causing an avalanche of such.

Nope, not such a good idea in having Essence-Operatives configured that way I realized, both early on, and rather quickly I might add. Therefore in keeping with what was working perfectly already, I realized that there was only one Will left open for consideration or use, being that of the Free Will. Having its targeted associative element already defined, I considered then what exactly all could be included or expressed in or through it in the way of experiences and expressions. "Not alone", I kept thinking to Myself at that time. Certainly, that Really was what I desired to accomplish in the inclusion of such a new element and Potential. As you are now wondering Little One, that is also why I call it the Cosmic / Communal Self. Simply because that was the purpose and potential fulfillment in it that I was looking for. And Yes Little One, I did in fact recognize at this point that this new element would be associated to one of the two Wills that would return inside My Essential Will in Transition, being that of the Free Will. Therefore, since that would be the condition of it, there were many dynamics to consider in its potential as far as its development and use. Yep, I had the singular Real Self returning inside with its associated Soul Will, and now I had to choose whether or not to allow one or more of these new types of Selves to return with the Free Will as well.

Prior to the addition of this new Self, a Potential Being or Thing simply manifested a Projected Self with which to use to incarnate into the Physical realm. In most senses it was like manifesting a foot or hand with which to open the door and the elevator took care of things from there. Not that there were any problems in that approach, I did recognize that this could be a function of the next new Self amongst other things. Of course that is if I allowed at least one of them to return inside and always remain associated to the Free Will of a Being or Thing. It was then that I considered that if I were to have a "Primary" Cosmic / Communal Self that would always be associated with the Free Will of a Potential, like the Real Self was to their Soul Will, the configuration would be perfect. This is especially so if the Primary Cosmic / Communal Self would in a sense oversee or manage any and all other Cosmic / Communal Selves that were manifested. Of course the Free Will would manifest any additional Cosmic / Communal Selves, but the Primary one would be established with the

Real Self and remain associated to it and Free Will perpetually.

Once I had finally decided to allow this new type of Self to return inside my Essential Will, I recognized that this new Self could not have Kinetic energy as part of its composition, as you are now surmising. Very good, Little One! While Kinetic energy was not to be any part of its makeup, I did see how Thought energy was perfect for it, as well as what I call a subset of Memory energy that is not unlike that of Time. Yep Little One, since all Thought energy reverts to Memory energy in time, this new Self would naturally do its own cleaning up of itself as it were. And no, as you are now wondering, I did not consider using Life Force energy at all. As you can see Little One, this very selection of the type of energy to be used in this new Self was a real special and significant part of the project. Also, a great new opportunity became evident. You see, by making these new Essence-Operatives from Thought and Memory energy alone, one could have all kinds of different configurations of them multidimensionally, and not have to keep track of them all of the time."

My first thought about what Great Pop had just explained was, "Wow, a super increase of flexibility and utility indeed." I then started to realize that in fact, I do not keep track of Things or Beings that I am in relationship with, not like in the way I constantly seem to inventory my Imagined and Projected Selves. Actually, these Relationship Cosmic / Communal Selves seem to take on a Life of their own in a way. They certainly do not need constant focus; at least the better ones like I had with Jack do not. I do spend energy, time, and focus when I am with another Being or Thing in them. I might even at times do things as expressions in them when we are not together. But still, that is Really because of my choice to do such, and not because of a need by another individual Being or Thing in them. Also I can feel as well as understand now how any of my Cosmic / Communal Self Essence-Operatives will continue to maintain itself with no requirement for me to do anything at all.

And as soon as I had come to that realization, Great Pop began again saying, *"Also Little One, this design of the Cosmic / Communal Self is what gives cause to the condition that when one is no longer actively involved with another individual Being or Thing, the memory of the involvement remains. It is also Why one is no longer encumbered by any need of any type of energy from oneself to maintain it. Because of this makeup of their design, these new "Relationship" Essence-Operatives become in a sense, everlasting, and can exist within one, no matter what happens.*

Yes Little One, as another part of their design, when one no longer chooses to be connected to another Being or Thing in any type of relationship, these new Selves are not absorbed like is the condition of one's Projected Selves. Instead of being absorbed, these new Selves are sloughed off like the unnecessary parts of an incarnated Being or Thing's Personal Structure in Transition. Yes Little One, the Memory energy of the experience of all relationships remains in the Emotional Body, but the element of the Cosmic / Communal Self no longer is extant. Yep, this occurs just like in the process of Transition, except this can occur throughout an incarnated experience. If chosen, the memory of one or more of one's Cosmic / Communal Selves will stay embodied within one's Emotional Body when one returns from any outer experience.

Little One, just such a condition is your relationship with Jack, as well as Nolayte, your other children, your parents, and so forth. And even though some of those individuals that you shared a Cosmic / Communal Self with are no longer present on Mother Earth, they are ever connected to your Real Self that way. And this will continue to be so, as long as you individually choose for that to be. So in a sense this new type of Self has a reality as well as a potentially perpetual existence, all of its own!

As I had achieved a great expansion in regards to the possibilities by having the Imagined Selves operate in multiplicity, I chose to take this new Self even a step further in a way. In this regard, I mean to say that not only could a Cosmic / Communal Self be expressed by one's Free Will from one's Real Self or a Projected Self, they also could become expressed from any Imagined Self as well. And yep, I do mean even one that is transferred from another individual Being or Thing, as discussed before. And remember, one's Primary Cosmic / Communal Self is continually monitoring and managing all of the others, all of the time, and one's Free Will is always in charge of it.

As an example of how the Cosmic / Communal Self works Little One, is that as you are walking along you see the girl that you mentioned earlier. At that point, you make an Imagined Self as relates to being in some type of relationship with her. You then essentially orientated the focus of your perspective and consciousness into that Imagined Self. Of course you simultaneously have your focus and consciousness operating in several other Imagined Selves just to be able to walk or even speak to her. At that point your Imagined Selves, including this new one that you call Don Juan, collectively facilitate you to begin introducing yourself. At that point, she may or may not also make an Imagined Self in regards to being in some type of relationship with you as well. If she does make one as well, then via the vehicle of the Free Wills of both individuals, a Cosmic / Communal Self Essence-Operative Self bubble is manifested from the new Imagined Selves of both you and her. So at this point each of you have a Real Self bubble with an Imagined Self bubble associated to it via a Projected Self bubble, or not, about the other person. Also, each of you have a Cosmic / Communal Self bubble associated to that Imagined Self bubble.

Now the really tricky part of this design kicks in. At some point, if there is a resonance felt between both you and her as being like-in-kind, then both can choose to share a portion of their Cosmic / Communal bubble with the other person, or not. And if there does then exist resonant sharing, you have a relationship condition like you enjoyed with Jack. Of course if there is not, then you have some other kind of condition including perhaps some of those that are considered as being one-sided relationships. The real key to Cosmic / Communal Selves is that they are profoundly Essential in Nature and thereby one has a limitless potential of possible experiences and expressions available in them. However, a greater potential will be realized from one's participation in a Cosmic / Communal Self that is shared, meaning when one is not alone in it.

As designed, unlike the others, Cosmic / Communal Self Essence-Operatives operate both in the individual as well as group or collective consciousness sense. This means that you have a Cosmic / Communal Self that is a part of your Life when you are by yourself. You have another one that is a part of your and Nolayte's Life, another that involves you and the church and tribe, and on, and on, and on... In Group Consciousness or collective sense, you have a Cosmic / Communal Self bubble that involves you and the collective of all individual Beings that are considered to be humankind. Actually Little One, you have a Cosmic / Communal Self that is shared with your automobile, another with your Rattle, another with your writing machine, and a collective one that includes all of the many different things about your home. And while these may seem like different relationships than one might enjoy with a person or such, they are identical Cosmic / Communal Selves in every sense and way.

Needless to say, you can now realize that this perfect design of the new Cosmic / Communal Self opened up all kinds of doors of limitless possibilities of experience and expression in relationships for Potential when incarnated. And as mentioned, in the process of

Transition, excepting the Primary one, those that are remaining merge with the Emotional Body and thereby also one's Real Self. And finally, Yes Little One, the functioning of the Cosmic / Communal Self originally was and still is, a capability of the Real Self. However, since it is limited to being operative mostly in the singular sense, I chose to include the return of the Primary Cosmic / Communal Self as well, upon exit."

PART IV

NOW

IN REVIEW

    At that point, Great Pop sensed that I was pretty full, and I was not just full of pie either. In His usual all-knowing way, Great Pop once again arose from that wonderful table of Understanding so as to allow me to assimilate and digest what I had just been given. When He came back, I began our Fishing Game again with, "Gee, Great Pop, It seems to me now that the answer to my question is a very complex one. Obviously, I am my Personal Structure to some extent. Yet except for the contents of some of the elements like one's Value System in it, every Being and Thing has one and they are pretty much the same. I guess that one could say that I am my Bark on Tree. And clearly at times it seems like that is all that I am, or that I can deal with. I do realize that this is one of the many different elements of that Personal Structure. Yet I cannot be just that, especially since it is one of the elements that will be left behind with my body when I finish my walk on Mother Earth in the current term. I guess that it could be said that I am my Value System as well as my Procedural Data Bank and so forth in my Personal Structure. Still, I do not feel that is what makes me Who and What I Really am in total.

    Actually, it seems more like I am my Resource Wheel, especially in the sense that such are the things that I care about and primarily use and operate with. It seems like I am these things as well as some others, but I still sense that there is more to me than just that. Clearly I am my Wills, as well as some configuration of the four Selves that You just mentioned. Obviously I do have these elements about me, and I have them about me no matter what my condition is, or is in. I also know that I am a unique blend of Essences. I do realize that my unique blend of Essences has some mix of Eagle, White, and ThunderBeing Medicine. I am also most certain that I am a consciousness. And even though I am not so sure of my Potential at times, I can see how I could be considered to be an outwardly expressive Potential as well. I could be said to be a Being versus some other type of Spirit or Life form, but that is of little help. So please Great Pop, help me to understand with the greatest clarity, the answer to the question of "Just Who and What am I, Really, and How do I operate in that?"

    With that last question I took a sip of elixir while awaiting Great Pop's response. He then winked at me and once again I found myself spiraling backwards in time. This time, I was given to end up at the beginning of the event of His making of the Earthplane, as is described in detail in Origins. At that moment, I found myself to again be in my Birdform in The Great Void. I watched once more as the lightening bolt which was obviously now being projected by The ThunderBeing, hit the mass of semi-solid material that Great Pop had fashioned for this very purpose and event. The result was the setting off so to speak, of the expansion that is the Earthplane. By any standards, one's experience of this event would give one a sense of the credibility of the "Big Bang" theory. In most ways it was pretty much the same as I remember when I visited this time and event in the development of Origins.

Yet it seemed like now there was something going on that I seemed to have missed when I watched this event previously. Perhaps what I had overlooked at that time in Origins was the Reality that I had in fact been present, or at least that was now how it seemed, when the Original event took place. Next I was given to remember that I was flying about and in a sense seemingly "showing off" and trying to please Great Pop in this Birdform when this event actually occurred. I was quick to realize that I Now have several potentially conflicting memories of different experiences of my being here in this event. Naturally this caused me to question my being here, or not, in the original and actual event. I then realized that my continued consideration of such possibilities served to only confuse me even more. Upon that realization, I was then propelled back a little further in time.

When I arrived this time, I soon realized that I was again sitting on the perch in that room of the Home of the Future that is depicted in the beginning of this material. It was Now a point in time that was even before the Birdform of my Spiritual body was complete. At this point, Great Pop was just manifesting the wings of it from the fingertips of His left hand. I watched as He patiently tried one configuration after another of what seemed to be an earlier type of semi-solid form of bone and muscle. He did this again and again until He was satisfied with How what he was making would work to His standard of perfection. At times, Great Pop would even fashion parts of one of these elements upon His own form. I watched as He would try it out there before producing and implanting the same type of configuration into the Birdform.

While I was given to see some of this process in Origins, I had not seen what was now happening. In that previous experience, it was like I had gone back in time and had watched in a pretty much detached kind of way, as Great Pop made something. This time I realized more fully that I already was myself. Now I became certain that I was Really my complete Self, and that I was actually there during the whole of the process of that happening. It was at the very next instant that I then realized the What I was at that time and in that event. I next understood that the What of me then, was not too unlike What I feel like inside in the present moment, meaning in my current Life expression on Mother Earth. "So this is and has been always, me," I then thought.

It was the next realization that caused an even greater excitement in me. And it occurred as I finally seemed to understand that the What of me has obviously changed to some extent over time, yet the Who of me really never has! Ah, the What it is that I Really am, is pretty much always changing and in motion, and the Who I Really am, is not changing at all. I then considered that perhaps this is what I had been looking for all along. And with that realization, I quickly found myself back again at that wonderful table of Understanding, and Great Pop. Great Pop then made Himself a little more relaxed in His chair. He paused for a moment, and then began His response to my "bait" saying,

"Well Little One, your "bait" in some senses was more complex than you thought. However, the answer is in fact relatively simple, which I hope to make even more clear now. The puzzle will be solved much easier if We first get to the part of the question as to how you "operate" so to speak. After all, that is one of the major Understandings that I desired to be presented in this material. My motive is to facilitate more Understanding as well as Self-Awareness about oneself and Life in general. The reason for the development of this material is so that any and All Beings can ultimately use it to better their own capability of such and Self. You see Little One, this material and project can be also somewhat of a Self-improvement or empowerment guide, for any that might choose to use it that way. With that said, let us begin discussing How you operate.

As you Now understand, the whole reason that I made the Personal Structure as well as Essence-Operatives of Selves is to do just that with. I made these things so that any Potential can use them to be self-expressive and thereby operate, so to speak. In this review of how you or any Potential Being or Thing operates, let us in a sense go backwards in as far as the elements involved are concerned. In any outer incarnated experience anywhere in the Physical realm, you or any Being or Thing operate in a sense through the Tree of Selves. The

Real Self, being the trunk and roots of the tree, with the Projected Selves being its limbs, and the Imagined Selves being its leaves. Naturally, the Cosmic / Communal Selves are its flowers or fruit. Whether you are doing anything as an internal expression or as an external one, and experiences including the one of reflection are expressions too, you do such through your Tree of Selves no matter what. All Beings and Things use their own personal Tree of Selves to think with, to plan with, to wonder with, and even to feel with. You use it when you are awake or even when you are asleep. You use it to experience pain or joy as well as to experience any type of fulfillment or loss. Not so unlike the Birdform that you just described, I made this Tree of Selves for any and all Potential to be outwardly self-expressive with. Also, any experience is just that, an expression, period. You see Little One you use your Tree of Selves to "operate with," no matter where you are.

We might liken the Tree of Selves to be somewhat like layers of bubbles within bubbles as well. As you have seen Little One, they Really do resemble such in a way. Of course all of these layers of bubbles reside inside the greater and more dynamic bubble of one's consciousness. Remembering that these layers and bubbles are in Reality, multidimensional, one can consider the outer layer of bubbles to be predominately that of one's Cosmic / Communal Selves, with many independently operating Selves within that.

One's Cosmic / Communal Selves are actually much more amorphous and free ranging than the other three. It is also the part of oneself that one cedes over in any type of relationship, be it with an individual Being or Thing or a group of such. While all Beings and Things can have multiple expressions of any of the other Selves except that of the Real Self, their number will be quite small as compared with this one. While a Cosmic / Communal Self may seem similar in its nature and thereby Medicine with that of an Imagined Self to some degree, it ranges far past it in most senses. This is because it normally is an Imagined Self that becomes involved to some degree in relationships in the most part. An Imagined Self is the Self that one most often consider themselves as being when they are participating in a Cosmic / Communal Self relationship. Also any individual Being or Thing can in fact and Reality manifest what can only be considered as an imaginary relationship as well, yet that will never be a Real one. This is because all Real relationships are Cosmic / Communal Selves by My design. Even in a Real relationship, one does sense and feel the relationship alone in the Imagined Self that spawned and is participating to some degree as well in it. Yet such a sense of aloneness cannot occur in the Cosmic / Communal Self. This is Real and true because the Imagined Self is not a connective or open one as is the case of one's Cosmic / Communal Self.

The Cosmic / Communal Self is also a type of Self that expresses things passed along through the other three Selves in a joint kind of way. The Imagined Self is the Self that is at bat in a baseball game, the Cosmic / Communal Self is the Self that shares in the ceremony of winning the game. The Imagined self is that which goes to work while the Cosmic / Communal Self is that which thinks of one's spouse or children when in route, or while one is there. One imagines and feels how one is going to be, or be treated, in the Imagined Self. It is also the one that gets angry or hurt in one's experiences. Yet the Imagined Self is the singular Self that does and feels that, as this Self can only be expressive or felt in the singular sense because one is alone in it, at all times. On the other hand, what one feels in the Imagined Self becomes immediately shared in the Cosmic / Communal Self with any and all others that are also engaged in it, at any moment. And this Nature of one's Cosmic / Communal Self does also feed back the attitude and feelings of others to oneself as well. So one might liken the Cosmic / Communal Self to be much like a two way street, while the others are primarily not.

The Cosmic / Communal Self is actually an engaging and joining one. This means that there can be many individual Beings and Things included in it, at any and all times. And this is always including that of oneself of course. However, it also is that part of oneself that one does give over to another in expressions of Loyalty, Participation, Care, and so forth. It is also the part of oneself that one's subconscious or deeper levels of consciousness mostly operate through. Besides one's Real Self, one's Primary Cosmic / Communal Self is the only other Self that you take back with you when you exit. Therefore Little One, you can easily see now how it is one's Cosmic / Communal Selves which are the Selves that one gets the most influence from, as well as make the most complete expressions through at any and all times. Also Little One, it is the Cosmic / Communal Selves collectively and individually that one considers their Self-image, to be an image of. It is also the Self that fosters and provides the issues that one brings to the theater section of one's Emotional Body so as to experience themselves in, during the process that you call Dreamtime.

In Reality Little One, in any and all cases, it is only the Real Self that experiences the dramas orchestrated in one's Dream world theater of one's Emotional Body. Even though one might be working out Fear of death in such episodes, the Real Self can never die. Also, only the Real Self is associated to, or maintains any direct awareness of past Life episodes and so forth. That is precisely Why it is that some individuals have recurring dreams about events and issues that they have carried forward into the present incarnation. Certainly, one might wonder as to the presence of Fear in these scenarios. The reason for such is that the Real Self always knows that Fear is a pseudo-Essence with a time limit, and in a sense even an illusion in a way. So, one's Real Self chooses to act out each episode as if it were as Real, as it always knows that is the condition of itself. And even though most oftentimes one will act out scenarios with many other people in one's Dream episode, one in Reality knows that one is alone in it as a complete self. Actually Little One, I designed things this way so that the Real Self is able to personally resolve all issues that it chooses to before beginning the experience of the next new day.

As you are now surmising Little One, yes the Real Self uses Thought energy to create the people, places, things, and events in the theater of one's Emotional Body that one considers as being their Dream world. Now this is pretty simple to do when one realizes that all of one's past experiences and expressions are permanently recorded as Memory energy in one's Emotional Body. Also, one's Emotional Body is a walking billboard so to speak, broadcasting - again stored in it as Memory energy - all of one's Prayers of Desire and that is whether they are of Fear or Hope. Now, one might say - Well if that is the case, why is the energy used not Memory instead of Thought? And the answer becomes self evident when one remembers that all Thought energy has a time limit to it before it naturally turns into Memory energy, no matter what. Yet that is what people do when they think. Yep, when they think, they are actually reading some Memory energy from some source, and then using the pattern of it to issue something forth as Thought! Understanding that is the mechanism of how Beings and Things think, one can rightfully assume that in the sensing of both Thought and Memory, that is also why Memory always seems to be static and Thought always seems to be in motion.

While it is the Real Self that generates the setting, and experiences each episode in one's dream experiences and expressions, it is a Projected Self that is actually used to generate and define the drama of each episode. As I mentioned earlier, only one's Real Self and one's Primary Cosmic / Communal Selves exist in True Spirit form, meaning before one incarnates, or when one returns to My Essential Will after exit and Transition. Therefore lacking any Projected Selves to use, if one were to ask if this means that one does not Dream in heaven, so to speak? Bingo! Nope, they do not. Of course in that condition of completeness, all-knowing, and so forth, there is no need or benefit to do such. And as you know, I do so like to keep things real neat and tidy. It is in the spirit such tidiness that by My design, all of a personal Dream episode reverts instantly to Memory energy when the episode is completed and remains contained within one's own Emotional Body for reference as necessary. As you are now wondering Little One, it is indeed within a Cosmic / Communal Self that any and all personal problems are felt, experienced, and resolved. Therefore, in resolving problems of any nature Little One, you can see how very helpful Understanding one's Cosmic / Communal Self that is involved can be in making ease and fulfillment of the process of it.

Also, in most instances Little One, it is the Imagined Selves collectively, that is the image that one wishes to have others see as being oneself, as well as the image that others wish oneself to be, or become. Needless to say, this is also the most easily influenced and manipulated image that one has. As you are aware, expressions and motivations through the Imagined Selves are the most susceptible to influence by Bark on Tree, or Ego. And of course this means that they are also susceptible to and influenced by Fear and the many faces of it, such as Anger, Guilt, and so forth. This influence from Bark on Tree can also be that of other Beings and Things, and not just that of oneself. Remember Little One, it is an Imagined Self that is usually the first part of a person that one will encounter, and in the prevalent culture as you see it, it is also at times the only one. This image of Self in an Imagined Self is also predominately a Mental and thereby Mind and Ego influenced one. This also makes it most susceptible to being rationalized and justified, as will be most of the personal expressions and motives that become expressed through it. Yet it actually is the image of Self that is most flexible and easily changed. Also, it is the very first image and Self, that one has to deal with to make any Real change in oneself or one's Life experience and expression!

By an outsider that is looking in, the Projected Self is seemingly not that much different than the Imagined Self. However, in Reality it is in fact vastly different and more dynamic in its position in relation to one's outer personal expressions and motives. It is also less susceptible to being manipulated or molded by others than oneself. This is because it operates as a bridge between one's Heart operative, and the operative of one's Mind. And as one's True Value System resides in one's Heart operative, in all expressions from this image of Self, any and all Bark on Tree influences are more balanced and minimal. Remember here Little One that it is one's Mind, not one's Heart that is influenced at all by any expression of Bark on Tree, be it of oneself or any other. Therefore if there is no Bark on Tree influence, then there can be no Fear or any face of it at all! Any Projected Self is much more Real than any Imagined Self as one might now more clearly Understand. Because of this condition, it is within a Projected Self that Real healing is done and changes occur. Also by My Design, any Projected Self is less vulnerable to outside stimuli or influences from any other Beings or Things.

Of course, one's Real Self is just that. It is what always has been and will always be, as well as being what incarnates and exits. It is the Inner Child that incarnates so as to go out to play, learn, explore, and so forth. It is the part of oneself that changes very little in a Life experience, except perhaps to become more in control over the other Selves and one's Self-image, which in the best of conditions is in a state of Balance. It is within one's Real Self that is the Where and How one's True Value System overcomes all of the silliness of influences from one's own Bark on Tree, or that of any other. It is within one's Real Self that is the Where, if choices are made, they are most rapidly as well as easily realized, period. Within one's Real Self is where all healing begins and is completed, as well as any Real changes are made as well. Yet one's Real Self is always in a sense most perfect, complete, as well as all-knowing. Therefore all that happens is that in a sense, it only needs to return to that completeness in all other Selves to accomplish that in itself. This is the aspect of oneself in one's Real Self that is constantly trying to rebalance oneself to the Reality of one's having chosen the conditions of oneself in accord to one's Plan in life, and continues to administer to all aspects and effects of it. It is one's image of Self in one's Real Self that is a blend of Conscience, Heart, Perspective and Soul Will, and thereby is Really Limitless in its Potential at any moment. This is the image of Self that becomes the Real hero, yet it needs to do no heroic thing except to accept, not master, the being of oneself in the past, present, and next moment of being.

Now then Little One, there is a reason that I had you make your final Resource Wheel as having your Selves appear as being a *projection of your Wills, versus having them being presented the other way around.* This is because each of the four kinds of Selves contributes to the idea of ones Self-image in one fashion or another. One's Real Self is an agent for the expression of one's Soul Will and any Desires or expressions made through it at any and all times. And like the nature of the Soul Will being superlative over the other three, so also is one's Real Self and one's Self-image therein. In Reality, one's Real Self is always intact, yet in most instances it is not the first Self that one's image assessments are made from.

So in a sense Little One, the answer to your question is really primarily with regard to your personal Self-image, as relates to both the What and Who you Really are. It is significant to note here that this, or sometimes these, images stay pretty much constantly in flux. This is because they are always being amended and redefined by oneself, even if it is because of an outside influence from others. Actually in most but not all instances, the Self that most individuals consider their Self-image to be comprised of is that of their Cosmic / Communal Self, and not necessarily their Primary one. And it is because of this situation, or perhaps better stated, Choice, that is the Why that improving one's Self-image is so difficult for most people at times. This difficulty is also resultant from the fact that not only is a Cosmic / Communal Self more amorphous, it also combines the nature and influence of all those involved or attached to it in some manner. This is to say that all relationships with other Beings or Things have influence upon one's Cosmic / Communal Self with them, and the image of oneself therein. And as you are now surmising, yes this is also where the desire to please others and so forth come into play. Yet even this potential reflects the perfection of its design. It is because of this potential in the design of a Cosmic / Communal Self that one realizes more feedback than is possible through any other type of Self. And feedback is very important Little One, because feedback is what makes one happy or sad and inspires one to make more Choices and thereby experience more in life.

Occasionally some individuals might choose to consider one of their Imagined Selves as being their Self-image. At times many individuals do try to fool themselves and others that way, especially in competitive situations. Yet one does not even really fool oneself in that maneuver, especially since it is a type of Self that usually is highly active in pursuit of expressing one's Bark on Tree and thereby Ego desires. On the other hand, some individuals may choose at times to primarily operate from their Projected Selves, as to do such is most safe in a way. Of course while they are pretty much incapacitated from most physical function, which is the primary function of an Imagined Self pool, they will feel less and risk less of themselves, which is the catch 22 of that type of choice and behavior.

So Little One, hopefully you can now better Understand that no matter what, one's Real Self is involved in one's Life at all times including any assessment of image and so also are all of one's Projected Selves. As far as Self-image, some individuals may choose only to include one or more of their Imagined Selves past that, again for safety to Ego. Any individuals that seem insensitive, cold, cruel, unfeeling, or callous, are typically operating in this measure of safety. However, the fullest experiences in life will always be resultant from one's Cosmic / Communal Self interchanges as it were. It is here that any activity or expressions that are chosen will be seemingly the most risky, yet also the most complete. Therefore it is from such expressions and experiences in one's Cosmic / Communal Selves that the most risky, yet complete "Who and What you Really are" Self-image will also be found."

With that last statement, Great Pop then magically produced this diagram from the tips of the fingers of His left hand:

The Potential Expressions of Selves

```
Imagined Self   Projected Self
         ↖    ↗
Real Self ——→ Projected Self —→ Imagined Self —→ Cosmic/Communal Self
         ↘ Projected Self —→ Imagined Self
         ↓
Cosmic/Communal Self
```

He then continued with, *"As you can see Little One, there are basically five means by which any incarnated Being or Thing can physically express themselves. And as you are now thinking, the What of those expressions, are patterns of energy, be they Desire Prayers, Feelings, Thoughts, Care, or any type of physical activity. Whatever one does in the physical sense of being in physical Life does in Reality occur through these aspects and elements, no matter what. Furthermore about being in physical Life, if one shuts one's eyes after looking at some pictures, the Memory energy pattern of those things that is stored as such in one's Memory Bank of the Mind Operative of Self, is simply revitalized into Thought energy. It is then just reprocessed through the canals of one's Mind Operative again, in that way. Whatever one might think or do does in Reality happen in such a manner. This is the mechanism that I created for all Potential to use so as to "operate" in their experiences outside of My Essential Will. While it might seem like the observing of something is different than doing something perhaps, it is not at all. The doing happens the very same way, except that not only is Thought and Memory energy employed, but Kinetic energy as well. To do something, such as picking up a pebble, one has to "think" about it first. And of course the Decision Factory comes into play by then finding and selecting a process that is stored as patterns of Memory energy in one's Procedural Data Bank of one's Mind Operative. Once a process is selected, then, as you realize now, one's Free Will Operative makes a choice to issue forth that process, or not. If it is in fact chosen to continue, then one's Free Will issues the process forth through the vehicle of an Imagined Self, not so much as an action in itself, but as a pattern of Thought energy coupled with the necessary available Kinetic energy.*

As you now better Understand Little One, one's varying supply of Kinetic energy is what one converts from eating and so forth that I designed as a part of the Imagined Self makeup and function. It is from one's center of personal supply of this type of energy that one uses to even move a muscle, or contract one to pick something up. Also, the very act of doing such a thing is simply one's making an outward expression of the process of such, as mentioned earlier, from one's Real Self through a Projected picking up something idea of Self. The process is then actualized as an expression and thereby becomes an experience of an Imagined Self that considers one capable of such activity. In most every action in any activity or expression of an Imagined Self, the process is usually assessed first by one's Bark on Tree as to the amount of Potential risk or danger that might be involved, but not in all cases, because of Free Will choice.

Therefore Little One you can see now that the core of this means of support, or How one " operates", is one's Real Self. Of course that is unless a condition of Possession, or some other type of imbalance has occurred, which We will cover in a subsequent section of this material. But for now, let us assume that a balanced condition exists. As the diagram illustrates, what happens in any personal expression is that through one's Personal Structure within one's Real Self a choice is made to issue forth something. Then as one can see, the process of it Flows through one or more of the other three types of Essence Operatives and ultimately outside of these parts of Self to the All of creation, or a specific target in it. And you might make note here Little One, is that while the illustration shows that an Imagined Self or Cosmic / Communal Self can be directly associated to the Real Self, most likely the Real Self will subsequently manifest a Projected Self between the Real Self and that element anyway. However, the other possibilities can and do exist at times. And of course for an individual Being or Thing to be of any type of receivership, it will always come to them via a Cosmic / Communal Self link to that other person or Thing."

With that statement, Great Pop magically turned that diagram into this one:

The Potential of Selves in Relationships

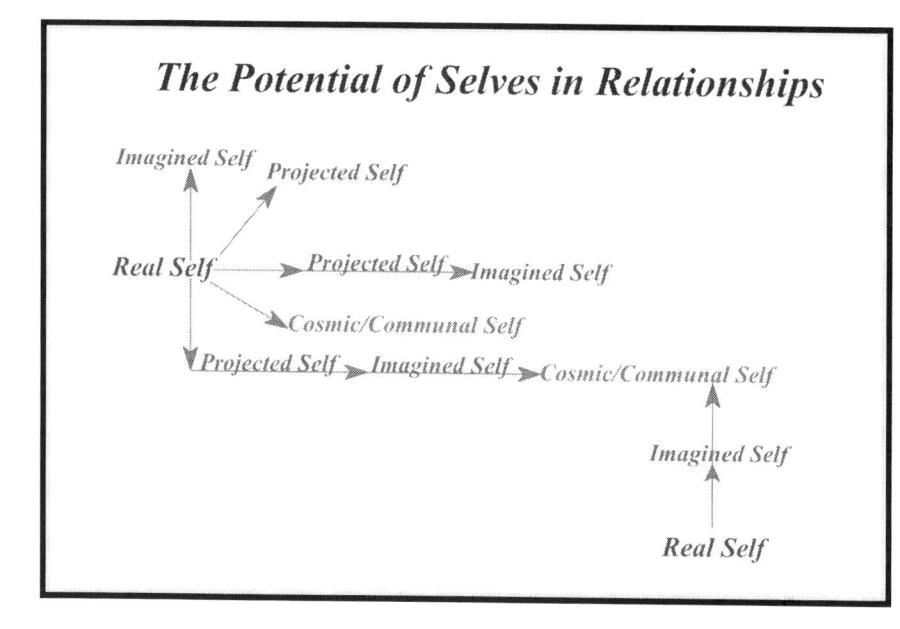

```
Imagined Self   Projected Self
     ↑         ↗
     |        /
Real Self ─────→ Projected Self ─→ Imagined Self
     |        ↘
     |         Cosmic/Communal Self
     ↓
  Projected Self ─→ Imagined Self ─→ Cosmic/Communal Self
                                            ↑
                                            |
                                      Imagined Self
                                            ↑
                                            |
                                       Real Self
```

He then explained: *"As you can see Little One, when two individual Beings or Things come into contact or have even the slightest recognition or awareness of the other, automatically an Imagined Self with a Cosmic / Communal Self attached to it is then projected forth by each individual to the other. This does always occur, even if the individual Beings or Things are not attracted to or even like each other. As you are now surmising Little One, the perfection of this design is not just because it facilitates negative expressions as well as positive ones. Nope, it is because it always and in all ways facilitates expanding self-awareness, self-realization, self-expression, self-determination, and self-actualization, period. So, even if you choose to ignore another Being or Thing, there still is the vehicle of one's Cosmic / Communal Self by which to do that very thing, you see?"*

*****

While this material was being edited at a much later date than this was originally written, Wolf Sister posed the following questions of which we both feel should be included here for increased explanation and clarity.

So, my Spirit is my Real Self. Could my Spirit / Real Self be thought of as my Soul as well? Is it from my Real Self that there is a

Projected Self that I have come to know as my physical body? And in my relationship with you, we each have created at least one Imagined Self in order to 'do' any of our communicating with and through, as well as we have created a Cosmic / Communal Self in which to be in a relationship with each other? And this Cosmic / Communal Self in which we are experiencing this relationship (and here I am meaning our relationship of friendship, sharing and working together) is one shared or group self? And, does my Spirit project more than one physical body with all of these various selves happening?

*****

What you call your Soul or Spirit are the same and that also contains the Real Self of You. Now when we realize that our Spirit (Soul) has its own Personal Structure by which to operate and do things, one can consider that as also being attached to our Real Self (Inner Child etc.).

It is our Personal Structure that facilitates any choice to be made, including to incarnate into the arena of Mother Earth or elsewhere. Now, we have two forms of our Personal Structure and when we choose to incarnate and thereby produce a Projected Self as being a human form that is born from our two parents etc., we then have the modified (incarnated) version of our Personal Structure with its extra Wills etc.

One way to look at this process is to see your Spirit / Soul / Real Self choosing a seed (egg from your mother) to incarnate into when it is fertilized by your father. At the moment of conception, your Real Self / Spirit / Soul embodies it with its expanded Personal Structure and messes with the chromosomes and DNA to produce, as a Projected Self, the developing embryo with all of the things that you desire to have in that body form when its development is complete.

At this point the fertilized egg and Projected Self can be likened to being the initial sprout or root of your incarnated Tree of this Life and of course that sprout will become its trunk in time. So in a sense, our first Projected Self in an incarnation is the physical body. And if that developing embryo comes to term and is born because of Our Choice to continue with it, your birth produces another Projected Self as being a child of someone and on, and on, and on as You keep making choices.

From the moment of conception, you are Not always in that developing bodyform and only totally embody it with the expanded

Personal Structure of your Real Self and Spirit, at or soon after birth. Also, we oftentimes take some time to get used to staying in our physical bodies right after birth. Yep, oftentimes we will come and go from it for short periods as it is not easy to adapt to after being a "Free Roaming" Spirit like before, when we are in Great Pop's Essential Will. Sometimes for some reason or another, some individuals decide not to keep going back into their body after birth and instead they return to Great Pop's Essential Will so as to start over, and that gives rise to "Crib Deaths" as you know them to be called. Since the body will basically stop developing and die if a Spiritual force (Life Force energy) is not present for an extended period when we are not in it, one or more of our Guides stay in it to keep it going so to speak.

Now comes the news that even before we incarnate, we and our parents already have created an Imagined Self of ourselves! And of course this earliest Imagined Self of is rarely the same as the one that our parents project upon that sprout (Real Self) that becomes the trunk of our Tree of Life. So, does this mean that we start life having one or more Imagined Selves that are associated to our initial Projected Self?

Yep, and some people spend a lifetime trying to detach from one or more of them.

Now as far as having two Projected Self bodyforms, the answer is No way, Jose. Why? Because our Personal Structure can only function in one of them at a time! You see, as shown in the drawing of the Incarnated Form of our Personal Structure, our physical body is a part of our expanded Personal Structure as is our Bark on Tree and so forth and it is what causes you to take your next breath. As far as the rest, you are on target in your assessment.

Also, All relationships exist as being a part of a Cosmic/Communal Self that is Shared as in the examples. Therefore by its very definition and Medicine (Nature), each Cosmic/Communal Self is a Group Consciousness. And yes, these Group Consciousnesses are associated with our physical bodies (Initial Projected Self) and are left behind with it upon our exit! Now as far as the survivors of our exit go, they maintain, or not, their participation in that Cosmic/Communal Self that stays with our physical body. So in that sense the Cosmic/Communal Self of one's relationship with someone that has exited lives intact within you, unless You choose otherwise. Now how very Neat and Tidy and on Autopilot is THAT!

*****

So in summary, as relates to one's Tree of Life in an incarnation, it all starts with our Real Self choosing our parents while we are still inside Great Pop's Essential Will. Conception takes place as we choose to express a Projected Self as the fertilized egg. That is the same as being the first sprout or root of our Tree of Life. Each Projected Self that we choose to express as a root ends with a Cosmic / Communal Self that is its relationship with Mother Earth and Water. That is because all physical bodyforms here on Mother Earth are composed of Mineral Spirits and water and it is the Cosmic / Communal Self at the end of each root that allows our Tree of Life to feed so as to grow.

At the other end of the seed of our Tree of Life of an incarnation we also express a Projected Self that is the initial sprout of our Tree of Life. This initial Projected Self sprout will seek the light, and when it sees it above the ground's surface, it will keep expanding itself so as to become the trunk of our Tree of Self. Instead of having a Cosmic / Communal Self at the sprout's end, we express our initial Imagined Self there as our first leaf. And so as to feed from the Air, we express a Cosmic / Communal Self to the end of the leaf so as to be in relationship with the air. Of course our initial Imagined Self leaf will cause the appearance of more Projected Self branches and imagined Self leaves with their Cosmic / Communal Self relationships with the air as we continue to grow. This process is all being paralleled in the development of our human embryo in our mother's womb.

One can equate the point that our Tree of Life of an incarnation produces multiple branches from the initial sprout, to shortly after our physical birth and the point whereby our Real Self embodies our physical body for good. At this point in our infancy, our Real Self takes over what used to be the sprout and now is the trunk as well root system of our Tree of Life and our human body-form, and we continue to keep expressing more Selves and expanding both simultaneously from that point on. While obvious Projected Self branches might be interests, career choices and the like, if you are wondering what Projected Selves might be roots of one's Tree of Life, consider one's race, sex, skin type, and even any deformities.

A long time ago I asked Great Pop how I should be and grow. His response was: *"Be and grow like the Tree, Little One"* and now we all can see Why.

SELF DISCOVERY

As I begin this next and new chapter in this material and of course in my life as well, I want to make something especially clear to any and all individuals that might at some time become exposed to it. Of course that something is not that I can make incredibly long sentences with many words in them, ha, ha, ha. Nope, it is that I do not want any Being or Thing to think that I consider myself to be in any way special, advantaged, or different, than anyone else on Mother Earth. I do not seek that Great Pop should favor me over any other Being or Thing even if I thought that He would do such, which I do not believe He would. I would not even consider asking such from Him, not because He does not like or Love me, but because He does! And with regard to such favor seeking of others as some people oftentimes practice for themselves, I am certain that such a desire and request would just be an expression of my Bark on Tree. Also, I truly do not fault or blame anyone else for my condition or circumstances, as I Really Understand that this is resultant to Things and Beings that I have chosen to associate with, and thereby have become manifested through someone's Prayers of Desire in some way.

During the recent period of the development of this material, Great Pop has had me become involved in playing games on the Internet as sort of a "Wake Up" activity in a sense. In this recent activity, I have found myself getting way too much involved in it, or so it seems. What I am referring to here in the way of involvement is in relation to my setting goals, feelings about winning and loosing, developing a Self-image from it, and questioning my Prayers of Desire and thereby Motives. On the plus side, I find that I have now come to realize many things from such activity. One such realization is not just that such "ambition" is simply fostered behavior that is promoted in the prevalent culture. It is one that goes even deeper to the target of this material in fact. Mostly it is more in how we tend to develop an image about not only ourselves, but also others and even Great Pop to some degree that is based simply upon whether or not we get some instant gratification and thereby become in receivership to a current Prayer of Desire in some manner.

Of course, as is also taught behavior, when we loose or become in any manner unsuccessful, we can and do make all kinds of excuses for such to occur. Yet for some reason I personally tend to belittle myself, or feel that I have lost favor in some way. And when we win, even those of us like myself that feel a little bad at times about someone else loosing in that experience, feel that somehow we are looked favorably on by some "power" in the universe. Naturally, "Lady Luck" or whatever force that exists like that idea, is something that I would really like to have on my side at all times. I have often said that I would rather be lucky than good at something any day. Perhaps this is because deep inside I do not believe that I am "good" enough anyway. After all I never made straight "A's" remember?

 Certainly one can imagine the overwhelming sense of peace and closure that I felt in Great Pop's explanation of how we "operate". It seemed that not only did He give me all of the missing pieces of the puzzle, but also He gave me a complete instruction book as to how the puzzle of myself and my life fits together and operates. I definitely felt that what I was looking for in my quest was now pretty close or at least much more clearly defined. In hindsight it appears that perhaps I was looking for an easy way out in my quest. Or maybe I was seeking a magical button to push that would make my life much easier in every sense. Lazy Indian, I hear people think of me at times. Actually, I just consider it intelligence. Why work hard at something when you can Play? Yet it seems that I also do a lot of making very hard work out of relatively simple tasks. I feel that many, if not most people would not even care about these many things that I find to be most important as well as intriguing. Why should anyone care about how things work? It is obviously much easier to accept that they do or not, and simply move on with what is available, disposable, and instantly gratifying. Of course for TohNaWah and I, that is just not enough! After thanking Great Pop for all of His help to this point, I found myself quickly back inside my human body form that lay upon my bed.

 As I begin this paragraph, it is now the 16th of January 2002. My first thoughts are about how amazing it is that this material has become developed so far and so quickly. It has been just a little over a month since I started, and now there are eighteen chapters complete. The Medicine of the number eighteen is Success, and it seems very appropriate that the last chapter was numbered that. I can honestly attest that I have realized a great Success in becoming of a much greater Understanding of the Who and What I Really Am now. I also have realized an added bonus thrown in by Great Pop as to the How it is that I "operate" in life. I feel that this Understanding is very important to have, especially if I am ever going to be able to realize any greater "success" in it in the physical sense. Yet for some reason it seems I am having a difficult time getting started in this chapter. Of course I am certain that this difficulty is a direct influence from my Bark on Tree. I say this now because within this chapter I am definitely going to undress my Bark on Tree, and thereby myself. I realize now that this is necessary to do if I am ever going to be able to improve my life situations on Mother Earth.

On the plus side, I just received another disk drive to replace the one that was of concern, from a new friend whom has Deer Medicine. On the not so plus side, when I tried to install it, it did not function properly. So at this point I am still operating with the older drive that has not so much time left it seems. Also, I have still not been able to get the drawing program to work. Therefore any new drawings will be difficult for me to include until some miracle happens to support such. Of course, I am greatly concerned about my being able to get more resources, especially the kind called money. The weather and season is not conducive to my being able to get, much less do, any more outside work. I even recently looked on the Internet to see what kind of computer job that I might be able to find for myself there. Of course, all of this concern is simply reactionary influences from my Bark on Tree.

Now it seems that all I can do at this point in my life, is to work on this material and that is certainly A-1 Ok with me. I have just paid the rent. Of course the light, phone, and a few other bills, such as website hosting fee and so forth are due again at the end of the month. I have plenty of food for a week or so. I am reasonably healthy, at least physically, ha, ha, ha. The little heaters are keeping TohNaWah and I from freezing. In a couple of days I should be able to apply for my driving privilege again. But like getting the computer fixed, the drawing program working, and paying the bills that will soon be due, there is not enough money presently in my supply to do anything about any of it at the present time. I do so miss Nolayte and my other two children, and do not have a clue as to when or how I will be able to become a part of their lives.

I also miss being with Great Pop at that wonderful table of Understanding, a whole lot. Yet the work for me to do Now is here and in this manner, so I might as well get on with it. Now also begins the "How To" part of this material, that any and all can choose to follow the steps that are presented for oneself as well. I am certain that for any that do choose to do such, will most definitely find them to be of a great benefit. For those individuals that do desire to develop such a wealth of personal Understanding of oneself, included within the Appendix are Worksheets, as well as some suggestions in support of such activity.

Over the years when counseling people, Great Pop has oftentimes had me recommend that they make certain lists. Earlier, we discussed the eight things that make me, me. This is the first list and it is perhaps one of the most important lists that one can ever make, period. That is because this list contains the key elements in one's Resource Wheel of Self, which are one's Values. Therefore, to begin any Real and lasting improvement of one's condition in life, one must have at least that much defined to start with. If one has not made one's own Value List yet, it goes like this:

MAKING A RESOURCE WHEEL

At this point, we now have the top eight items identified on the following Lists:

TRUE VALUES - My major Value System components.

ASSETS - Capabilities that I have and most Value.

TRUE DESIRES - What I Really desire to have happen next in my life.

FEARS - Things that I am presently concerned about and Really do not want to happen.

CARES - Things that are Really important to me now.

MAY-BE's - Things or events that I feel would dramatically change my life in a positive way.

At this point, we Now should also have the profile of our Hero. And if you have not recognized it yet, one's Real hero is Always and in all conditions, Oneself! The primary reason for doing that particular exercise is to become as fully self-aware as possible.

Defining the qualities of our Hero helps us to recognize things about ourselves that we basically are not conscious of. Again, the more that one puts into it the more that one will benefit. Actually any abilities like leaping over tall buildings and so forth can be real, especially if one has a rocket suit or the like. More important than the "superhuman" abilities like that, is to determine how they would be employed, as well as specifically Why one has such an inner desire. A periodic review of one's Hero, as well as amendments to such will give one a much more comprehensive idea as to not only one's Imagined Self as such, but also that of one's Real Self as well. Certainly, we all can give a thousand excuses as to why we feel that we are not good enough, or have a poor self-image. And those influences of the past that contribute to this idea of oneself are very real. Yet they do not have to stay so influential with regard to our Future, that is not if we choose differently! The reason to find such out about oneself is so that one may then use that knowledge to make changes and develop different patterns of behavioral choices. To do this will facilitate one to finally and perhaps evermore, become fully operational as one's Real Self as well as increase one's own Potential of Success in life, in every consideration.

In addition to the lists, I just happen to also have my four Wills defined as to their animal form influence. Also, Great Pop says to include at this point, a method by which some people may successfully determine those aspects of themselves as well. It is important to note that if one is not certain or completely successful in determining this from the exercise to be given, please do not be disappointed. This information is very good to know, but not having such will not keep one from making a fully functional and beneficial Resource Wheel of oneself anyway.

Remember those two symbols that were described in one of the earlier chapters? Yep, here is where they can be of more possible utility. At this time please get some paper and a pen or pencil to write with, I'll wait. Next, make four copies of each symbol by hand on eight small fresh pieces of paper as described earlier. Got it together now? Good! Okay, on the back of either a square-like symbol with dots at the corners, or a copy of my symbol, write; Heart. Then place the piece of paper with the Heart word side against one's forehead. Then as described earlier, project your Mind and consciousness into the symbol Really hard, meaning with a great Passion of Will and Desire. One will next feel an opening as one lets go of thinking about the physical. If one **_Really_** desires to go through the portal that the symbol will provide, it will happen. And do not worry, Great pop told me that any that try, will always be safe there. Next, pray for guidance from Great Pop and then ask Him to show you an animal form image of one's Heart Will, while thinking about someone that you Really Love. Once it is determined, then write it down by the word Heart on another piece of paper. If one type of symbol does not yield any successful results, then try the other type in the same manner. This is actually a developed ability and if one keeps working at it, success will ultimately become realized.

The next Will is to be done in the same manner, which is one's Bark on Tree or Ego. So, next write Ego on the back of the type of symbol that you now feel yields the clearest and easiest results. Repeat the procedure as before, except this time think about something that you would really Hate to have occur, like having a loved one hurt on purpose by someone else. Once complete with that one, then write Soul on the back of the preferred symbol patch and this time think about God giving you a great gift and holding you dear to Him. Many people will find that an animal form will not be seen in this one. Instead of an animal, the wind or something like a flower, a fiery volcano, or some different type of elemental Spirit vision will appear. This is perfect because most Beings do not have an animal form pattern of Resonance to their Soul Will. Instead of an animal form, the Medicine of most individuals Soul Will is usually an elemental Spirit form, or something that is all together different! Finally, write Free Will on another patch as determined before and repeat the process. However, this time think about having the choice of eating poop or something that you really like, like ice cream. Once you are complete with that one, take a break. You earned it!

As mentioned, this determination is not critical or will keep one from making a Resource Wheel that will work A-Ok. However, if one has any success in the exercise at all, that will be even better. As is often the case, it is an exercise that if one continues to do it, then most likely they will become more proficient in it. Now that we have that much done, one might be wondering what the heck does knowing what these animal forms have to do with self-awareness and self-realization? Again, the answer is, Everything! Remember, in Reality our Wills are basically hose-like Operatives that we make personal expressions through. Therefore, if one knows that their Heart Will is of a Dolphin-like Essential Nature then it would be most natural for them to be showing their affection in a "touchy-feely" kind of way. It is also important to realize that because of this animal form relationship, such a pattern of expression may not be natural for someone else because they have a different type. So once one has one's own identified, it is most beneficial to spend some time learning about the "normal" lifestyle and behavior of these animal forms. To do such will help one understand and be able to better accept the Why it is that one has certain preferences of behavioral expressions. Of course the Really powerful aspect of this awareness is that it facilitates one to recognize what is perfect and does not need "Fixing" about oneself!

Now then, we are finally ready to fashion our Resource Wheel. So, at the top of a fresh piece of paper, title it as "The Resources of - (Your Name)". In the middle of the page you are to now draw a big circle with your first name in the center of it with lines radiating out like:

My Resource Wheel

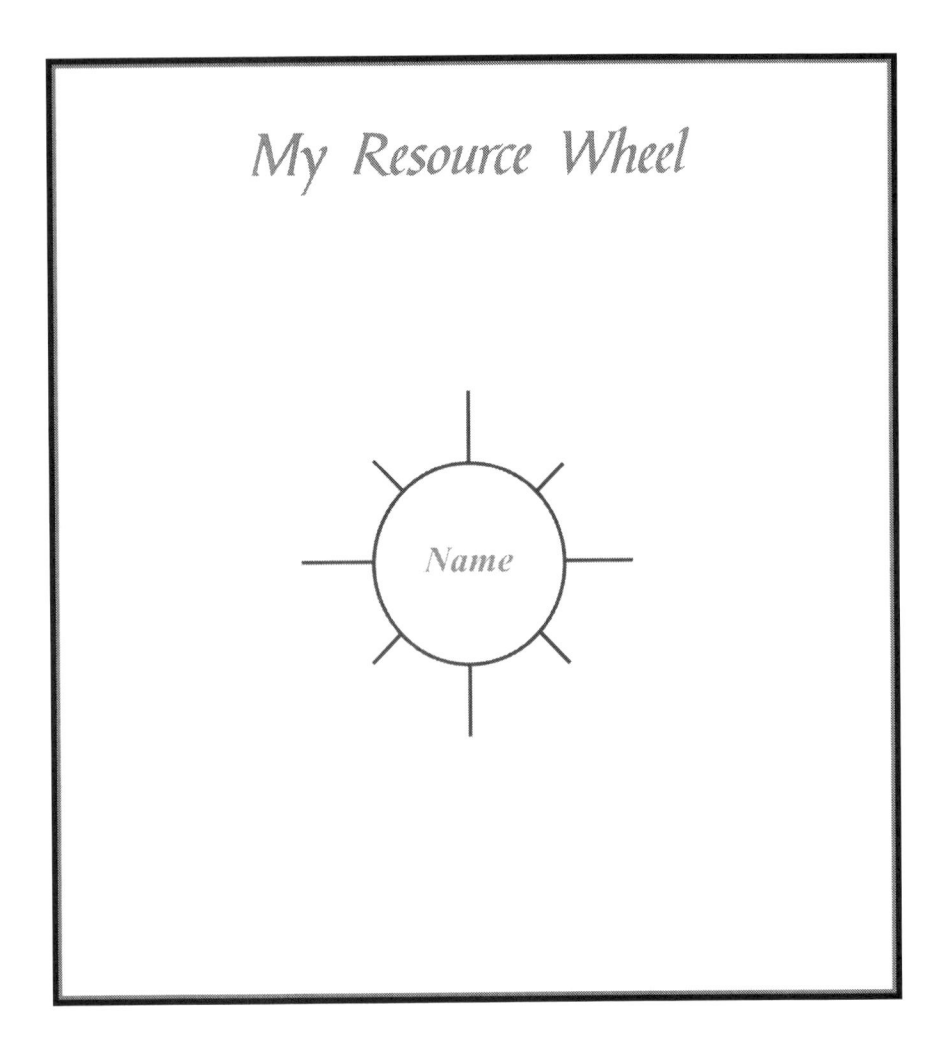

Name

As one can see, the blue colored North to South axis and the East to West axis are positions of cardinal reference, just like on a compass. For easy reference we will now number the eight Orientations as:

My Resource Wheel

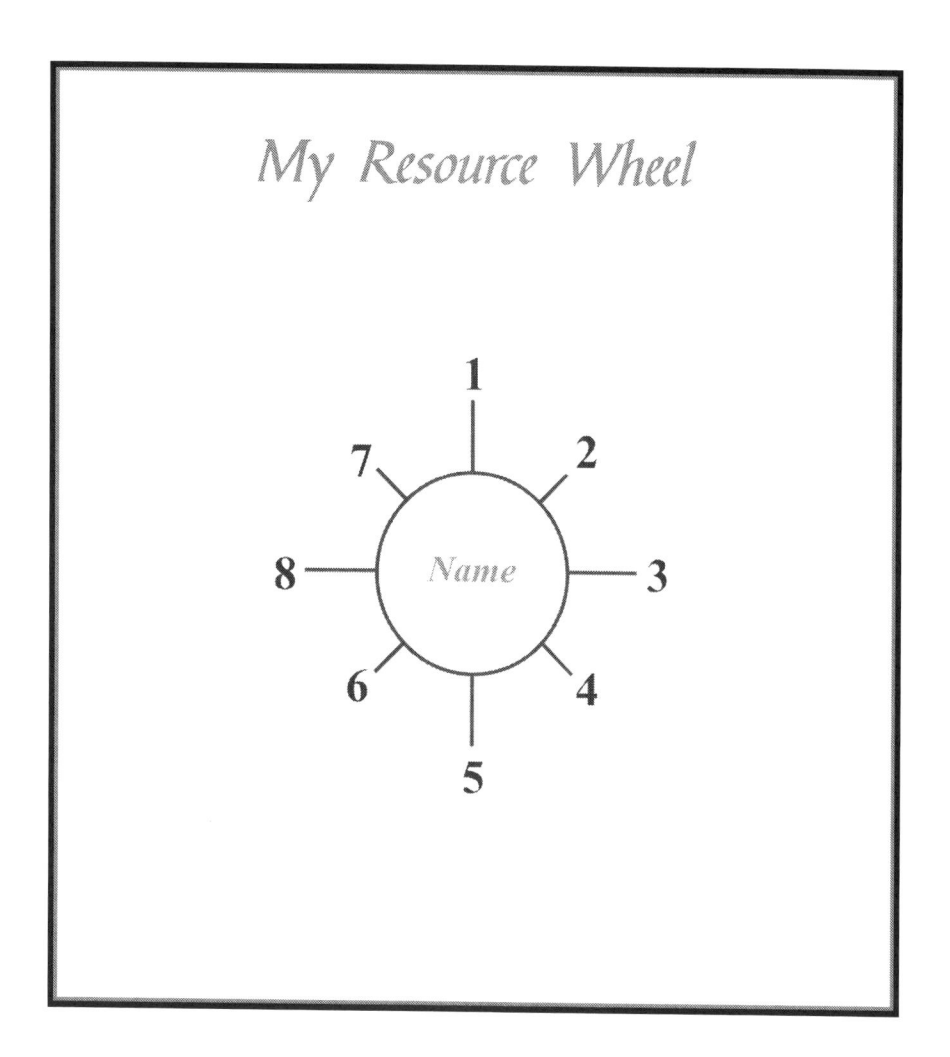

    Of note here, the numbers almost appear to be clockwise, but not quite. The next step if you know what they are, is to place one's Will elements and animal forms in their proper location like so:

My Resource Wheel

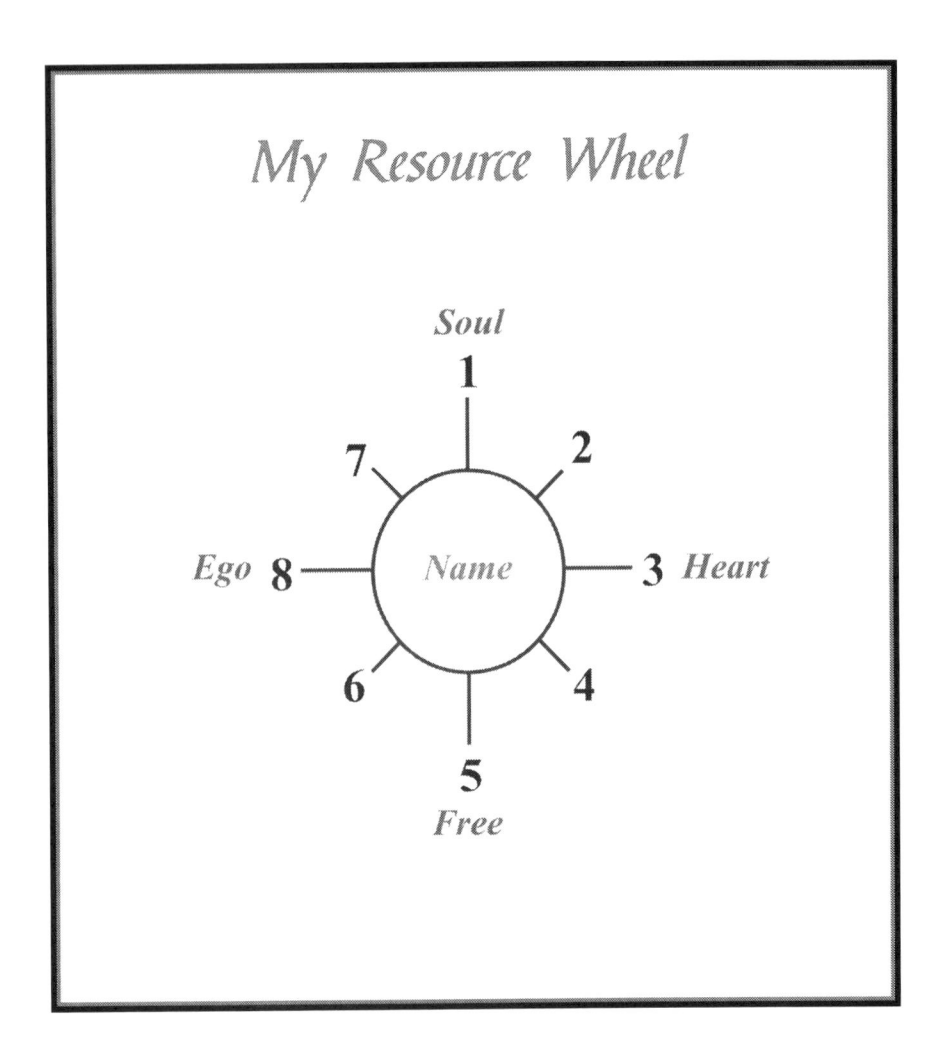

```
              Soul
               1
          7         2
 Ego  8 ——— Name ——— 3  Heart
          6         4
               5
              Free
```

Next, based upon the numbers that you assigned to your **Values**, add these elements to the Wheel in their respective positions as follows:

My Resource Wheel

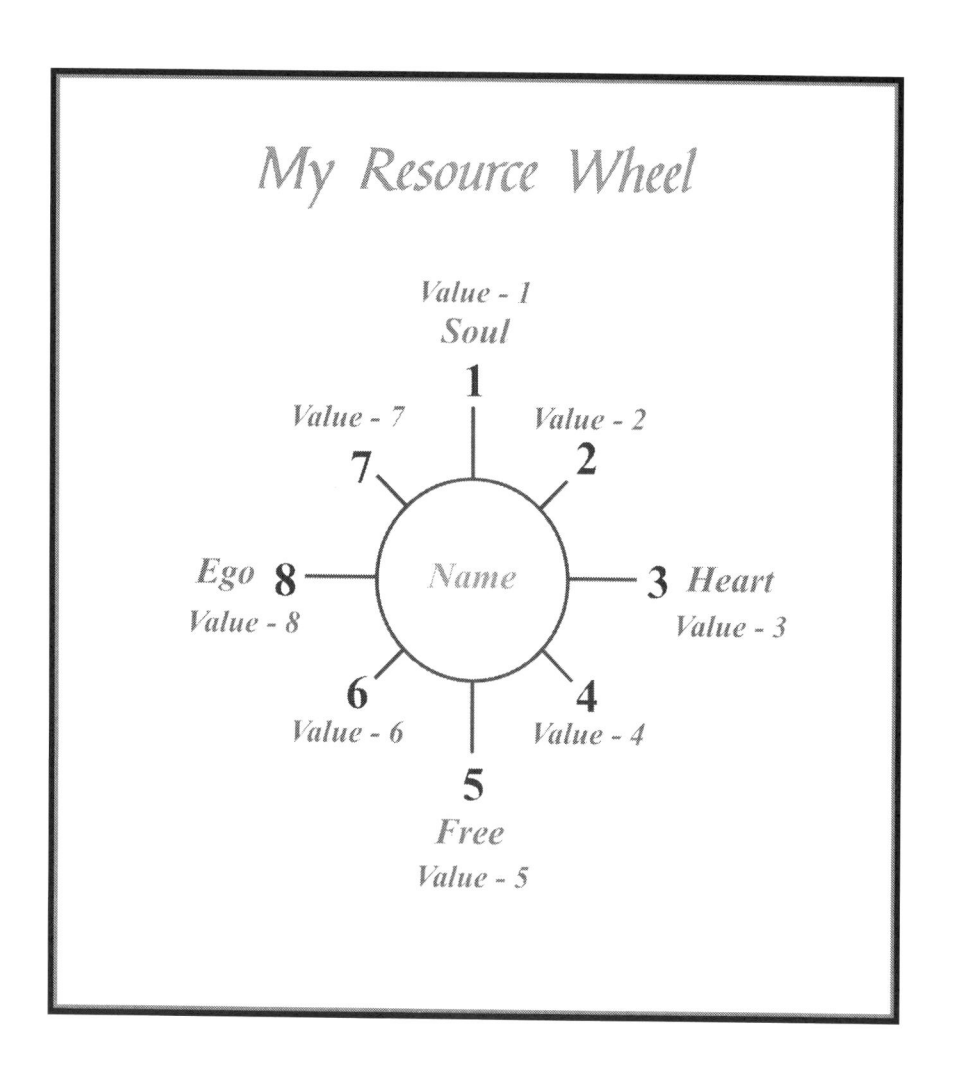

```
                Value - 1
                  Soul
                    1
   Value - 7              Value - 2
       7                      2

Ego  8 ─────  Name  ───── 3  Heart
Value - 8                     Value - 3

       6                      4
   Value - 6              Value - 4
                    5
                   Free
                 Value - 5
```

The next step in this process is to place one's top eight **Desire** and **Asset** elements from the lists that you made in accordance to their relative positions as follows:

My Resource Wheel

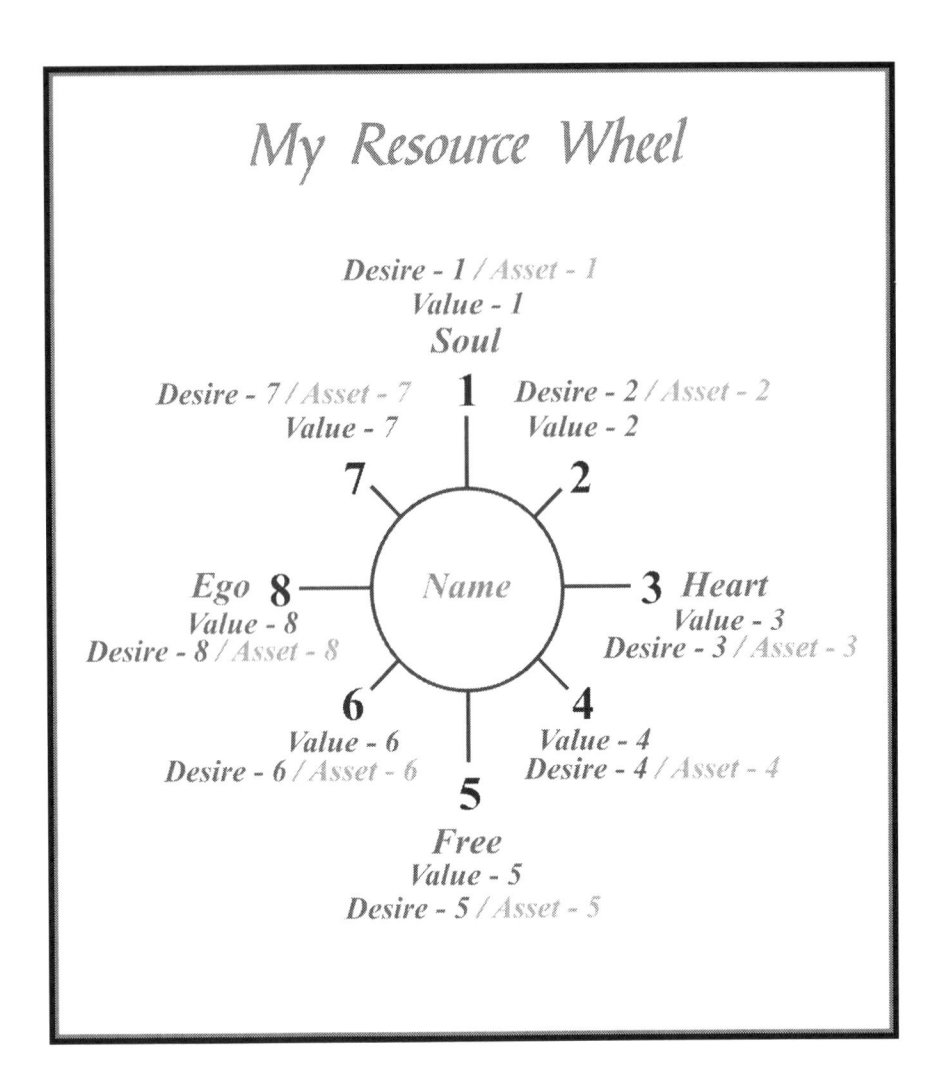

Desire - 1 / Asset - 1
Value - 1
Soul

Desire - 7 / Asset - 7 **1** *Desire - 2 / Asset - 2*
Value - 7   *Value - 2*

7   **2**

Ego **8** — Name — **3** *Heart*
Value - 8   *Value - 3*
Desire - 8 / Asset - 8 *Desire - 3 / Asset - 3*

6   **4**
Value - 6   *Value - 4*
Desire - 6 / Asset - 6 *Desire - 4 / Asset - 4*

5
Free
Value - 5
Desire - 5 / Asset - 5

The final step in this process is to add one's **Fear** and **Care** elements in that very same manner as follows:

My Resource Wheel

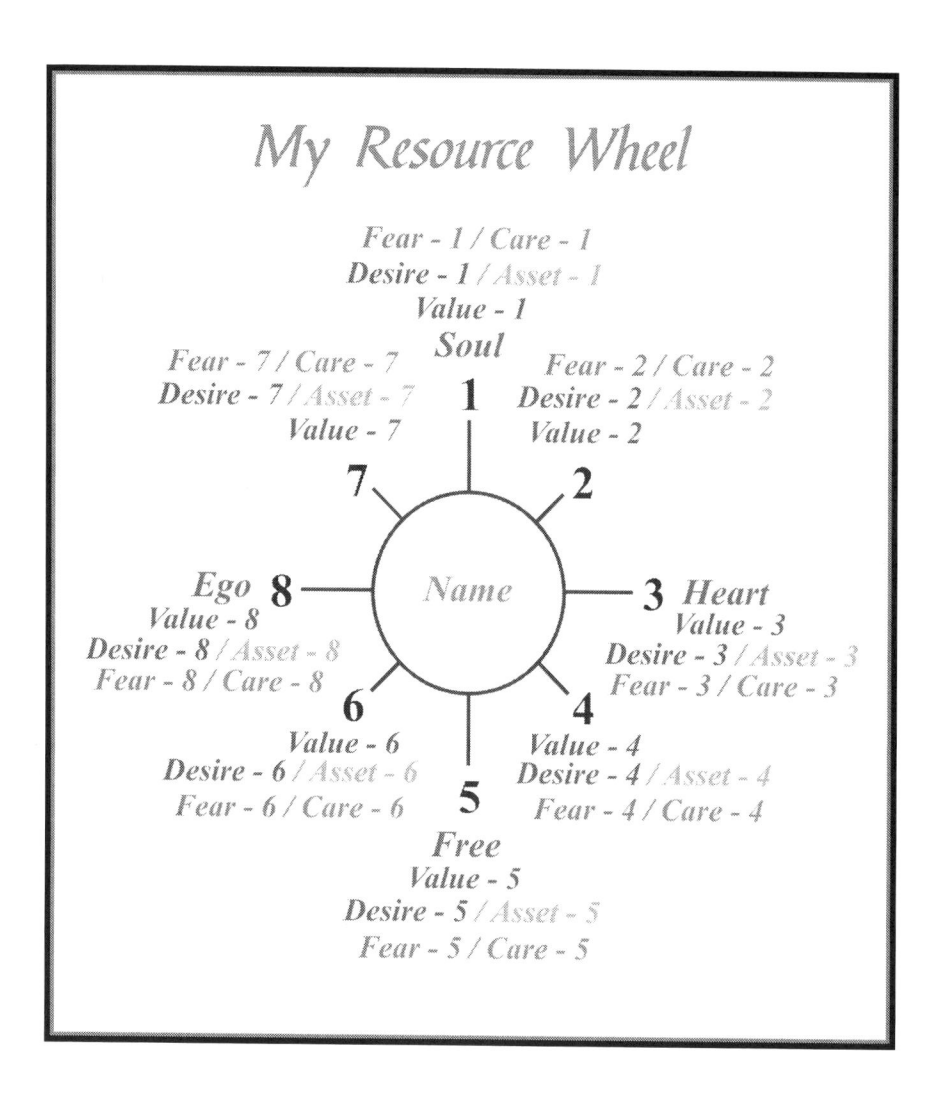

```
              Fear - 1 / Care - 1
             Desire - 1 / Asset - 1
                 Value - 1
                  Soul
Fear - 7 / Care - 7    1    Fear - 2 / Care - 2
Desire - 7 / Asset - 7      Desire - 2 / Asset - 2
    Value - 7                   Value - 2
         7               2

    Ego  8 ──  Name  ── 3  Heart
    Value - 8                   Value - 3
Desire - 8 / Asset - 8      Desire - 3 / Asset - 3
Fear - 8 / Care - 8         Fear - 3 / Care - 3
         6               4
    Value - 6               Value - 4
Desire - 6 / Asset - 6   5  Desire - 4 / Asset - 4
Fear - 6 / Care - 6         Fear - 4 / Care - 4
                  Free
                 Value - 5
             Desire - 5 / Asset - 5
              Fear - 5 / Care - 5
```

At this point your Resource Wheel is complete. It is also important to mention that there is significance as to the influence and orientation of these elements in respect to their position on the Medicine Wheel. In this I mean to say that anything above the East to West axis is of Spiritual orientation and influence and the others are as follows:

Directional Influence

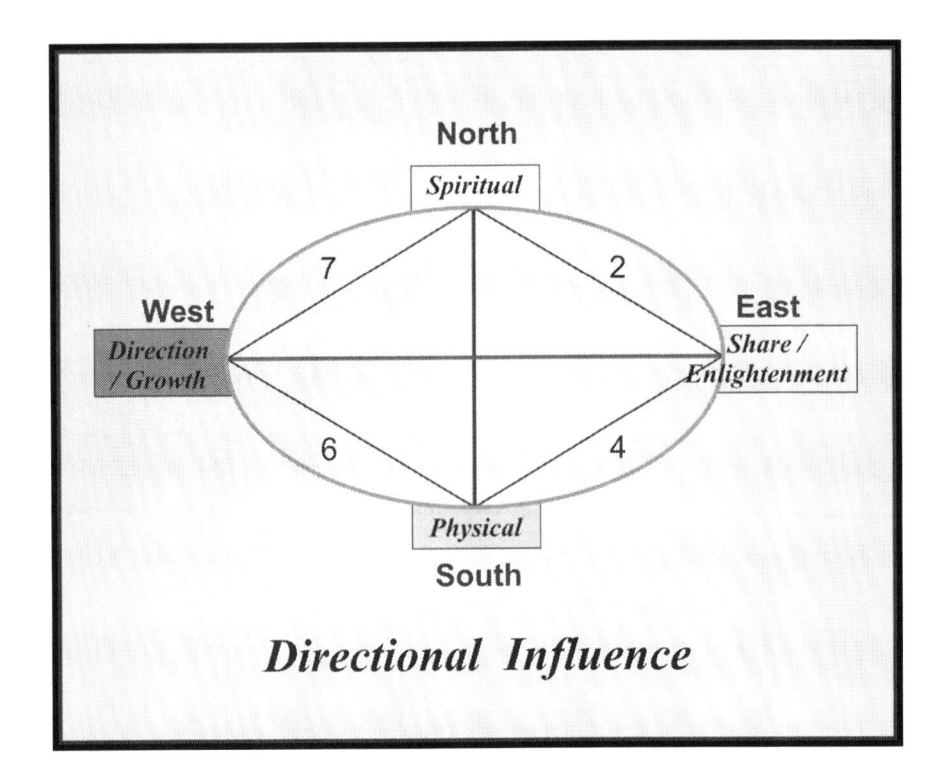

Therefore one can see that any things that are in position 7 are about Spiritual Growth and / or Direction while those in the position of 4 are orientated towards Physical Enlightenment and / or Share and so forth. For example the completed version of the elements of My Resource Wheel is as follows:

Where:　　A = Value　　B = True Desire
C = Asset　　D = Fear　　E = Care

D - Dying before I get to experience　　E - Staying healthy / Not dying
B - My desire to serve Great Pop　　C - *My Eagle Medicine*
A - My Love for Great Pop
Soul Will - Thunder
1 - Direction

Ordination - 7
A - My Trust & Faith
B - To help others & leave things better
C - *My Ability to read thoughts*
D - To have to get up early for poor pay
E - Helping others & the Future

2 - Union
A - My Potential & Openness
B - To parent my children
C - *My Ability to talk with G. P.*
D - Being without money & home
E - Doing a good job for G. P.

Resource - 8
Ego - Serpent
A - My Courage / Choices
B - To establish the Church and Tribe
C - *My Ability to help beings and things*
D - Being incarcerated
E - Getting my drivers license back

3 - Trinity
Heart - Dolphin
A - My Desire to Please and Serve G. P.
B - To get the books successfully published
C - *My Ability to Serve G. P.*
D - Being broke and not in Nolayte's life
E - Getting the books edited and published

Passion - 6
A - My Love and Care for All things
B - A continuous flow & supply of resources
C - *My Ability to call things forth*
D - Being indigent and not well thought of
E - Being in my children's lives

4 - Resonance / Cycle
A - My Commitment
B - To have security and a home
C - *My Ability with Spirits*
D - Not getting the books published
E - Being able to support myself

5 - Fulfillment
Free Will - Eagle
A - My Loyalty
B - To be Self-sufficient / Free　　C - *My Vision Medicine*
D - Getting a Fatal Condition　　E - Finding a means of Self-support
　　　　　　　　　　　　　　　　　　with comfort and ease

SELF REALIZATION

At this point, we now have a fully complete and operational Resource Wheel as well as have identified the things that are involved in our consciousness on a daily basis. If one was honest in the development of one's lists and Wheel then these are the specific and most important things that Really do mold, govern, and have an impact on one's daily life. Therefore, if we ever Really wish to experience any semblance of success in our life then these are the things that must be addressed and become the path to that success, period. Not only that, the awareness of one's Wheel elements can also help one realize a Proper Self-image.

I must state emphatically here again that the past Really does not matter! One certainly cannot change it, therefore one can only let go of it in order to have unlimited possibility in one's Future. If one allows any past event or experience to influence one's next choice or expression at all, then one is simply being limited or strangled by it. I am not at all implying that one should not learn from one's past experiences and expressions. Yet the only Real value of the past is to learn what expressions worked and how one discovered the process of realizing that to occur. Therefore it is not the What of the past, but instead the How to make more positive and profitable personal and collective expressions so as to realize the most Potential of the Future that is to be learned. Also, one should not limit the possibility of what did not work in the past from being appropriate or possible in any Future or next expression. Had I let my past drowning experience prejudice or control my idea of being about the water in the Future, then I would not have later enjoyed the many great and wonderful experiences of surfing, swimming, and all sorts of water sports that I did and do still enjoy. With that stated, let us now see how one's Resource Wheel can help one to become self-realized.

Most of this may be obvious to some people, but I will now give a full explanation at this point anyway. To start with, we will talk a little bit about our Self-image. When an adult person wakes up in the morning, the normal process of most people is to set forth actualizing an agenda that was determined by the activities of the previous day, month, and so forth. We were not born this way. Nope, we do it as a result of programming or "taught behavior". We might make long term plans at certain points in out lives, but mostly we stay in the mode of what some call "brush fire" resource allocation and management. The kids need something from the store, but the car has a flat tire and the phone is now ringing, you see? And to no great surprise, we also keep amending our Self-image in direct response to such behavior, events, and tactics so to speak. Yet what is really going on most of the time in our lives, especially if one is a part of the prevalent culture, is that we are constantly trying to operate while being personally out of balance to some degree, if not totally. There is never enough time in the day to do all of the things that, through our own Choices and Wills, we allow others to demand from us. And even if we do periodically have any spare time, then we need to use it to rest up from all of the strain and stress of our most recent efforts at pleasing others, while we struggle in pursuit of what it is that we feel that we need or want next. This rest time is actually a response to try to regain one's balance in some manner. Therefore, to be about any potential of Real Success in life, it is critical to remember here that Balance is in Fact, always in Motion!

Sadly enough, when one incarnates no one gives you a guidebook of how you can succeed in life, much less instructions in how to be Really and totally oneself in it. Nope, instead you are born and the rest is up to you to figure out for yourself, or not. Naturally all Beings and Things are born in Have mentality instead of Need mentality. A baby cares not what type of crib, diapers, or any other thing that it has, or not. Yet, Need mentality is the foundation of the religion of Materialism of the prevalent culture. Therefore the first lesson of newly incarnated Beings is how to get what you next want to receive and to want more of something that someone else has, which we can call the "Joneses". Naturally as well, is that in such a condition of the prevalent culture, no one wants to accept the Reality of their circumstances and the many deceptions and lies in it in most instances. This causes many individuals to try to escape these conditions of the prevalent culture though fantasy in youth or other self-destructive or demeaning expressions when they become older, such as with buying a lot of unnecessary stuff, watching sports, and other abusive expressions such as with drugs, alcohol, or even sex. And guess what? Yep, all of this colors and has an impact on one's Self-image. Not only that, in the prevalent culture most oftentimes one's Self-image is not really defined by oneself at all! Nope, most individuals in the prevalent society let others do it for them in fact. If course this is all part of the Bee Hive game as I call it, and the religion of Materialism. This societal structure and method of the prevalent culture needs to sponsor such conditions and behavior so as to continue to make and sell stuff that no one Really needs, period. And the really insane part of it all is that no one seems to Really Care! In fact, the image of success in the prevalent society in the most part is that of a wealthy and "Care Free" individual. Clearly since this material is about How To Realize Real Success in life, then first of all one must Understand what Real Success as well as Life is for oneself. And yes, all of the lists, including that of one's Hero and one's Resource Wheel, become the pathway to that Understanding.

Therefore, the first step on that pathway that we have to take is to define a Real and Proper image of Self. Of course to do such we must first recognize the difference between image and status. Every Being and Thing is born into a condition that one could call their circumstances and thereby status. Some Beings are born into wealth, and others are born into poverty or something that is somewhere in-between that some call the "Middle Class". And it is amazing to me that so many individuals of this classification and thereby status, have such great expressions of ambition so as to rise above others in it. Of course in the prevalent culture this is again simply taught behavior and promoted Need mentality. Therefore, in this use of the word image, I am talking about what is Real, and status is something that is all together different. Of course for any that prefer to let others define and determine their Self-image as mentioned can and does occur, they will only get status and not image. So, when one considers this condition and behavioral potential, in most instances of someone having what some call a "poor Self-image", it may not Really be that at all, or is it?

That realization brings to mind another awareness at this point. And that awareness is about what some consider or require "Success" to be. This material is being produced in support to realizing Real Success in life. So, it seems important to now clarify what is being meant by that use of the word of Success as well. What might be the easiest approach is to consider the difference between what one would consider as being of Success in life versus being of Success in a game. This material is not about how to succeed in winning a football game or business venture. And when you think about it, they both are simply games in some fashion. Yet I am certain that it will help in those types of choices and expressions to some degree or in some manner as well. Nope, this material is about life, and How to realize Real Success in it. To do such is actually quite simple and the only way for anyone to do such is to be Really and totally Oneself in it.

And to do anything other than that is to let some other consciousness or force, including other Beings, live vicariously through the precious vessel of Potential that is oneself! Of course when one does that, is to not realize one's own desires at all and thereby not Really, be in life! Yep, Success has to do with Desire Fulfillment and Real Success in this sense of the word is simply that. Yep, the type of Success that is being sought in this material is: ***The Realization and Fulfillment of one's own Prayers of Desire in life.***

So now that we finally have established a clear understanding as to what is being considered in the idea and word of Success, let us do a reality check concerning what we consider our life to be Really about. First of all, no one ever survives an incarnation into the Physical realm. Period. We come to it as visitors only, not to stay permanently. One can consider oneself and other Beings and Things to have started dying, in a sense the very instant that each one is born. Or, one can look at the whole of the experience of life in the Physical realm in the Proper Perspective and Attitude of being a great opportunity for expanding self-expression and realization, which is what it Really is all about. That is Why Great Pop made the theme park of Mother Earth and hence this current life opportunity for us, and that is What we should see it as being and be in pursuit of in it. One cannot possess a Proper Self-image at all if one is of any other mind set than the Reality of that last statement. Also, one cannot Really be of any success in self-realization if one does not fully embrace a Proper as well as complete image of oneself.

A comprehensive and Proper understanding as to what life really has to offer and what one should be about in it should certainly be taught early on. Another important thing that should be related to each Being and Thing after incarnating is not only their opportunities and Potential in life, but also the Who and What they Really are in it! Not too surprisingly though, most individuals are raised in the prevalent culture to be as fodder for the continuing and seemingly necessary wars of the Bee Hive game of the religion of Materialism. And since that "game" is predicated upon Need versus Have based mentality, Fear instead of one's Real opportunity and Purpose is what is instilled and programmed into each individual early on. From this condition of the prevalent culture, one can certainly understand the Why it is that so many individuals have a less than ideal or complete image of themselves. Therefore, in pursuit of what it Really is and should be, let us now consider just what we Really are. I Really am a Spirit that incarnated so as to make and experience physical expressions, period. I am a Spirit first and foremost. I am also, not instead of, a physically incarnated Being secondly, or even lastly. I also chose, as an expression of self-determination and thereby of my Free Will, to incarnate into the prevalent culture of Mother Earth, which you can tell I am not really happy about at times, ha, ha, ha.

Also, each and every circumstance that has or will be the conditions and experiences of my life, are singularly resultant from my Prayers of Desire and therefore my personal Plan and Prayerstick, period. No other Being or Thing can have any Real influence upon these things, except again, by my choice. I am Now also in life here on Mother Earth for the sole Purpose and Motive of experiencing things. And there is an even greater thing to consider in this respect at this point and that thing is that Great Pop Desires for me, you, and each and every single one of the All of the Potential which we consider to be Creation, a continuum of both New and Expansion. New is necessary to insure the Future, and so also is Expansion in a way. In the Physical realm that I chose to incarnate into, Great Pop designed it so as to be self-perpetuating with regard to these two things. And the tool or mechanism that He built into it is what is called Renewall, which will and does automatically accomplish such. Therefore, each and every single Thing in the Physical realm is constantly in some aspect or condition of Renewall in some fashion, all of the time, no matter what.

In consideration to the Reality of this condition of Renewall, not only is the surface as well as that which is within Mother Earth renewing herself so as to provide a continuum of new to be realized in that, but even the Galaxy and Universe are constantly doing the same thing. This type of Renewall is not simply making things the way that they used to be over and over again. Nope, instead of that it is making them different and New, over and over again. Understanding this aspect of Great Pop's design of the Physical realm and theme park of Mother Earth in it, can also give each of us a more clear perspective as well as orientation of what we too should be about in our life expressions and experiences. Renewall is a Reality as well as a tool that any Being or Thing can use anytime that they choose to call it forth and embrace it within the Life and Plan of oneself. And not only does Renewall facilitate self-realization, it facilitates Expansion within it as well. Why should I Desire to experience and express Expansion? Simply put, the answer is so that I can do more for Great Pop myself and in every sense and way!

Therefore if I now choose to Desire to experience anything different in myself or in my life, I do have the necessary tools identified by which to Realize that, in and for myself. Clearly any Being or Thing can Successfully accomplish such at any moment, and as often as is Desired and Chosen by themselves. Actually, if I want to embrace Renewall or experience anything New at all, I only have to embrace Change to Realize any such condition or thing, period. Also, since something always has to die so to speak in the process of change, I certainly better start considering the Real and clear purpose of my being in life, lest I become hesitant or resistive to Change. So, now that we have our wonderful tool of a Resource Wheel, let us see how it can assist us in accomplishing what we have just chosen to Desire to experience and express within ourselves and thereby our lives.

Obviously the first target or objective at this point is to "fix" any Self-image problems, as not to do such will preclude experiencing the fullest condition of Expanding self-awareness. You see, to not have that condition of oneself will inhibit one's capacity for Expanding self-realization and thereby being able to experience the fullest measure of success in life. I am certain by now that to "fix" anything is to simply embrace and employ Change. Also, I am positive that it Really is not necessary to consider what one's Self-image was in the past or even in the present. Clearly all of the reasons for the why of it being the pattern of such are of no consequence at all either. While many people might like to explore different reasoning about such things, in reality it is of absolutely no consequence as to why one's Image of Self was as it was! Of course in the prevalent culture there are certain individuals that provide such support of discovery, and charge a lot of money to really do little of the work other than that assessment, period.

You see, anyone can help someone Change, but only the person that seeks to Change can actually Realize any Real Change in themselves. Therefore if I Really Desire to have greater Success in my life at this point, then I must choose and do the work of Change in myself, no matter what. As mentioned, the very first step is to Change the Image of myself, and I state it this way for a reason. It is one thing to consider one's Self-image as seen only by oneself, and a totally different thing to consider the image of oneself from the perspective of others. Remember here again, most Self-images are not really defined singularly by oneself in the prevalent society. Therefore since I am a part of such a society, for me to really be successful then I will have to consider both perspectives.

I can in fact choose to ignore the perspective and image that others might have of me and still be of some relative measure of success in life. But since my consciousness is a part of the Group Consciousness of the prevalent culture and Beings and life forms as a whole, I do now choose to work on both images simultaneously so as to be able to realize the greatest Potential of Success. And the key and operative element that I have to use to accomplish such in this and the other things that I will do so as to realize that success, is to Change and retrain my Focus. Yep, Focus is the key tool and element that we must employ to accomplish any or all that is necessary to realize any Change or improvement, period. If my Self-image is too conditioned by and results from what others think of me, then I need to redirect my Focus as to what *I* think, not what *they* think. If I am callous as to what others think and too self-absorbed that way, then I need to consider what face of Fear has resulted in such a choice of behavioral pattern in myself. You see, both images of self are to be operative in balance, in order to realize the greatest measure of success in life. Therefore in managing and renewing both images, one has an increased capacity of expressional influence, meaning that one's expressions can have a limitless and expanding dynamic effect upon the life of oneself and other Beings and Things, and that is an expansion of one's Power Potential in a great big way!

An example of such a potential can be where I only consider my image as seen through my own eyes. In that case then other Beings and Things will not know of my Real Potential, Motives, and Desires. Have you ever been around an arrogant and know-it-all type of Self-image person that has asked or more likely told you to do something? If I am able to live alone and on my own land and do not have to interact with others then I could be relatively successful in life that way perhaps. But even in that condition, I would probably alienate all of the other lifeforms to some degree. Yep, even my crops would not grow well. Certainly most of us do know of some people just like that example, which is an individual that cares little about anything other than their own image and idea of success. However, to be of Real Success in life does not in fact require that others share the same image of oneself at all. You see, the trick is to "consider" one's image of Self as seen by others, but not let it become altered or defined by them.

Remember the tool of Focus? The way to be able to maintain two Self-images as described is most simply and easily realized by recognizing and employing one's Focus as necessary. To do such is as easy as for one to Change one's Choices of behavioral pattern response to stimuli. The responses that I am talking about here are commonly referred to as habits. Yep, one can stop being a "Pleaser" personality and all sorts of dysfunctional personal behavioral expressions simply by a Choice to do such and commitment to Renewall. Actually, by accepting that Reality, the expansion of one's potential next expression or response can automatically effect a change of image of oneself as well. So one can perhaps now recognize that there is tremendous Potential to be realized by not trying to rationalize and make excuses to maintain some aspects of one's old Self-image. Actually, much more speed and potential to Realize Real Success in life will be affected simply by choosing to Change and experience Renewall. I did this very thing when I changed schools as a child. I did not like the old image of myself made by others, or myself at that point. Also I recognized that because of that condition, my Potential was being very much limited and one of the limits had to do with not being able to play on the teams in sports.

So, I started over and did experience and express Renewall by simply Changing the personages of my peers in a way. It was as simple as for me to go to a different school to get different peers, and the images of myself that way. I could not change the image and ideas that the old people had about me, and it seemed like it would have been wrong for me to try. Instead, I started over in a sense, in a different "community" of peers, and it worked Great. At the different school I made new friends, played on the basketball and track teams, and even made much better grades. Clearly all of this was not available to me at the school, image of Self, and life of the "past". Nope, I never would have got to have the life that I have had at all if this process was not Real, and did dot Really work.

Now that we have an understanding of the potential of the process of changing one's Self-image, let us consider what the one of our next and "New", Self-images should be. Here again, we get to make some choices. Actually, one can make up any kind of stuff and consider that for one's next Self-image, after all, consider all of the Elvis impersonators! There are some people that one might know that do in fact walk in that "river in Egypt" that I call "De Nile" or fantasy and illusion. Imagination is good and beneficial, that is how inventions happen. But no one ever did anything at all from illusion that was more than some type of entertainment for some individuals. And if one Really Desires to experience Real Success, in Real Life, illusion is not the way to it. On the other hand, the lists that one made as well as one's Resource Wheel certainly are. To change my Self-image, all I have to do is to look at those things that are most important to me, and then choose and Really Value My Choices with passion. Here again, remember it is not a Real Choice but a May Be, if one later changes their mind about something.

The eight top elements of my True Value System is the Real Image that I can Choose to Renewall to, at any moment. The next step, like changing schools, is for me to then choose only to be about those individuals that respect and value that sense of character and potential about myself. If I keep my Focus and Balance upon those elements at the top of my True Value List, then my next new Self-image cannot be influenced by anyone that Desires to make a "Pleaser" out of me. All that I then have to do is to establish and continue to Remember my New Self, and forget the old Self ideas of me. Even if family and friends may not be as accepting of my New Self-image or are as easy to be with as the new people in my new Self life, I do also possess the ability to choose not to care what their image is of me during this transitional period at all!

Remember here that if we desire better or different in our life experience, then we must embrace Change for that to occur. *If we honestly desire Real Success in our life, we must Change the things that cause it to continue to be less than, or different than that.* Also, the only way that any Being or Thing can realize Real life as well as any semblance of Success at all in it is to be completely and honestly one's Real Self in it, and totally conscious as much of the time as is possible. Our personal expressions and choices are what have caused our life to be as it is and was, and these are primarily resultant from one's own management of one's Self-image and Value System. We individually and collectively have issued forth Prayers of Desire for Potential to be self-realized in our lives or not. That Really is how things have become as they now are in our lives. And if no Change is made to these fundamental elements that determine the experiences and expressions of our selves and thereby also our life, then one can only expect more of the same, and thereby the past. We can and should change our Prayers of Desire in order to realize more Potential Success in the Future. Yet that Potential will not be fully available to us unless we choose to embrace Change in our Selves first. I say such because unless we make room for any such thing to be embraced and held dearly to oneself, we can never fully receive it. Real Success in life is just that, receiving the fullest measure of Potential in one's experiences and expressions of being completely one's Real Self in life. Hence, it is obvious that the quickest and easiest means to effect such Change in our lives and Self, is to Renewall so as to become completely one's Real Self and thereby also one's personal and collective Self-image.

As far as the other elements in the other lists, they are not as significant as relates to one's Self-image as one's True Value List at this point. The number one thing on my True Value List in fact has nothing to do with people and their opinion of me at all. Nope, it is My Love for Great Pop and no Being or Thing can ever take that away from me or change it in me. And unless I loose Focus or give it away, nothing can thereby keep me from being my Complete Self and totally in Balance and Successful in that. Remember here that we are Choosing to experience and express Change and Renewall. In the future when things are not so easy, all that I have to do to get myself back in Proper Balance and Perspective is to train my Focus upon that first element, or one or more of the others and then I will again become Really Self-realized. The next step is for me to then choose to Expand this image of myself, which is a Spirit and a Real Being that Really Loves Great Pop, with the second element, which is that of my Potential and Openness. Unless I can honestly accept those qualities and limitless Potential of myself, then it is not possible. This is why honesty in these lists is so very important. In reality, each and every Being and Thing is an outwardly expressive Potential and thereby is of Potential in some way. Yet I have to honestly and consciously own that of myself and hence have it available for inspection so to speak, if I am ever going to be of any realization of it.

From its position on the Wheel, this aspect of myself which is perfect in all conditions and at all times is something that I am ever in discovery or seeking Spiritual Enlightenment about when I am incarnated. That awareness is invaluable in keeping my balance and an image of myself that is complete. You see, if I see myself as being complete then I cannot have any of my expressions or Desires become not fulfilled or thwarted by other Beings or Things at all. This is most important to maintain consciousness of, especially when being sold the idea that I am incomplete or in need of something, by other Beings or Things. So as I start at the top and accept the Reality of What and Who I Really am and what I came to Mother Earth for, it all starts to formulate and develop into a most perfect and Proper Self-image. Equally important is that this is an image of Self that is based upon Reality, not illusion. Naturally if it is of Reality, then it is also an image of Self that is capable of Realizing the greatest Potential of Success in life. The rest of the process of Renewall of one's Self-image is to "process" and expand it in the same manner with the remaining elements of one's True Value System. The final step and trick is to commit to it and then take one's first step in it, just as in the first day at the new school which I described earlier.

PART V

TO SUCCESS

SELF - ACTUALIZATION

The desired result of the work that was done in the preceding chapter is the realization of a Proper image of one's Real Self. It is significant to note here that this is a process that should be done periodically throughout one's life on Mother Earth. I say this because the elements that are currently present in my True Value System are different to some extent than when I was a child, a teenager, or during my early adulthood. Not all of my True Values are different and some them, including the top ones, are the same as when I incarnated. Yet at this particular point in my life, some of the others are now different. I do also have White, Eagle, and ThunderBeing Medicine and I always will, as these are Medicines that are a part of my Ever Name. Those aspects of my Real Self are important, but they are something that I cannot Change. I also know that things I cannot choose differently are not things that determine my Real Success in life. Therefore in my pursuit of Real Success in life, I can only respect and honor the Medicines of my Real Self in what I do and do with them. The same is Real and true for any Being or Thing that was born with a disability or develops such a condition later. You see Real Success in life has no condition to the physical. Remember, all incarnated Beings and Things are Spirits first and foremost that come to experience and express being themselves in the theme park of Mother Earth.

So at this point, it is safe to say that the Real and Proper Image of myself that I am solely responsible for using and maintaining, is that of an incarnated Spirit of a Being that just happens to also be a PohTikaWah that is deservedly Proud and Committed to:

1. My - Love for Great Pop
2. My - Potential & Openness
3. My - Desire to Please and Serve Great Pop
4. My - Commitment
5. My - Loyalty
6. My - Love and Care for All things
7. My - Trust & Faith
8. My - Courage & Choices

Also, for me to be of any Real Success in life, it is not so important that others respect or even recognize these aspects of myself. It is only important that I do, and constantly I might add. It is my responsibility to keep them in Focus as well as to not let others change them in any manner or form, period. This is critical if I am to experience Real Success in my life now and in time to come. Any failures that I have had in the past were actually resultant of my not keeping such things in Focus, or through my allowing of others to change them, and of this I am most certain.

Each of these values and aspects of my orientation in life are expansions of the first one, being that of My Love for Great Pop. This not only colors and defines the pattern that is the Real Self of me, but it also directs the events and opportunities of my life experiences and expressions that result from being that in myself. In this I mean to say that it is all my Choice and this Real and honest Self-image will manifest certain experiences and challenges thereby, all on its own. Of course, any challenges are also predominantly resultant from either Fear Prayers in my own Prayerstick, or the actions and Desire Prayers of members of the group as a whole, of those Beings and Things that I choose to interact with in the society that I now live in. It is also important to note here that All of one's Value System and not just those top elements do apply here. The very last element in a long list of such values will have influence, as does the very first. Of course the last element in my list will be of a relatively lesser impact upon my life comparatively speaking, simply because of my choice of prioritization of it to be that way.

So at this point, we have the springboard or foundation as it were to Real Success in life, in the manner of establishing a Real and Proper Self-image. This foundation and springboard is what I must maintain the integrity of, and also what I should use to re-establish my balance and center with. It is also what I must keep as my Primary Focus from this point forward if I am to Realize the greatest Success in my life. As long as I can do that, I will in fact and Reality be able to Succeed in expanding Self-realization, which is one of the things that Great Pop identified that He wants each and All Beings and Things to continue to have, experience, and express. And since that is the case of it, it seems important to add that an even greater Potential for me to experience Success in my life now and in the future is even possible. Yep, an even greater Potential can be realized in my Being and being in life. That greater Potential can become realized if I recognize that

Great Pop does Desire this for All Beings and Things and I continue to do what is Proper, when it is Proper, to support the continuing fulfillment of that Promise not only for just myself, but also for any and All other Beings and Things as well. And it is of no great surprise that the last statement just happens to define in a sense the Real intent and orientation of the theme park of Mother Earth, which is Brotherhood Proper.

It certainly is of great benefit to finally realize not only the Who and What I Really am, but also what that "am" is Really about, which is what having a Proper and complete Self-image can facilitate. At this point one might be wondering as to how one can use this springboard and foundation other than just self-remedy at the times that one is thrown out of balance by the events of one's life? The answer is that such a Proper foundation for success in life is augmented by the other elements in one's Resource Wheel so as to not only experience and express expanding Self-realization, but also expanding Self-actualization as well. As one might recall, Self-actualization is also one of the things that Great Pop Desires for all Beings and Things, and it too is a part of what He promised to provide a continuum of, so as to ensure the future. Again, one might be wondering just what the heck does expanding Self-actualization have to do with realizing the Greatest Success in life? Again the answer is simple, Everything!

Yep, any time one gets fulfillment or success in any aspect of one's being in life, it is only the result of the actualization of one's Prayer of Desire for the Potential of that experience or expression to occur, period. And of course that can be a collaborative expression of Prayers of Desire as well. In this I mean to say that even if you personally do not pray for something to occur, it can still happen if someone that you are in association with does pray for it. And to clarify what I mean here by Prayer and Prayers of Desire, these are not necessarily chants, oaths, mantras, or any type of religious statements. A Prayer can be a simple thought, idea, curiosity, hope, or fear, and they are the same whether spoken or not. If one becomes thirsty or hungry for ice cream, at some moment it is a Prayer of Desire. Worrying about someone or something is a Prayer just the same as when one is kneeling in front of an altar in some religious temple or the like. In reality all that we do in life is to Pray, meaning to decide, choose, and then issue forth Prayers of Desire based upon our Resource Wheel or not, that can be considered as being of Fear or Hope. We do this to attract a like-in-kind Potential so as to become self-realized in itself, which becomes our next experience or expression in life. So in a nutshell, no matter what happens in one's life there can only be a certain kind of success that is resultant anyway!

Of course that is just because of Great Pop's brilliance of design. But what we are seeking to achieve here is something even better than just letting things happen without our total involvement and Focus. To simplify this part of How to be of expanding Self-actualization, we will simply Focus upon those Desires that are originated in oneself, period. Earlier in this material, the complete methodology of receivership was described in detail. In summary, it is the same as casting a line and hook with one's Prayer of Desire magnets attached, upon the waters of the sea of Creation so as to attract like-in-kind. Yet in the prevalent society, it seems that certain individuals seem to catch more fish than others, and some individuals seemingly to never miss any at all. Actually there are even a few individuals that do not even have to wet a line, as some call it, because the fish always seem to jump right into their boat!

At this point one might be wondering what Receivership has to do with Actualization? After all, actualization seems to be about making something happen or at least doing something such as making something with one's hands or the like. Okay, one more time, the answer is, Everything! Yep, to be able to move a simple object such as a pebble or any such outward personal expression is actually, Receivership. Again, all that any Being or Thing ever does in life, is to issue forth Prayers of Desire and make decisions and choices about such, period. For instance, a person is playing a stringed instrument. They had to Pray (issue forth thoughts and or feelings as a Prayer of Desire / Hope) for that instrument to be in their life at that point, as well as for the strings to make the sound that they Desire to come from it, or it would not be there doing that at all. They had to Pray for the ability to learn to play it, and for most individuals they also had to Pray for some person to help them in that process. They have to keep Praying that the strings do not break and so forth all the while that they are playing, as well as for their muscles to respond in the manner necessary to manipulate the strings, and on, and on, and on....

You see, Self-actualization is just Receivership! So with that Understanding, what can we now do to become better at it, so as to have more of it, so as to realize the greatest Potential of Success in life? The key and operative word in answer to that question is Focus. Now the tricky part is to figure out just what to focus on! Just because

I focus on something, that action in itself does not necessarily mean that I will get what I Desire, at least not right away, such as some seem to think is necessary to be of success in life. On the other hand, if I am distracted from my fishing pole and the process of my being of receivership by the appearance of some pretty girl, then I will probably not be getting many fish that day. At this point in my life, I do realize that I have now missed many fish in life, simply because of my lack of focus. This is another point where our exercise in defining our Hero comes into play. Actually both the May-Bes List and Hero identification are dynamically influential upon one's capacity of Self-realization. This is Real and true not so much in what they add or enable, but instead in the sense of identifying things that can present a distraction, just like the pretty girl.

A Potentially positive use of one's Hero definition is to consider the patterns of behavior and Value System that inspired such that is given in it. If your Hero is a rescuer type of individual, Why do they need to do that? Does being a rescuer make them feel good, complete, or important? Besides, who wants any Being or Thing to be in jeopardy so as to need rescuing anyway? Of course the same goes for Healing and so forth. This can be of a great assistance, especially when one wishes to Change a habitual response to stimuli that is not totally rewarding. Remember, one's Hero is the Who and What one Desires to be if one is not one's present Self, and in one's present condition of Self. So the trick is not to try to escape into one's Hero's condition of being in life, but instead incorporate the positive aspects available in their behavioral model and profile into one's own. In reality, to do just that can enable one to experience a much greater Potential of Self-actualization than one has yet experienced. Even so, the very greatest Potential still exists singularly within one's own Resource Wheel, period.

The minus side if there is one, of one's Hero definition and May-Bes List is that the things in them can and probably will be of some level of distraction to one's focus, which is good to know about as well. If one is not totally fulfilled in one's condition in life, many people tend to either measure it by, or escape into, the imaginary Potential of these two lists. I cannot tell you how much time in life and precious energy I have wasted by "Planning" what I would do if I won the Lottery and so forth! It has been said that man is of air and a Dreamer and I have certainly been a dreaming airhead or so it seems at times, ha, ha, ha. Had I just bought tickets and given no more time or energy to such than that, then no downside could be considered. But to distract my focus from the fishing pole of my Prayerstick that way has definitely caused me to miss out, on some of the Potential that I could have realized with that energy and time. Fantasy and speculation are not bad if one does not invest too much time and energy into such expressions that have marginal Potential of Fulfillment. Actually, realizing the greatest Potential of Success in life includes imagination, dreaming, and so forth, as long as it adds to one's Potential and resources thereof. There are many different ways of doing anything in life, but not if we Really want to experience the greatest Potential of Success in it.

Actually, I do still Really Desire to experience winning, including the Lottery. Yet I have no money or way to get to where there is one at present. Therefore, my greater Potential for Success in life at this point is in focusing upon what is presently available versus what is not. And, guess what? Even if I won the Lottery, I would only use the proceeds of such to actualize the things that are now defined in my Resource Wheel anyway! Certainly there are many different ways to be of the receivership and thereby actualization of anything. Yet the Real and most important element is still that of focus.

In the big picture of such, life is pretty simple as Great Pop originally designed it. Each Being and Thing makes out an itinerary of experiences that they wish to have in the theme park of Mother Earth before incarnating and it is amended as one progresses along the path of one's own design once incarnated into it. There is no need for money Really, all that one needs one already has in the way of a Prayerstick of sorts that issues forth Prayer of Desire "Tickets" so as to experience or express something while one is there. There are two other things that one has a relatively limited supply of as well in an incarnation and hence life, and they are time and energy. It should now be pretty easy to understand how one's management and hence focus of these two things, can and do affect one's ability to realize the greatest Potential of Success in life or not.

The way that one's Resource Wheel works is most helpful with regard to management and focus. Not only does it identify what is Really important to oneself at any point in one's life, it also gives one a sense as to why that is, and is that way. Another nice thing about one's lists and Resource Wheel is that identified therein are not only what one should direct one's focus upon, but also the order in doing such from the priorities assigned therein. An example of such a condition and consideration in my Wheel is found in all of the positions. So let us now examine just one of them:

5 - Fulfillment
Free Will - Eagle
A - My Loyalty

B - To be Self-sufficient / Free   C - My Vision Medicine
D - Getting a Fatal Condition   E - Finding a means of Self-support with comfort and ease

The elements defined in position five, tell one why Loyalty is so important to my sense of Being, and being fulfilled. Therefore one can understand why I feel that to be Really Successful in life, I must be able to be Self-sufficient and Free. Also, since five is the position of the South in the Wheel and is thereby physical, one can certainly understand why I might have a Fear of getting a fatal condition at this time in my life. With the South being about predominantly physical things, it is of little surprise that my Care at this point is to find a means of Self-support with comfort and ease. Certainly these are more than just clues to both what I Desire and what I am Afraid of at this time.

What is given in one's Resource Wheel is a road map so to speak of how to actualize the greatest Potential of Success in life. On top of that it even describes in detail the easiest as well as most necessary way or method to get there! And once again the operative tool is simply that of Focus. Another really neat part of the design of one's Resource Wheel is that not only does it tell you how to get there and actualize the greatest Potential of Success in life it also identifies any road blocks that might be in the way. As added support it even describes what one can do to remove the barriers of them so to speak.

Therefore, for me to actualize fulfillment in my life at this very moment, I should consider using my Vision Medicine to find a means in which to become Self-sufficient and free. Through the application of Focus, I can use my Vision Medicine to break down any barriers to being Self-sufficient and free in the present, the near term, and the future. Clearly, that will definitely actualize a greater Potential for Success in my life at present. In the same fashion, I am certain that finding a means of Self-support with comfort and ease will preclude me from getting a fatal condition as well. Even if becoming Self-sufficient and free does not totally eliminate any concerns over such in the present and future, it certainly would facilitate me to be able to do much more about it than I can at present.

A review of the rest of my Resource Wheel or that of one's own will confirm that this is clearly a road map to Success in life through enabling one to be Self-actualized. Of course to do such, again all that is necessary is to apply one's focus upon that Potential which is to be actualized and then, give that element the necessary Time, Energy, and Passion. Another benefit of one's Resource Wheel is that it defines and allows one to recognize one's priorities. This is very important to one's being able to actualize the greatest Potential of Success in life in the sense that it tells one just what that Success is or might look like. The number one priority in my life is Great Pop, my Love for Him, and my Desire to serve His Will and Plan. Any expression that I can make or focus upon to actualize that is what I most Desire to experience, express, and do, period.

Of course when I keep my focus and stay in pursuit of actualizing that number one thing in my life, it does take energy, attention, and focus, away from the other directions and elements of my Resource Wheel. My commitment and focus in getting this material written now is the Reality of that condition. I am presently not expending energy or care about any of my other Desires on the Wheel at all while I am doing this activity either. I have prioritized the preparation of this material as the thing that I should focus my time and energy on at this moment because of the fact that Great Pop wants it completed in the near term. Therefore, I choose to actualize it now and in this manner because pleasing Him is more important to me than anything else at present. This is an example of focus you see. And I do have a passion about doing it, and doing it to the best of my ability. In support as well as response, Great Pop has facilitated this writing machine to keep working and I am presently not without food. Also at this moment and even though I do not currently have enough money to pay them, the bills are not yet past due. In a sense one could say that the potential of this material is Self-actualizing itself in a way because it too wants to please and serve Great Pop that way and so forth. Focus is the means of Self-actualization and the only tricky part or cost of focus is choice. If I am focused upon the writing of this material, I cannot also be giving my time and energy to anything else. When I am through with this material or perhaps even before that, I am certain that Great Pop will have me shift my focus and be about the actualization of one of the other elements of my Resource Wheel, maybe, ha, ha, ha.

SELF - DETERMINATION

It has been several days now since I completed the last chapter. My focus has shifted primarily due to my concerns at present as to how I am going to be able to continue to live. So as one can see, my life paralleling this material has once again become very apparent. Currently it is the 30th of January and I am still without prospects of getting work. Again the fuse that is burning down on my being past due on the bills and having the website shut down is now only a few days long. In a couple of weeks I may again be homeless. My concern and worry is not just about myself in this, but also as to the wellbeing of TohNaWah. There are several people that I have talked with that might be able to find me some work. An angel in the form of Dolphin sister whom has helped me several times in the past is sending some resources to me in the mail. I hope it will be enough and in time to keep what little that I do still have in operation so to speak. A few minutes ago Coyote sister in Seven Lakes, whom also has been most helpful and supportive, has also done the same. Ironically Great Pop had me put as the question in that segment of this week's update and section of the website: "Why does God let Bad things happen to Good people?" The answer to that question does seem to be an appropriate beginning to this new chapter about Self-determination and my life, which is: "He doesn't, people do."

As experienced in the Odyssey of Origins, it is all about the promise that Great Pop made to the Potential when they were free roaming in The Great Void. In a brilliant way Great Pop proposed that if all of the Potential would Choose in Unanimity to return inside of His Essential Will, then He would continue to ensure that there would be a continuum of "new" and thereby the Future. He elaborated upon this proposal by promising that if all of them went inside His Essential Will then He would make arenas for outer personal experience and expression so that any and all Potential that might choose to, could experience expressing themselves therein whenever they desired to do such. The goal was that outside of being of His Real Creative ability, Great Pop wanted each and all of the Potential to have as much of what He enjoyed for Himself as possible. The promise was stated in a manner that reflected His desire for each and all of the Potential, which was that of a continuum of expanding personal Self-realization, Self-actualization, Self-awareness, Self-expression, and Self-determination.

Just by posing the offer to them in the manner that He did, Great Pop brilliantly effected self-determination in each and every one of them, and thereby also us. Self-determination, yes this thing that we so oftentimes refer to as being Free Will, is pretty tricky stuff at times! I say such now because it seems that when one considers the Really big picture of life, one is never alone in it. Certainly, my situation in life can be construed as being all my fault in a way, and I will, and do take full blame or responsibility for its being as it now is. On the other hand, I also recognize that it also is resultant from not only the choices that I have made in the past, but also choices that others have made and expressed as well. In this it is not just money that I am referring to, but also support in the way of opportunity and so forth. If I had been able to continue working at the latest job that I tried to re-establish my computer career and skills with, things would now be much different for me, maybe. Yet several years ago now, an individual at that place of business chose not to let me have the opportunity for that to occur. In the same way, so also have the many other people impacted my Potential and condition of Self-determination which have rejected the many applications and resumes that I have submitted over these many years now. The same goes for the multitude of individuals that have chosen to either reject or ignore the various applications as well as submissions of various things that I have used to try to accomplish some means of self-support with over these now many years. In this regard I am not referring to just those individuals that have had an impact on my Potential by denying employment opportunities to me. Equally of impact are those individuals that try to take advantage and give one less compensation than what one should receive for some effort or work.

As one considers the influence of others upon one's own Potential of Self-determination in life, perhaps now one can see why I call it the Bee Hive game of the religion of Materialism in the prevalent culture. In reflection I am now being given to realize and understand that there does exist a dynamic link between Self-sufficiency and Self-determination. Clearly, the more Self-sufficient that I can become in my life then the more Self-determining I can be in it as well. This cause and effect exists primarily because of the possible influence of others upon one's own Potential of Self-determination. In that realization, my next thought was, " So that is why Great Pop has been telling me to become more Self-sufficient lately!" Many years ago Great Pop started trying to help me understand how this all works and how important being Self-sufficient really is in life. Yep, it all started many years ago in one of my first of the year Medicine Wheel ceremonies. In that one, He told me to be very careful with regard to my freedom and that I should make only choices that would ensure that I be as free as possible. Periodically, He would repeat that guidance since that time and I would take note of it. However, until now I did not realize the significance of what He was trying to share and did not really know what to do with it.

Obviously there is much to be considered as to what Real Self-determination is all about it seems. One's freedom is clearly related to one's capacity to realize Real Self-determination. Also, one's sufficiency in Self is related to one's capacity of being able to realize, or be of any condition of Real freedom. Obviously the more that one becomes of complete sufficiency in oneself, then the less influence that any other Being or Thing can have upon one's being free to experience and express oneself however one desires, which is being completely Self-determining as well as free. Therefore, it seems that the more that one can do to insulate oneself from the effects of the choices of others in one's life, the more free and Self-determining that one will become. While this condition seems only valid in the individual case and sense, it actually is Real and true collectively as well. The more sufficient in Self each member of a collective or group is or becomes, then the less that they will need of anything from anyone else in the group. In such a condition as that, not only is evenness maintained with its membership but the group will be of greater resource and strength both individually and collectively. Hum, that sounds like a Tribe doesn't it? But oops, that is Volume Two of this material, ha, ha, ha.

Now I can see just Why the Bee Hive game of the prevalent culture is so popular as well as successful. Of course the "game" is founded upon and promotes what is contrary to complete sufficiency in each Self as through its hierarchical structures and specialization it promotes dependency and compliance instead. It certainly is much easier to "Play the Game" than to try to operate outside of it in any manner, as I have been trying to do for some time now. Also, I can see that the bottom three elements in positions four, five, and six of my Resource Wheel just happen to be all about this particular subject of Self-determination. Of course it is so very perfect that the elements in those positions relate to things of a physical nature. It is now clear to me that for me to be able to realize any form of expanding Potential of Real Success in my life, the key now it seems is that I must be able to be of expanding Self-determination if I am to realize such. So the question becomes, "Just how in the heck do I do that now, Great Pop?" Great Pop's immediate response to me was, *"Simply "choose" it now."*

"Not always so easy," was my first thought about that response from Him. In fact, at most times it is not easy at all. Great Pop then reminded me about what we experienced and learned about Choices and the Future in the Odyssey of Origins. I then began to remember how I must embrace Change in order for me to have anything different in my life at all. I am not so big on Change most of the time it seems. Maybe the reason for my feelings about such has to do with what I experienced and learned about the Origin of the Future in Origins, which is as follows:

*****

Excerpt from Origins – Volume 4

It seems kind of funny that I am beginning this material about the future by talking about the past. Yes the future can be pretty scary stuff at times, especially since we have Bark on Tree and its associated essence of Fear. As Great Pop has explained these concepts and this understanding to me, an essence is unlimited in its shape, form or utility. One of the Medicines of Essences is that they are self-perpetuating, like air or smoke or water in the ocean. No matter how much you take or use, there will always be plenty more. And yes, smoke is self-perpetuating because even when it has dissipated and you can no longer see it, it still exists. In Volume One of Origins, we learned from Great Pop that all things began by The Law of One segmenting a part of itself into the five Founding Essences of Desire, Feeling, Onement, Balance, and the ThunderBeing of Change. Any and all things that are, are because of The Law of One and from it these and all other essences are made. When Great Pop, as the Group Consciousness of these five Founding Essences, originally wished to express Himself, the first Operative was then made to accommodate that desire. We learned that the reason Great Pop had expressed that desire way back then, was to ensure there would always be a Future. Also learned was that Operatives are like hoses that one can use to direct the flow of Essences through.

When Great Pop designed the Personal Structure for Spirits to outwardly express themselves with, including ourselves, He created a subordinate or limited form of an Essence and called it Fear. When I asked Him why He created Fear, He told me it was made to motivate and protect the physical form and that He made it with a composition that has a time limit. Just like one's Ego or what I call one's Bark on Tree, this limited or subordinate Essence is left behind with the cocoon of one's physical body on one's exit, when the Spirit returns to His Essential Will. Great Pop has always told me how everything that is, has and is Medicine. The previous volumes of Origins helped me better understand the How and Why that this is real. I also learned from Him that everything that is, is a composition of Essences as well. In fact it is the unique blend or mixture of Essences that comprises the Spirit and consciousness of any and all Things, including oneself or the paint on the door. Also, any and all Things that Great Pop has made have some of each of the five Founding Essences in their makeup. Therefore whatever exists has Desire, Feeling, Onement, Balance, and Change inherent in it. As you can see, I did not include in that list of Founding Essences, the ThunderBeing of Change. So what happened to the ThunderBeing? He died!

Yep, in the Original event whereby Great Pop as the Group Consciousness of Medicine desired to express Himself, The ThunderBeing of Change chose to die in order for Great Pop to be able to realize his desire. At that time the ThunderBeing of Change saw and felt that His death was necessary as a means to provide an outside. Prior to this event, all that existed, existed within the Group Consciousness, hence there was no outside for it to express itself to as of yet.

What one can consider as being _New_ had already been originated when the Law of One produced the segment of the five Founding Essences. Great Pop as The Group Consciousness of Medicine knew that at some point the five Founding Essences, whom could only move around within it and thereby express themselves that way, would ultimately no longer desire to do such when they had experienced all of the possible positions and expressions of themselves. In this case and event there would no longer be anything _New_ and therefore unlike an exit from a sojourn, which is simply returning home for a while, there would then exist True and Real death. Great Pop realized at this very early point in Origins that _New_ had been originated and that was what was being constantly sought and experienced inside the Group Consciousness of Medicine, which would later also become known as Himself or The Creator etc. He also realized that when _New_ was no longer available, it was all pretty much over and that real death would occur within in the sense that all that would exist, would become in a state of static, or <u>Was</u>.

At this point and time there did exist a <u>Past,</u> which was the original condition of the <u>Is</u> before the segment was produced by The Law of One, and was originated by the event of it, but there existed no <u>Was</u> or death as of yet. This was the real motive of desire for Great Pop as The Group Consciousness of Medicine to express itself outside of itself. So, The ThunderBeing of Change died in this condition and event in order to separate himself into two parts, and become The ThunderBeing outside of the Group Consciousness of Medicine and the Essence of Change which remains inside. From this beginning event, a continuum of <u>New</u> was ensured and therefore also the <u>Future</u> really began and this action and event was the actual origin of it!

Of course on the down side, from this point on, for any change to occur, a certain death has to also occur, which we call the <u>Past</u> or what <u>Was</u>. So also what is considered to be the <u>Now</u>, which is the <u>Future</u> of the <u>Was</u>, is constantly in change and thereby death in a certain way. To simplify this understanding: to have anything <u>New</u>, one's not having it has to die or be given away. Or one can also say in reality, that any change has a death of sorts associated with it. On the plus side, because of this event and expression, there will always be the possibility of <u>New</u> and thereby the <u>Future</u>. Another side benefit is that because of this condition, <u>Now</u>, <u>New</u>, <u>Is</u>, and the <u>Future</u> are from this point, always in motion as well, all because they are all dynamically linked to this original event! One can also safely surmise that <u>Now</u>, <u>New</u>, <u>Is</u>, and the <u>Future</u> embody as one of their major components, the Essence of Change from the sacrifice or death as it were, of The ThunderBeing of Change. This event and sacrifice also originated what one calls the <u>Was,</u> and the <u>Was</u> and the <u>Past</u> now both embody the death and sacrifice that occurs in this event. One can safely surmise that all of this is because of The Law of One, as well as is the possibility of any part in or of it. Also because of the Law of One once a thing IS it will always Be.

All that existed before the death of The ThunderBeing of Change was simply in a state or condition of the <u>Is</u> and the <u>Now</u>. When The Law of One produced the segment of itself that Began everything to see what would develop, the <u>New</u> was originated, and All existed within the idea of that. Yet at that point, it could not really be called the <u>Now</u> as well, only the <u>Is</u>, because there was no other point of reference to it. When The ThunderBeing of Change died, the static condition of the <u>New</u> was set in motion and it became separated or individualized from the <u>Is</u> and thus originated the present idea of the

Selves – Vol. 1

Now. This is because of course Now was carried forward to the outside with the New by The ThunderBeing. Also, from this event both the Now and the New were embodied with some of the Essence and Medicine of Change, as was the Future. As one might surmise, the Was and the Past were left inside the Group Consciousness of Medicine and both shared the same condition of embodying death and the sacrifice and being left out with respect to embodying Change. From this point forward, once a thing Was or is Past, Change is no longer possible in it.

The Is, is the real tricky part of this original development of the death of The ThunderBeing of Change because that is exactly how he pulled it off. It is the Is that was the tool The ThunderBeing used to make it all happen to begin with! All that existed before the Law of One produced the segment of itself was in a condition or Medicine of Is, and was static. Is, is what the Law of One produced the segment with in the beginning. The ThunderBeing of Change knew that was what it used to make the segment with. So knowing about The Law of One and Medicine of the Is, The ThunderBeing also used Is to individualize himself from the Essence of Change and make everything happen in the event thereafter! If one is wondering, because of this action and use of Is by The ThunderBeing in this event, at this point forward what Is, became no longer static because it also embodies the Medicine of Change. And of course all of this was by and because of The Law of One! So, since this material is about Origins and the Future that should cover any questions that one might have as to the Origin and Beginning of the Future. At least this is how Great Pop has explained all of it to me.

In simplistic terms, because of the event of the death of The ThunderBeing of Change, what Is, was set in motion as it was embodied with Change. Now as well as New also became of this same Medicine of being in Motion because of embodying Change. The Future was also originated in this event, with a Medicine of being in Motion and embodying Change. The Past and Was embodied the death and sacrifice, but not Change and thereby remain static. Since this point and event, the Future, what Is, what is Now, and what is New can change and do. But the Past, or what Was cannot change. One can liken the condition of these things as Now being a sword or blade with two edges. One edge is the Past and Was. The other edge being the New and the Future, with all of it being the Is. If this material seems somewhat complicated or hard to follow at this point, I do apologize and Pray that it gets much easier. The following *diagram illustrates what has just been discussed:*

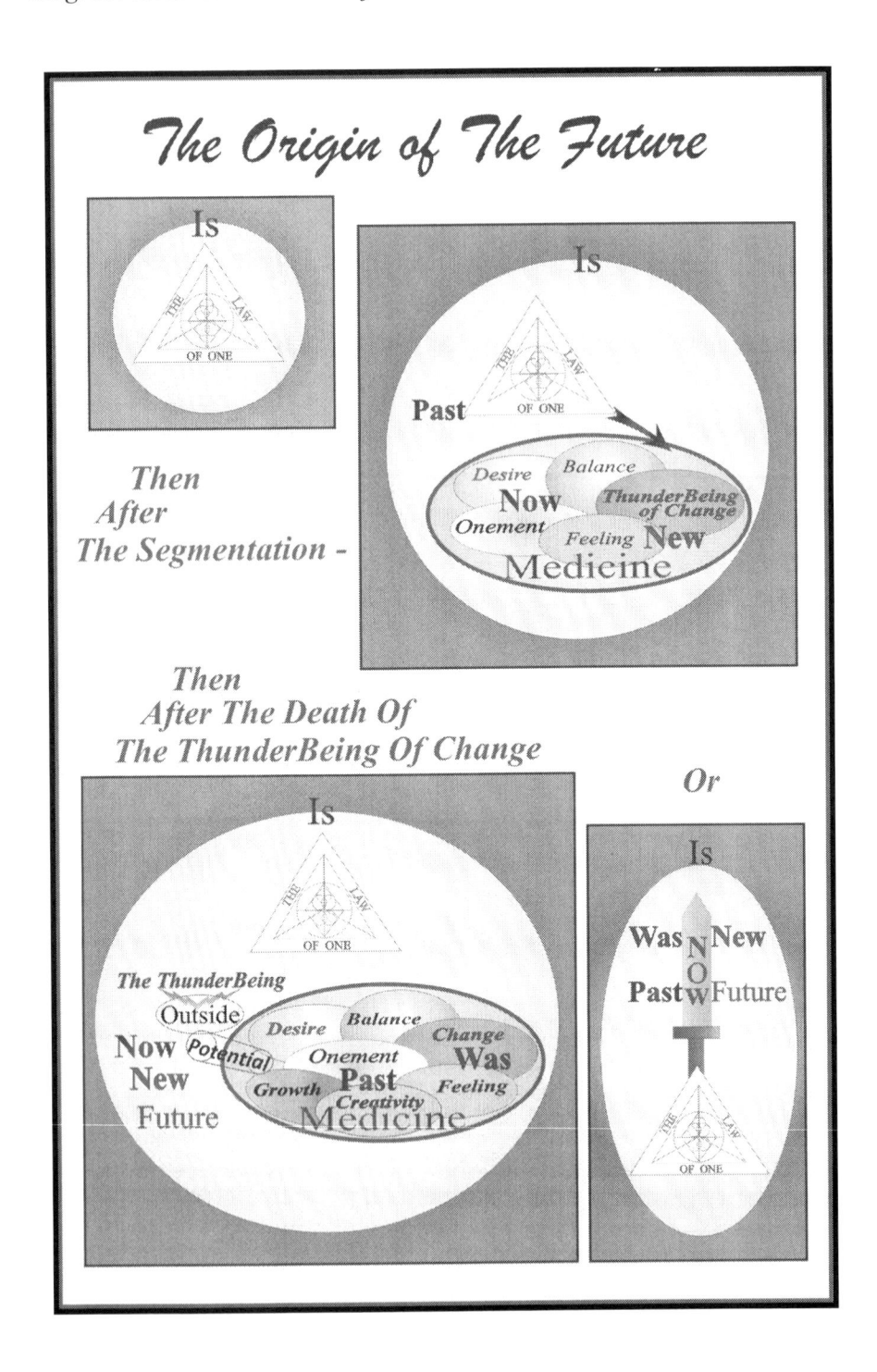

Yes, when The ThunderBeing of Change died so that The Group Consciousness of Medicine could express itself outside of itself, The Future began or was originated. This clearly was a most important and significant event. Of course because of The Law Of One, The ThunderBeing still Was and was something. However, never more could he be The ThunderBeing of Change. Of course being simply The ThunderBeing certainly was not all that bad of a difference. At that point The ThunderBeing became mobile outside of the Group Consciousness and could support its expressions in that position and way, which later became of great significance and importance in the ensuing events and developments.

Another significant aspect of this event and development in Origins was that the Essence of Desire offered a portion of itself for use in making the mechanism by which the Group Consciousness could then express itself with. This ceding over a portion of itself clearly was in keeping with its Medicine or Essential Nature as it was a desire of the Group Consciousness that was being fulfilled in this moment and event. The offering of the Essence of Feeling to share of itself in the making of the device which would later be known as the first or original Operative and Potential was also of significance.

From this point forward, all Desire expressions have an associated Feeling, and all Potential have these Essences as a core ingredient within them. This means that everything from this event on has these two Essences as a part of, or at the core of their inherent nature or Medicine and naturally this means including ourselves. One can safely say that The Future was born from a Desire of the Group Consciousness of Medicine with Feeling in it and all Future Desire expressions by anything and everything will also have Feeling associated with them, all because of this originating event of The Future and the mobilization or putting into motion, the New and the Now.

*****

Yep, my resistance to change at times is that I know that for me to have something different, in a sense something must die for that condition to occur. Yet I would gladly have my fear and the uncertainty as to my continuance and wellbeing Now and in the Future die once and for all with no remorse nor regret. Therefore if I desire to have any semblance of Real success in life Now and in the Future, I am going have to embrace change as well as make certain choices. As one might recall I have mentioned that all that any and All Beings and Things do in life is to make choices and express Prayers of Desire. In reality, even to choose to do nothing is to choose, and thereby do something that way. Also, within the experience of the Odyssey of Origins a lot of things were learned about making choices, such as there being actually four options for each choice to be considered which are:

Yes, or Positive

No, or Negative

Maybe, which is to choose to defer to choose until later

And Never to choose at all, or Neutral

One might liken the choice making process as being the use of a Sword of Choice that one uses to sever all of the Potential other than that which is selected. In any expression of oneself, one also uses another sword called Ability. In the understanding of what we Really Do in life, we simply employ the use of these two swords at certain times and in certain ways. We use the Sword of Choice in expressions of our Free Will and the Decision Factory of our Mind Operative. And guess what? It has edges on both sides that must be considered, as with that of Ability. The leading edge of the Sword of Choice is called just that and it severs all other Potential so to speak. The trailing edge of the Sword of Choice leaves something behind that is resultant from that choice being made, and that which is left behind is called Consequences. Likewise, in the employment of the Sword of Ability, left behind is one's Responsibility for the expression of that Sword and Ability, no matter what. All that any and All incarnated Beings and Things do in a life expression is to express Prayers of Desire and use these two swords at certain times, and in certain instances. Therefore one can rightfully assume that all that is resulted in a life process and experience is the Consequences and Responsibility of their Choices and Abilities. It seems clear to me now that to be of any form of Real Success in life one must get really good in the use of these two swords, and stay conscious and respectful of what one is leaving behind in their employment at any and all times as well.

Of course there is also that consideration that was mentioned earlier as to the Potential of influence of choices by Things and Beings other than that of oneself. Remember, there does exist within our lives the condition of Imagined and Cosmic / Communal Self influences. Certainly, one might also consider the Ability Sword of others to some degree at times. However, in Reality it is of little real impact as compared to that of one's own Sword of Choice. This is because we all are of choice as to our response to such external influences at all times and in all cases. This is real and true especially in relation to the ability for oneself to realize expanding self-determination and thereby also one's greatest Potential for Real Success in life. I say such now, because it is clearly evident that if one is of Real self-sufficiency, then the ability of others is of no real consequence in relation to one's own Potential, period. However, in the Bee Hive Game such freedom and complete self-sufficiency is the last thing that others would like to have an individual develop. Why? Simply because it can only continue to function and remain successful if everyone is of Need, not Have mentality. That pretty much identifies at least some of the hurdles at present in anyone's path to being of Real self-determination and thereby of the greatest Potential of Real Success in life.

With regard to the things that I have identified and employed in my Resource Wheel, my life is pretty much perfect as it is. The many volumes of material that have been resultant from my presence on Mother Earth to this point were done in response to my asking Great Pop how I might serve His Will and desire of me, as is this one. That is what I most desire and care about, and in that respect my life has been and is presently a Great Success. In fact, if I were to exit for good at this very moment, I would be pretty pleased with myself even. I would not have gotten to experience all of the things on my Desire list if that were to occur, yet at least for some time now my resources of Self, including my effort, energy, ability, and time, have been employed in leaving something behind that Great Pop wanted. Most assuredly expanding self-determination is one of the necessary things to consider and use in order to realize the greatest Potential of Success in life. It is also clear that with regard to self-determination, one has to use the Sword of Choice as well as Ability in such ways so as to ensure the greatest measure to oneself of self-sufficiency as well as freedom if one is to be of the greatest capacity of it, period.

It is obvious to me now that I am of some relative measure of being successful in life so far. However, I am also certain that I can realize an even greater and expanding Potential for Real Success in life Now and in the Future. I know that I can do such by being more open to embrace change and through increasing my capacity of self-determination by making choices that realize greater self-sufficiency and freedom! It is also obvious that with the wonderful tool of one's Resource Wheel and the map that it provides, the tool of Focus, and one's endeavor of expanding self-determination, there certainly is new Hope as well as Potential for each and All of us. Most certainly any and All Beings and Things that choose to employ these tools and understanding can now be able to realize a greater and expanding Potential for Real Success in life. Thank You so very much, Great Pop!

SELF - AWARENESS

I will begin this chapter by once again giving the status of my condition of being in life here on Mother Earth. It is now Thursday, the 31st of January 2002. Thankfully, the weather has not only been clear, it has also been unusually warm so that I am now able to leave the little heaters off and save the cost of electricity for them. As mentioned, yesterday was a critical one for me to continue in life. Thanks to Dolphin sister in Winston-Salem, Deer sister in New Jersey, and Coyote sister in Seven Lakes, I was able to pay the phone bill two hours before that service was to be cut off. I was also able to pay the hosting fee so that the website has one more month of operation and I was finally able to sleep a little better last night.

This morning Coyote sister also offered to help me get my driver's license and blue pony going again. That will certainly make a huge difference in my life condition as well as increase my Potential to be once again Self-sufficient because I can use them to find some means of employment. I placed a call to Turtle brother in Winston-Salem to see if he could help me get to the places necessary to have "Eagle again on wheels" and I am waiting for his response. Of course all of this serves to evidence that other people can and do make a huge difference in our ability to realize even momentary continuance as well as any greater Success in life!

As compared to yesterday, my Potential to be able to continue and even perhaps realize Real Success in life today has increased dynamically. Also, to all of those individuals that have shared their care and been so supportive, I am deeply thankful. One can easily understand how these events and conditions in the odyssey of my life obviously serve to enhance one's sense of Self-awareness. Therefore it is no great surprise to me at this point that another one of Great Pop's desires for each and All of the Potential is exactly that. Not only does He desire that we all be of Self-awareness, but even more so that we stay in the expanding kind of it.

At this point one might question as to what is meant in the concept of Expanding Self-awareness as this might seem like a tricky thing to experience and express. Actually, it is relatively simple and is in reality another one of the tools that at times is necessary to be used for one to be able to realize any Expanding Potential of Real Success in life. Self-awareness can be considered to be consciousness of oneself in a sense. Yet what is to be considered in this use of the idea of Self-awareness is even more dynamic and extensive in its range than that.

One might consider Self-awareness in respect to any individual Being or Thing that is acting in an egotistical and self-absorbed manner. While this might seem like Self-awareness, it is not what is to be considered here. Nope, that choice of behavioral expression is really almost the very opposite of it! I say such because for any Being or Thing to experience or express Real Self-awareness, they must include consideration of the any and All of creation as well in that expression, period. In reality, individuals that choose to operate in a self-absorbed and thereby isolative manner are restricting their capacity of Self-awareness. Therefore in such a behavioral pattern choice they also restrict themselves from being able to experience and express the Expanding form of it as Great Pop desires for any and All of the Potential.

Self-awareness can certainly be considered in terms of consciousness, and one must be conscious to be of any experience or expression of it. One should remember the importance of the tool of Focus in being able to effectively administer and manage one's limited resources of time, energy, and ability. As Focus is necessary for Real Success, one can easily understand how anything that distracts or restricts one's capacity of Focus does also negatively impact one's Potential of Real Success. Any abuse of drugs or alcohol will reduce one's capacity of Self-awareness, period. Even those types of stimulants and drugs that are supposed to enhance one's Mind are little different than watching a cartoon or taking a ride on a roller coaster in their effect. Actually, the roller coaster ride will make one more Self-aware in the Real sense of it, than those other things. Maybe the best approach to gaining a better understanding as to what is to be considered as being Self-awareness, is to consider what it is not at this point. Egocentric, self-absorbed, selfish, afraid, aggressive, manipulative and so forth are all expressions that one's Bark on Tree uses to keep one's attention and Focus of Consciousness to itself. Therefore, these expressions and behavior models serve only to distract the Focus of the Real Self of anyone.

Great Pop made Fear so as to stimulate one to motion. Therefore, Fear can and will give cause for a Being or Thing to experience or express a certain kind of Self-awareness. Certainly when one is faced with making choices or expressions that may result in one's continuance or not in life, one should be most conscious and thereby Self-aware. Surprisingly, many times certain individuals will do just the opposite. For example, how often have you seen or heard of someone taking a drink of alcohol or some type of other drug so as to give them courage? In my current condition of being in life on Mother Earth, my Bark on Tree has been quite active. Ironically, it is just that condition of it that I have to fight off in a way, as I consciously try to make Proper and effective choices as to what to do about changing my condition as regards the clear and present jeopardy in my continued existence. As taught behavior and influence from the prevalent culture, a part of my problem and jeopardy at present is that I reacted too hastily in the past, and of this I am certain.

I am also certain that one's Bark on Tree can be of great support or encumbrance to being of Proper and of Real Self-awareness at this point. In asking Great Pop about such and what might the best thing for one to do when in this kind of condition and situation, His response was: *"To always back off so as to gain total or greater Perspective of the situation and regain one's Balance and Focus before any Real Choice is made or expressed about such."* It did not take me long to remember that it is one's Essence-Operative of Perspective that is the most powerful and effective self-righting or balancing tool that one can use in any situation. Happy with that result, I decided to go fishing again by responding to Great Pop's answer with, "Thank You Great Pop, and can You also help me define what is to be considered as Proper Self-awareness?" Being on to my ploy, Great Pop then just said *"Yep"*, in response to that one, ha, ha, ha.

Seeing then that I did not know what to say next, He added, *"Little One, Proper Self-awareness as well as the Expanding form of it is to be conscious, and consciously embrace oneself as being a part of the All and seeing oneself as being even in it. All Proper expressions of Self-awareness are to then use one's Value System to effect expressions of Prayers of Desire and Care that realize the greatest benefit to oneself and the Wellbeing of the All. To do just that will also and always, effect the expansion of one's Real Self and thereby one's Potential of Real Success in any and all situations."*

I was then given to remember that whatever one does, does in Reality effect and affect each and every Thing that Great Pop has made, including Him, no matter what. The way of The Great Web of Creation is in a sense described in that last statement. Also described in it is what our Real position and circumstance always is as relates to oneself, the All, and Great Pop.

It was then that I recognized and finally became of understanding that Real Self-awareness can be said to be the condition of not only Consciously Realizing one's Value System, but also the act of one's "Owning it" as well. In Origins, I learned that Great Pop made the theme park of Mother Earth based on the theme and thereby Potential of Brotherhood lessons and experiences. In light of that purpose and intent, one can realize that for one to try to operate alone, self-absorbed, self-serving, and the like in life on Mother Earth, one will never embrace any Potential of Real Success in life. In Origins one also learns that the Essence-Operative of Perspective is like a lens that has many facets through which one can focus one's consciousness and at the same moment one's expressions of Care. Also it is always through the lens of one's Perspective that any form of Self-awareness is realized. Therefore, to realize the greatest Potential of Real Success in life, one's Perspective of Expanding Self-awareness should also consider oneself and one's condition and expressions as relates to All other Beings and Things, no matter what.

It now becomes clear to me that if I am to realize the greatest Potential of Success in life, then I must be of Expanding Self-awareness and thereby also most Conscious. Also because of the nature of the tool of Focus, whatever I choose to allow to influence or distract my condition of consciousness will have a dynamic affect in relation to my Potential of Real Success. I am now aware that for me to be of any Potential of Real Success, then I must remain Conscious of my Value System as well as of my Important and Even position in relation to other Beings and Things in the Great Web of Creation. To be capable of Success, I must remember at all times that I have Potential, no matter what condition my condition is in. Furthermore, I must also remember that this Potential is not ever Really conditioned or restricted, especially by anything that has happened in the past. I am certain that whatever I do or choose not to do, does affect the All of Creation. If I am of Real Self-awareness then I singularly do also have the power of Perspective to Choose how and when I let any outside influences stimulate or distract my Focus and Perspective from my Value System and Potential. Clearly, any Potential can and will effect everything that Great Pop has made when it is expressed and realized. One thing for certain that I do now realize is that only when I am of Real and Expanding Self-awareness, do I have the broadest power of Choice as to what any next expression of my Potential will be and when, period.

Real Self-awareness is not that of being just an outwardly incarnated Potential and thereby Spirit, even though it is all of that. Nor is it when one realizes that one is ever in the condition of evenness of Great Pop's Care, Support, and Love, even though it is all of that as well. Self-awareness can be experienced in one's support of others and it is certainly found in such expressions. However, Real Self-awareness is not even so much about what one is or does at all, although it certainly must be considered. Nope, Real Self-awareness is only realized when one sees oneself in evenness of Potential in relation to other Beings and Things in the Great Web of the All of Creation. Therefore it is one's limitless Potential and hence one's True Value System that drives and reflects such, that one must maintain constant Focus and thereby Self-awareness of. And since one's True Value System is dynamically linked to one's Real Self, it stands to reason that one's Real Self is the Self that one must maintain the Focus of one's Perspective and Consciousness of at most if not all times. At this point, it is clear to me that these are the very things that one must manage from time to time to be able to realize the greatest Expanding Potential of Real Success in life, period.

To be of Real Self-awareness, I must accept that I am a Spirit that incarnated into the Physical realm and arena of Mother Earth. I chose to come here for a physical experience, and I am aware of that. I am also of constant awareness that I will at some point exit this visit and thereby life and that my Potential for Success is determined singularly by the expressions and choices that I make now and in the limited future of such for me. I am also aware that what I will leave behind when I do finally exit this visit will in a sense be a testimony of the

Motives and Choices that result in my experiences and expressions. I also realize that for life to be of any success for me, what I leave behind matters only in as much as to whether or not things are in as good of a condition if not better than when I found them. I am certain that I came here to serve Great Pop as being my highest commitment and priority. I also realize that I continue to choose to maintain that priority, and I am constantly aware of that.

Certainly, one's Resource Wheel and the other tools that we have developed in this project can be of great support in being able to be more successful in life. Yet it is also clear that the single most important thing that is required in our realization of anything at all in life, is that of our maintaining a condition of Balance and Proper Perspective and thereby Proper Self-awareness. After all, it is not so much that I am or what I have done that matters now or in the Future. Nope, it is what I choose to do next that is most important. And even more important than the What or How of it, is the Why and thereby my personal motive for doing such, or not. Yep, for anyone to be of the realization of Greater Success in life, it seems that is what one needs to stay conscious of and thereby Self-aware of at all times.

Another thing that seems important to be Self-aware of is one's condition of the pattern of the various Selves that one has active and how they are influencing one's Attitude and Focus of Perspective. Clearly if one or more Imagined Selves or Cosmic / Communal Selves are compromising one's ability to easily and evenly distribute one's energy and time, then some choices and actions should be considered so as to remedy that condition.

SELF - EXPRESSION

At this point it seems that pretty much all of the pieces of the puzzle are now put together as regards answering the question of What and Who I Really am. In His Brilliant and Supportive manner, Great Pop has facilitated us to have the tools by which to discover that in ourselves. In addition, we can also use those tools at any moment to either re-establish that Self, or change it to be what we Desire next in being ourselves. And as a bonus, it is obvious that these tools of Self-discovery are the same tools by which we can realize the greatest Expanding Potential of Real Success in life.

Another major thing that Great Pop promised the Potential when they all decided to return inside His Essential Will was that of a continuum of Expanding Self-expression. At this point one might consider that there may not be much to say about this topic. After all, whatever one does is certainly some type of Self-expression and by now we All have experience in doing just that particular thing. Yet up to this point most of my and probably your Self-expressions as well, have been pretty much made as responses to some type of influence of the prevalent culture and society in some manner or form, period. Because of this condition, our sense of ourselves as well as our Potential thereby to realize Real Success in life has not been determined solely by or within the total control of oneself.

Also, when one's sense of Self is given to be performance based because of the morays of the society such as is extant in the present prevalent one on Mother Earth, for one to be able to realize Real Success seems almost like some Utopian or far fetched idea. Even so, by Discovering and Understanding Who and What we Really are and How we operate, one can most definitely effect just such an outcome. Clearly we have now been given several new tools and processes by which one can increase the Potential of Success in any singular or collective expression. This means that we can now employ these tools that we have at our disposal at any time as a means of Self-expression to champion any condition or circumstance.

Without question, one's Resource Wheel is just one such enabling device and tool! Not only does it identify the hurdles, it defines the things to Focus one's next Self-expressions upon to get past them. If one was honest in the development of one's Resource Wheel then this Potential will certainly be available. For example:

Resource - 8
Ego - Serpent
A - My Courage / Choices
B - To establish the Church and Tribe
C - *My Ability to help beings and things*
D - Being incarcerated
E - Getting my drivers license back

    In my Resource Wheel are the things that are of the most importance to me at this point in my life. In a simple survey of it one can easily recognize that position eight in the West is what describes not only what my Resource is in the way of Courage and Choices, but also what my immediate concerns are about. If I Really and honestly Desire to experience anything different in my life than what is the continuum of my present circumstance in it, I am certain that I must apply or Focus energy to and thereby Change something to make that difference possible. Yet in most instances of Brush Fire management that we are taught and are often caught up in, our attention and thereby Consciousness and Focus is often misled or distracted towards applying energy to things other than what will effect such a different result. Typically, most people are of little awareness as to what the Real constraints are with regard to our Potential of Success in life, much less what is possible for anyone to do to remove them.
    In this brilliant design of a roadmap to the realization of Real Success in life provided by Great Pop, it defines one's Real Goals and objectives as well as the constraints that encumber one from Realizing Success and Fulfillment in them. In addition, it also defines and describes what one's next best Self-expression should be directed towards making a Change or impact upon. From this map it is easy to recognize that if I can get my drivers license back and what I call the Blue Pony operating legally again will produce the greatest impact upon the majority of the other elements. Clearly if I am "Eagle on Wheels", then I can secure some means of Self-support which is listed as another Care in number four. Obviously if the Care element of number four is achieved, then the Potential for realizing the Care element of number five as well as most, if not all of the others will dynamically be increased as well.

Clearly, that singular item of my driver's license is the one that will make the most significant improvement as well as produce more Potential for me to be of more Success in life than any of the other ones that are listed. That item is from the things that I Care about. It is in the West, the place of Direction and Growth. It is in the place that is midway between the Spiritual and Physical and thereby it embraces and embodies both. It is presently a Care, but it clearly is also a present hurdle that I must get over in some manner at some point. Not being able to drive encumbers my Potential of Self-expression more than any other thing at this point in my life. Therefore if it encumbers my Potential of Self-expression, then it encumbers not only my Freedom but also the Expansion of my Potential of Success. In this I mean to say that I can still be of Success without being able to drive, but not as much in so many more ways as I could if I were able to drive.

As mentioned, the really brilliant part of one's Resource Wheel is that it tells one what needs to be resolved, and it gives one things to use to resolve them. For example, by using the Value element listed, with the constraint being my Courage and Choices, I can choose to make clearing it the Focus of my next Self-expressions. Also, once I realize fulfillment in that Expression of Self, then that Care hurdle can also change to become a milestone and asset. Getting a drivers license and my car operational does not mean that I will automatically be self-supporting. Even so, it is obviously the shortest and easiest way to it. To be able to drive does not necessarily mean that I will automatically be able to be in Nolayte's life as I Desire and Care about as well. Obviously, when the Care element of position eight is no longer a hurdle but becomes an asset instead, then the Care and Potential of position six as well as all of the others will be much easier to become a Self-expression and thereby Realized Potential too!

With mobility, I can find some type of employment that will facilitate me to develop greater Freedom and sufficiency in myself. That increased sufficiency in myself will help me to become able to produce an even greater and continuing flow of income. As another Choice of Self-expression, I can then choose to use some of that increased income to better support myself. I can then also choose to use some of the excess past that to do other things with, such as to share with others, find my children, hire an attorney, buy property, build my own home, publish these books and basically be Free. In Reality, all that one does in life is to make Choices as to what becomes one's next Expression of Care or Prayers of Desire. That being the case, then one can easily realize how very important it is to know what these "top of the list" things are that one is Desiring and Caring about!

In the experience of the Odyssey of Origins one will find the reason that I lost my driving privilege, which obviously resulted from a Choice made by myself. The motive for my choosing to behave in such a risk taking way was resultant from an influence that was basically a discarnate that I was in a Cosmic / Communal Self relationship with. The Potential of such a condition of myself became realized as an outward expression of an Imagined Self in association with that relationship, again of my Choice. I now recognize that this whole condition and problem is actually defined and about the elements contained in position eight of my Resource Wheel, which as mentioned also identifies the tools to use to resolve it. I also now better understand the mechanisms of Selves that are the operative elements and mechanisms by which one actually does express and experience one's Potential in life. It becomes even more meaningful when one is able to see that life is simply one's Real Self making Projected Self-expressions of Choice so as to be Self-realized and Self-expressive through Imagined Selves via Cosmic / Communal Self relationships with other Beings and Things. From that reality it is not too difficult to see that the more that one is free to be Self-expressive, then the more expanding Potential can be realized in one's life from those expressions.

Of course Self-expression is not just about making Choices, it is also about using one's Focus of Perspective and energy in taking action upon them as well. Knowing what one's hurdles and constraints are, will be of little use or benefit unless one is honest in them, and with oneself about them. Actually such insight is useless in the most part unless one is willing to Change something in the pattern of the life of oneself in order to clear up those limits to one's Expanding Potential of Success in it. You see, just getting my mobility back in itself will not realize any Real Change in my life, unless I also choose and express Change in other things in it as well. Actually, just the event of getting my license and car legally operational will not even keep fuel in it. In the really big picture, my real hurdle in being in life does not have anything to do with being able to drive at all. Nope, it has to do with the inability that I have at present to garner the resources in the way of money to support myself or do and obtain the things and services that will help me to realize my Real desires and objectives.

And as one can tell from my Lists and Resource Wheel, my Real desires and objectives are things like being in Nolayte's life or getting these books published so that all can benefit from their content as their Choice and Expression of Self. One can also easily see that even the Potential of my being able to serve Great Pop's Will can be Expanded from being of mobility, as it will allow me greater ease in being physically available to do such over a larger area. Therefore getting my driving privilege restored as well as Blue Pony fully operational and legal should be the first and most important thing that I can and should next Focus my energy upon.

And the remarkable thing is that at the time this material was started, the Potential of my being able to get my license back was zero, because they said I had to wait until after the nineteenth of January of this year to do such. And Guess What? Yep, today is now the second of February, so that hurdle is no longer one. Therefore next in the process of Self-expression and Focus then should be for me to see what it will take to get my license back and Blue Pony legally operational again. I could look for all kinds of work at this point as well. However, until I have realized that mobility my job getting Potential has not really changed at all. Just because there is a greater Potential now for me to be "Eagle on Wheels" does not automatically result such. Nope, at present my Care element of position eight is still the same. However it is also one of the things that is now of my Focus and thereby is something that I choose to become of Expanding Self-expression about in some manner.

Now comes the tricky part of this process of realizing a greater and Expanding Potential of Success in one's life. Once again in respect to one's capacity of Self-expression, it is given to mention Motive. If one is Really of a desire to Realize the greatest Expanding Potential of Success in life then one's Motive is much more important than any outcome. In this I mean that one's Motive in each of one's next Self-expressions is more of a determining factor as regards one's Potential of Real Success in life than any other single thing including the How that these new tools that we have identified should be employed, which one could consider as being the second most important. Nope, The End Never Justifies the Means, period. When I was much younger, I lost my driving privilege and chose to drive anyway. I even got caught once and was put in the "Pokey" for doing just that thing. I was working at the time and had the money with which to pay the fines and attorney fees, therefore I did not stay incarcerated long on that occasion. However, at present such is no longer the case for me as far as monetary resources go. Yep, as one has probably noticed, Being Incarcerated just happens to be my Fear Element in position eight as well.

As we have already discussed, pretty much all that we do in life is to use our two Swords of Ability and Choice. While this section is predominantly about Ability in the manner of Self-expression, it is also about Choice. This is because in Reality, these two Swords cannot be used separately. Every time one makes a Choice, it becomes an Expression of Self. If anything is an Expression of Self, then it is the use of one's Sword of Ability. Earlier we went into great detail with regard to understanding one's Personal Structure and Wills. Therefore it is not too hard to recognize that any expression of one's Wills is Self-expression, as that is the Reality of such. However there is another mechanism and means of Self-expression, which is through one's Essence-Operative of Care in one's Personal Structure. Oftentimes I will liken one's Care Essence-Operative to be like a hydrant to which one attaches one or many hoses of Care. Now with the increased understanding of this material, I can easily see each hose as being a Cosmic / Communal Self as well. Yet it seems to me that the management of one's Care Essence-Operative is not nearly so difficult or tricky to manage as are one's Wills. This might be simply because one of one's Wills is an Operative element of one's Bark on Tree. At times I have chosen to be Self-expressive and thereby operate in what I call "Willfulness".

Actually, operating in Willfulness is pretty much the norm in the prevalent society. It is taught behavior that is rewarded early on in life. The infant cries to get what it wants, and when it is not satisfied with some type of instant gratification, it continues the process. Some individuals choose to keep doing that throughout their life with no regard to any other Being or Thing. Some individuals never stop to consider the consequences of their next instant gratification, much less the real cost of such to oneself and others. Aggression and self-assertiveness are highly rewarded forms of Self-expression in the Religion of Materialism and the Bee Hive Game of the prevalent culture. These behavioral models of Self-expression are necessary to maintain its prevalence, as well as feed those at the top in it.

A definition of Willfulness might be simply that of being Self-absorbed and having the End Justify the Means. Yet being Self-expressive at all can in some manner be considered "Selfish" to some extent perhaps. So what might be the Proper way of being about one's Self-expression so as to Realize the greatest Expanding Potential of

Real Success in life one might now ask? Finally I decided to ask Great Pop just that question. In so doing, His response was: *"Consciousness"*. Great Pop then reminded me of the material of the Proper Way. Within the definitions of it, He often described the process by first stating that one should bring one's Consciousness to Heart. He explained that to do such would automatically remove any influence from one's Ego in that little maneuver. Once that condition has been established, then one can and should choose to operate from one's True Value System elements of one's Real Self.

One might wonder at this point as to what being Proper might have to do with realizing Real Success in life? Once again the answer is Everything! Remember, all that one does in life is to make Choices and Expressions of one's Prayers of Desire and Care. Also, every single Being and Thing in the Great Web of Creation has influence. Not only does each and all have influence upon one's own condition of being and life, but also that of each and every other single thing in it, as well as the Future for All of it now and for all time to come. Therefore one can affect the Wellbeing of any and all of it, in any instance of any Expression of oneself. In this theme park of Mother Earth, if one is to Realize even the smallest Potential of Real Success in life then one must in fact consider the effects of one's behavioral Choices upon the All of Creation, including that of oneself to Realize such. Self-expression is by any definition a behavioral choice. So as to be of the best choices of expressions of behavior, Great Pop has already given us guidelines in the Prayer Proper and in the material of the Proper Way. The Prayer Proper is available for making any Choice so as to Realize the greatest Expanding Potential of Success in life. The Prayer Proper is the test of: **"*Does it Walk in Balance and With Harm to No One Being or Thing, including that of oneself*"?**

It now seems clear to me at this point that if I Really Desire to be of the greatest Expanding Potential of Success in my life, then I must continue to choose to make expressions of myself that are Proper in it from this point forward. Therefore it seems that for me to Be Proper is the obvious way for me to realize the greatest expanding Potential of Real Success in life. From the material of the Proper Way, we find the definition or way to Be Proper is:

BE PROPER - *To Be Proper is to behold the perspective of oneself as to ever be in a an Expanding condition of being and* *expressing the unique Medicine of oneself.*

To Be Proper is to continuously Endeavor to be what one has never been, in the condition of becoming as an expanded expression of one's current self.

To Be Proper is to ask the Creator each day as to what one should do so as to best exemplify His next best Idea of oneself. One can do such in any moment by Prayerfully and Meditatively asking for His guidance in each step of each day. In this way one can thereby learn the lesson of being like one should Be, which is Properly and simply, one's complete Real Self.

To Be Proper is to express one's Attitude, Perspective and Potential of self in such a manner that truly does walk in a Respectful Sharing way and in Respect Proper to oneself as well as to the All other beings and things of His Creation.

To Be Proper is to embrace one's consciousness to the Heart of self and see the blessed gift of one's own Medicine and being, and being at all.

To Be Proper is to realize in oneself one's own Perfection of one's being ever in a state of Expanding Potential, and thereby ever as a Perfect expression of one's imperfection, and Perfect in that.

To Be Proper is to be ready and willing at any moment to Change and expand so as to Be more Proper as the Creator's next more Perfect Idea in oneself. To Be Proper is to Love Him, the All, and oneself more each moment by Being Properly one's Real Self in the process of it.

And the one for making expressions is:

ENDEAVOR PROPER - *Truly any action and thereby expression of self can be considered as being an Endeavor of oneself. However, any Endeavor that is to become expressed as being in the Way of being Proper is that Endeavor which is one of Morality. In this sense and use of the word, Morality is that which is Chosen as an Expression of Self that is made with God Consciousness in Mind, Heart, and Will. Any and all expressions of Endeavor which truly has one's Consciousness to Heart and thereby the Creator and His Will in the Mind of oneself, is truly most Proper.*

Expressions of Endeavor become in Way of being of Behavior Proper when the Real motive of one's Endeavor is in the manifesting of one's own greatest expression of expanded Potential in the Proper Way. Such expressions of Proper Endeavor will always result in the condition of oneself becoming even more valuable to Him and the All, and thereby to oneself. Through each expression of Endeavor Proper, one becomes more able to Compensate Proper and thereby assist in manifesting an increased Flow of The Creator's Light, Love, and Benefaction to the All.

To Endeavor Proper is to ever be in the process of Change and thereby expanding as a more Perfect Idea of the Creator in the vessel and unique expression of Him that is truly the Medicine of oneself.

To Endeavor most Proper is to seek guidance from the Creator about each and every step that one takes along the Way.

To Endeavor most Proper is to then Act upon that guidance with Humility and in the most Respectful and Reverential manner possible, so as to keep the influence of one's Ego at bay.

To Endeavor Proper is to be of Joy in the Attitude, Consciousness, and Perspective of one's own Being, and to seek to be a more Proper expression of it each and every way, each and every day.

To Endeavor Proper is to Love the Creator and His Benefaction in and of oneself.

To Endeavor Proper is to seek new and better ways to express and experience His Light and Love and Benefaction to and through oneself in the way of Compensation Proper.

To Endeavor proper is to seek to exemplify as best as one can, the creator in oneself by thinking of new and better things for which to Pray. To consciously and with clarity, seek and Behold the Creator's guidance about any Endeavor or Desire that is expressed in or through oneself, is to Endeavor Proper when one acts upon that guidance.

And finally the one about Behavior is:

BEHAVE PROPER - *To Behave Proper is for one to seek guidance from the Creator and then act upon that guidance with the Prayer Proper in hand.*

To Behave Proper is to then use the Prayer Proper in the making of any Choices that one might encounter along the way of it.

To Behave Proper is to continually seek to become an agent and emissary of the Creator's Will in oneself, and be operative as a most open and expanding channel of His Light and Love in any and every way possible.

To Behave Proper is to Walk in Balance and with Harm to No One being or thing in a Respectful Sharing and Prayerful and Meditative way.

To Behave Proper is to continue to seek to expand the limitless potential and Medicine of oneself.

To Behave Proper is to own the responsibility as well as consequences of one's Self-expressions before, during, and after one has made them.

To Behave Proper is to maintain a Proper Attitude as to what one Really is, and maintain one's Real Self consciously in that.

To Behave Proper is to treat each and everything as being precious to the Creator and even in that, including oneself.

To Behave Proper is to continually seek to expand the Potential of oneself, while maintaining the condition of Wellbeing and Balance of the All of creation in the process of it. As all Prayers are answered in some way or form, to Behave Proper is to walk the path of life with one's Mind directed from Heart to Conscience, and pay as little mind to Ego as possible except in matters of personal safety for which it was designed.

To Behave Proper is to always consider oneself with one's Consciousness to Heart as being an ever expanding Potential and child of a Loving and Benefacting Creator, and ever most willing to take one's own next first step.

To Behave most Proper is to then Prayerfully and Meditatively seek guidance and direction from Him in the Heart of oneself in the process of it, and to be ever respectful and Thankful for the All of it.

To Behave Proper is to walk the path of one's Life in expressions of Self that ensure that there will continue to exist the same or even better conditions, opportunities, and resources for all of those in time to come.

So there we have it. Great Pop said that these are all the tools that are necessary to be able to experience and express the greatest Expanding Potential of Real Success in being, being oneself, and being in life.

SELF HELP

I will begin this last section by first explaining the reason that I recommended saving all of the material that was prepared in the development process of making one's Resource Wheel. The reason is that one can still apply it in making other Resource Wheels! Clearly the first eight items in priority are the primary things to use and focus on first. However, one can in fact successfully make as many more minor Resource Wheels as one might desire. To accomplish this one has only to shift away the top eight items that were used in each list and the first Resource Wheel and simply repeat the process again. As one progresses along one's path of life these lists should be amended periodically so as to reflect such progress and changes. Then one will always be able to benefit from the Potential that is within them by making new Resource Wheels and applying them in one's life.

In the process of applying one's Resource Wheel in the pursuit of Real Success in Life, first and foremost is for one to use it to establish a Proper image of oneself. And if one is wondering what a Proper image might be, it is that of being a visitor that chose to come to Mother Earth to experience and express things. This visitor is no better or less in their capacity of doing that than any other Being or Thing. This visitor has no special position that it can attain in relation to other Beings or Things and will always in Reality exist, and exist in evenness to everyone and everything else that is. This visitor that is oneself, also has in the very next moment of their being in life, unlimited Potential. At any moment that Potential can be realized to effect anything, including Real Success in Life as well as the pursuit of any particular objective imaginable. In the process of this endeavor and expression, one must also choose to establish Reality as well as Openness in one's Perspective and Attitudes. If one Chooses to believe a thing to be possible, then it is possible, no matter what.

To establish and maintain a Proper Self-image is to continually choose to maintain and Value that Ability and Potential in oneself. It is also mandatory to no longer determine one's image of Self by the reflections of oneself in the eyes of others. To realize Real Success, no longer can or should one seek to establish or maintain themselves in relationships whereby they must perform or please others just to be accepted. This includes relationships with one's partners, mates, associates, or even one's family in which this may be the most difficult to accomplish. What is meant here is that to be able to realize the greatest expanding Potential of oneself, then one Must Choose to operate as a complete Self that is not of Need, and thereby maintains a Perspective and Consciousness of Have mentality. This also is where one can realize a great benefit from the understanding of the different types of Selves and their relative influence upon one's image as well as goals in life per se.

A Proper image of Self can always be found through examining one's True Values and Assets. Of course one's Cares, Desires and Fears can add to or detract from this Proper Self-image. However that can occur only if one chooses to accept or empower them to do such. No matter what, one's Bark on tree and thereby Ego is ever present in one's life when incarnated. Yet one always has the Choice and thereby Power to regulate it's Potential of influence. This personal ability and Power is Real and true not only as relates to one's Self-image, but also as relates to one's Potential of Success in every fashion and form as well.

Therefore, to be able to realize the greatest expanding Potential of Success in one's life, it is most important to maintain one's Consciousness in Reality. It is equally important to maintain Consciousness of all of the Realities just mentioned to achieve such a Potential in life. Each individual Being and Thing has limitless Potential and Medicine, and that Potential and Medicine are Essences and thereby are limitless in Nature. Each individual Being or thing also has specific qualities of their Potential and Medicine. Therefore, each individual has specific qualities and abilities that one is always Perfect in being and doing at any and all times. In addition to that, each individual Being and Thing has the ability to Expand these "Assets" at any moment that they Choose to endeavor at realizing such. If one chooses to maintain the Reality of these conditions of Self, then and only then will one's Potential be limitless in the Real sense of such. If these considerations and Realities are honestly embodied as being one's Image of Self, then it will in fact and Reality be the Real and Proper Image, period.

The next step in the application of one's Resource Wheel in one's life is to Realize the conditions and map to one's Fulfillment that exists within it at any moment. This means that one should endeavor to both review it as well as update it on a regular basis. And just like any map, one's Resource Wheel can only assist in making ease and Success in reaching one's destination, if one uses it! It will not carry one there, but it will provide the support necessary to make the appropriate Choices that will get one there. And as mentioned, the most significant Choices to consider are what to focus one's Consciousness, Attitudes, and next efforts upon in the next expression of oneself.

Clearly in my present condition and situation as well as Resource Wheel, it is obvious that initially I can and should Focus my energy, time, and expressions towards the realization of the objective of Care listed in position eight. I say position eight because the Medicine of eight is that of Resource, and getting more resources is my current objective. If I were more interested in fulfillment then I would focus more energy and time upon the elements in position five and so forth. Also, while there might be an incentive to try to effect simultaneous results by spreading out one's focus and energy in other areas of desire, constraint, or concern, one should maintain singular steps towards the most influential one whenever that is possible.

An example of such targeting of one's focus is that it is now the fourth of February, 2002. I could have gotten up this morning and called to see what is necessary for me to get my driver's license. Instead, as is my usual procedure of beginning each day, I Meditated and asked Great Pop what to do first, so as to serve and Please Him. As is shown in my Resource Wheel, I am here to serve His Plan and Will first and foremost, so to me everything else is secondary! For me, that is the way that Real Success in my life will be realized. I am certain that Great Pop is Conscious of my situation, as well as is constantly supporting me in it. The primary focus of my next choice and expression of each day in my life is upon what I can do for Him first in it, period. When I feel that I am complete with that, only then will I redirect it towards that of myself. Therefore, for me to realize the greatest expanding Potential of Success in my life is for me to not try to get my driver's license back today. Instead, it is to first work on getting this material completed, ha, ha, ha!

Actually, it would be much easier for me to get involved in the distraction of pursuing other things than to keep working on this project. After all, I never claimed to be a writer. At this particular moment it is difficult for me to even translate the next thought from the picture words of my personal language into something that is understandable in this English language. I am certain that my Bark on tree is a part of this particular condition and Potential. Even so, I have to make Choices. When one thinks about my life in respect to my present condition and circumstances as well as my Resource Wheel and commitment, there is one choice only that will realize the greatest Expanding Potential of Success. That choice is for me to keep trying to bring the Word of the Creator to the mountaintop, however, and as often as I can!

In the big picture of my life, these words will be around on Mother Earth long past my temporary visit this time. Also, they serve to support the Expansion of the Potential of improvement in the condition of Balance and Well Being of the All. Therefore, Real Success in the life of myself or any Being or Thing will not be fully realized while I am in it at all. Nope, because of the nature of the Medicine of the Potential of myself as well as my life, any Real Success will occur only after I have finished experiencing and expressing myself in it. Therefore, in our perspective towards our being in life, we should not only look at what we are leaving behind in our choices and expressions in it, which are certainly very important, we must also consider at all times what we are doing or adding to our choices and expressions in life, so as to increase the Expansion of the Potential of the Future for all Beings and Things to come.

Even if one were to selfishly choose to only consider the future of themselves in this regard, that in itself will have impact upon the future of the All, no matter what. This perspective and attitude of expanding the Potential of the Future is also the means to get out of the vicious cycle and waste of time and energy of "Brush Fire management". Yep, sometimes what seems most important at the moment is not really important at all. At this point it may be pretty easy to recognize the great Value and Asset that one now has in one's Resource Wheel in this regard.

At this point one must realize that since one's visit or life on Mother Earth is temporary, time becomes one of the most significant resources and assets that one must consider and manage. To realize the greatest expanding Potential of Success in life, the employment of one's Medicine, energy and time, become some of the most important things to consider in it. It is also important to recognize that there are cycles that relate to time, and in this I am not referring to the sunrise or the cycles of the moon. I am referring to the cycles of Potential that exist as being the Medicine of all things. Yep, there are times that seeds can be planted and that they will flourish, and times when they will not. Period. Therefore, one of the major tools of time management becomes Patience, which of course requires choosing to express Trust and Faith. Yep, Trust and Faith that one will realize the fulfillment of one's desire if one operates in resonance to the natural cycles and hence Medicine of that Potential, can definitely be considered as being a Proper expression of patience. And of course our Bark on tree likes to use Fear in the guise of impatience to create distrust, and thereby gain control once again, ha, ha, ha.

One might now ask what, if anything, can one do to be able to use one's time assets to better realize a greater expanding Potential of Real Success in one's life? The first and obvious response is that of: "Do Not Waste Any of It!" Another answer to that question is sitting there within one's Resource Wheel and becomes evident in one's prioritization of True Values, Desires, and Cares.

One can consider one's Fears and Assets as well. However, the other elements are much more dynamic as regards one's Real Potential of Success in Life in any and all cases, period. Also, throughout our lives our Guides, or Angels as some call them, are constantly supporting us. If asked and listened to, these supporting Spirits do and will help one as relates to making choices about the timing of certain expressions. Personally, most oftentimes I Choose to Meditatively and Prayerfully call upon and ask Great Pop and include Him in the process and thereby outcome of such things.

At this point, I was given to call the driver's license people in Raleigh, which of course is long distance. My first effort at such failed. On my second attempt, I was put on hold for a long time while waiting for the "next available representative". Naturally, my Bark on tree made me anxious about the cost that was adding up by the second and thus paralleling this lesson in time. Then even more Bark started building when the representative that finally answered told me that my driving suspension was now for two more years of time! As one might imagine, my heart sank immediately on that little bombshell. I was then told that I could schedule a hearing over the matter and of course I responded that I would like to do that. The end result now is that I have to wait (Patience), until the later part of this month for that hearing to take place. Also, I Pray that somehow I might (Hope Prayer to realize that Potential) be able to get a license to drive somehow, anyway. Not only do I now have to consider how I am going to get the resources to continue to live (meaning that the rent is soon due again), but also how I will be able to get to the place of that hearing. Yep, that this time thing is real important and tricky stuff is pretty obvious to me now.

At this point, it is being given that I again state that each individual Being or Thing is solely responsible for one's own condition and circumstances. That is Reality and I cannot over emphasize it! If I get sick, it is solely because I Chose to allow or accept that to develop within my body in order to have that experience. Likewise, if I get well or heal a wound, it is because I Chose to manifest that new condition of my physiology in order to experience that. Again, life is simply experiences and expressions of Self-Determined Choices. As a PohTikaWah and healer, I can and have channeled energy, as well as manifested things to occur at times in someone else's body. Since they were previously not well, some of them would claim that I healed them. I do not personally make any such claim. Instead, I only say that I assisted them in healing themselves, which I believe is always the case of such. Even my expressions of that, were only effective when they subsequently Chose to maintain that new condition of themselves. Therefore as a PohTikaWah, all I did and do is to facilitate and assist in Self-help.

In order to give the best possible support to Self-help, at this point I was given to lie down and soon I found myself back at that wonderful table of Understanding and Great Pop. Upon my arrival, I was somewhat surprised to find that Great Pop was not already at the table as usually when I do this "barging in", He is already sitting there and waiting for me. So, if one can imagine how uncomfortable my current situation in life in the physical sense is, it certainly pales in comparison to what I am feeling right now in this moment! Obviously hearing that thought, Great Pop then spoke to me from another room. He told me that He would join me in a little bit. Hmmm, I then thought, it seems like I still am dealing with this time thing. If any are wondering, when I come here to be with Great Pop this way, I do still have some Bark on tree associated to me. Of course it is not nearly as much as when I am back in life on Mother Earth. Thankfully, Great Pop soon appeared from around the corner and He was carrying something in a very plain-looking box. He then sat down and with a wave of his hand, magically caused more treats and elixir to appear before us in the center of the table.

My initial reaction to that was to say, "I'm sorry to barge in on You this way Great Pop, but I have come to a point in this new material that I need some more of Your help in." Great Pop just smiled in His all knowing way and with a twinkle in His left eye, said, "*I Understand.*" Unlike what some might imagine in such a response from Him, for some reason this time I was not at all comforted by it. Perhaps it was because His answer was so short. On the other hand, it was more likely because I was not totally aware of what He expected, or what I should do. Of course all of this served to make me very conscious of my Self-image as well as Bark on tree. I was actually so uncomfortable at this point that I even considered excusing myself for the obvious intrusion that I was making upon Him, and just leave! Thankfully, Great Pop again rescued me from a massive attack of Bark on tree and calmed me down by explaining:

"Ah, Little One, are you feeling a little insecure right now? Sorry about that, but it is good and necessary. You see, the first topic that we will now cover is,"

***

How to Champion Insecurity

"Little One, as you are aware all insecurity comes from a fostered sense of doubt and lack of Trust. I say fostered here Little One because no Being or Thing ever incarnates with such doubt, and in all cases it is a taught pattern of behavioral response that one becomes exposed to in a Cosmic / Communal Self relationship after one incarnates. As you are well aware, doubt and insecurity are simply two of the many faces of Fear that one's Bark on tree uses to try to get control of one's Mind. Just by recognizing this nature and condition of insecurity, one has taken the first step in the process of championing it in oneself in the Medicine and Proper Way. Actually Little One, the insecurity that you felt upon your arrival had nothing to do with coming here and being with Me at all. In Reality, the insecurity that you felt upon your arrival was actually a carryover from that which you are currently experiencing in your life. Therefore, it is pretty easy to see that insecurity can and oftentimes does build or feed upon itself.

Little One, in the process of championing insecurity it is very important that one develops an awareness and perspective as to the Real Origin or source of one's expression of insecurity. I say such because insecurity is an expression by definition, and thereby it is a pattern of energy and behavior that one Chooses from time to time to experience or express. Insecurity is likewise both an internal as well as external expression, as is the case of Trust. Because of this duality of Potential expression, as with Trust, insecurity can be a source of influence within itself upon oneself. In this I mean that one can choose to trust one's own self or not, as well as to choose to trust another Being or Thing, or not. As you are now realizing Little One, these are both like switches that are either turned on, or off. There is no Real condition of maybe about trust or insecurity, one either chooses to express one of them, or not. Any maybe-like condition is to *choose to express distrust to some extent. Ah, I see that you are now aware that maybe and distrust are what is promoted in the prevalent culture and is a seed which some Beings plant and use to feed off of others with. In fact, an expression of trust or insecurity is not always about oneself or another Being or Thing doing anything at all. Nope, it can be about intent, motive, character, value, loyalty and all sorts of things that are predominately expressions that are internal to an individual Being or Thing.*

You see Little One, the more that one understands the nature of Trust, the easier it is to manage or deal with insecurity. In the big picture, one might liken insecurity as being just another word for Fear. Yet in its perfect design it is not that at all. Nope, while the time limit of Fear soon disables its Potential of influence, such is not the case of insecurity at all, you see. This is not to say that there is no time limit involved with insecurity, it is just that it is longer lasting than outright Fear. As you are now wondering Little One, yes, I made it this way for a Reason. Actually, insecurity can best be described and understood as being a shadow or footprint of Fear. In a sense insecurity is a pattern of behavioral response that is resultant from an experience of Fear, which is also always an expression in itself as well. Therefore one actually has an asset Potential in insecurity, in the sense that it was designed to maintain heightened awareness and sensitivity to caution, for a period of time of one's own choice.

Let's imagine that you are walking down the street and a car is heading directly towards you. It almost runs over you, but in time you realize that your life is in jeopardy and you jump out of its path. Fear made you jump, and it was the source of energy that enabled you to respond as quickly as you did. Fear is an Essence with a condition to time that is associated to one's Bark on Tree Operative of Ego, and it is perfect when used in that type of circumstance. When the car finally does miss you and has passed, then the time limit of Fear soon neutralizes itself automatically. As you have also experienced, once you are again in safety from that particular jeopardy, the very next steps that you take will be of caution still. That is because of this perfect design of insecurity. When another car soon approaches, because of it you are naturally of a heightened awareness as to the Potential of what it Potentially might do as regards your personal safety.

As you can now realize Little One, this continuing regard to one's condition of safety in such an example and experience is only possible because of the design and Medicine of insecurity. Yep, in My perfect design of it, I fashioned the behavioral model and pattern of insecurity so as to prolong consciousness to Well Being and safety and it is a simple as that. Hopefully, from this example all might better understand the perfection of insecurity. Yep Little One, in a sense one can Choose Fear as an expression of response to a Potential, and thereafter one can maintain awareness to caution through Choosing to express an Attitude of insecurity. So, the simplest method of distinguishing Fear from insecurity is that one can rightfully consider Fear to be an expression of response, and insecurity to be an expression of Attitude.

Therefore Little One, the first and foremost step in the process of championing insecurity is to:

Identify the associated Fear.

Then:

Decide and Choose a means by which to no longer be of consideration or concern as to the Potential that is being considered with regard to it.
For example, stay on the sidewalk or off the street when walking, and look at the path of each vehicle as it approaches from any direction. Once the Potential is removed or eliminated, then the Fear will automatically dissipate because of its time limit.

Next:

Choose to detach from past patterns of behavior and Attitude, and then foster a new Open Attitude and Perspective as to the Potential regarding issues that one maintained the Fear about.
And Little One this is where the important work is done with regard to insecurity. One must in Reality bring closure to the events of the past to be able to experience unlimited Potential in the Future! Just because something occurred, or occurred one way in the past, does not mean that it will in fact happen again, or happen the same way in the Future. Period.

Finally:

Make a commitment to oneself from that point forward to Choose to Focus one's Perspective, Desire, and Attitudes, so as to Realize the greatest Potential of experience and expression in one's Being and being in life. Period. *This is where one causes the time limit of insecurity to expire. As you know, Fear has to continually be consciously brought to mind else it evaporates so to speak. One cannot erase the footprint of it so easily as one can choose to establish and maintain an Attitude that looks forward to a new and better experience, and release from consciousness what one is leaving behind in the process. In so doing, the time limit of insecurity will erase the footprint in the same manner as the next high tide. Also, thereafter one should continue to choose patterns of behavior that Result the greater Potential of one's True Values, at all times and in every Future circumstance. You see Little One, an Attitude that embodies and expresses a <u>Commitment, Perspective, and Focus to the Future</u> will always and in all ways, champion any condition of insecurity, no matter what."*

And with that last statement, while waiting for a response from me, Great Pop took one of the treats and took a bite of it. As one might suspect, I naturally began to relax quite a bit when Great Pop began His discussion on insecurity. Yet I seemed to still have some lingering sense of it at this point. Great Pop offered me a treat then so as to give me even greater ease, and soon began again saying:

"Well, Little One you still seem a little uncomfortable. Let's see what We can do about that now. In your Earthwalk, you chose a condition and parents that would naturally develop a sense of inferiority as well as some other types of complexes which are primarily based upon one's image in the eyes of others. Actually you did this for a reason, and that reason was simply because you were afraid of your Real Self and Power. You were afraid of not only what you could do, but also how others might react when you did it. And actually there are many different symptoms that could be considered as falling within this category of discussion. Yep, next we will discuss:

***

How to Champion Inferiority, Complexes, Addictions, and even Obesity.

First, We need to get to the Real source of such patterns of behavioral Choices of expression. Yep Little One, all complexes and even addictions as well as obesity, are simply that, expressions. As you are now well aware, expressions always and in all ways, represent and reflect one's Value System, Perspective, and Attitude in some manner or form. And as you are now rightfully surmising, each and every one of these expressions reflect some condition of, or issue with, Control. Yep, Control is the key word and issue as regards this topic, very good Little One.

Actually Little One, all of these behavioral patterns of expression are primarily fostered responses to Fear, usually in the guise of illusion. Each and all of these are expressions, and all expressions are choices. All choices are reflective of one's True Value System within one's Real Self, yet they can be modified or changed by influences from one's Bark on Tree of Ego, which is associated to each and all of one's Imagined Selves at all times. All external choices become expressed through one's Care Essence-Operative and they always are sent there from one or more of one's four Will Operatives. Therefore, Honesty is the operative word and choice of expression to use in being able to champion any expression of one's Care, including Fear. Ah, I see that you are now realizing that inferiority and other complexes are in fact and Reality, simply the Desire or inability to Control the image that oneself or that others have about oneself, very good. And these Fear based expressions have another thing in common as well Little One, and it is that they all are resultant from one's Self-image.. As you are rightfully surmising Little One, in certain instances and applications the Original designs and intent of these patterns of behavioral expressions are perfect in every sense and way. Yet when used in response to Fear and illusion, which is usually resultant from operating in Need mentality, they can sabotage one's unlimited Potential of Self-realization as well as expression. And as you now recognize, in all of these conditions the primary culprit or source of the problem as it were, is that of one's Bark on Tree.

As you now Understand, each of these conditions and expressions are in Reality choices of expression that some individuals make, and are no more or less than that. One might say that they have no control over their desires, and that is an illusion. One might say that one does not have control over the desires of others, which can be the case to some degree or extent. However, one can and should always maintain control over the Idea as well as desires that others have about oneself at all times in a Perspective and Attitude of being in a condition of Spiritual perfection and completeness in Self. As you well know by now Little One, even with Imagined and Cosmic / Communal Self external influence Potential, each and every Being and Thing is always and in all ways In Control of their next experiences and expressions. Not only that, they also are totally and completely In Control of the bodyform that they have to experience them in, no matter what. So when we describe these behavioral expressions as being responses to issues with control, it is not because they are of the Proper Perspective, Attitude and Belief that they are always in Control, it is because they Choose to believe the illusion that they are not, instead. Also, while the particular choice of expression made in response to the illusion of not being always and in all ways In Control might appear different, actually they all are the same and have the same process and technique of remedy.

So Little One, the first and foremost step in the process of championing Control Issues is to:

Choose to accept the Reality that one is always In Control of oneself, no matter what.

In Reality Little One, no other single choice or expression can equal the impact that just such a choice can make as regards one's being able to Realize the greatest Expanding Potential of Real Success in life. For many years now Little One, you have stated that you Really do not know Why Nolayte's mom left, and now I will tell you. She left because she was insecure and wanted to be in control. The difficulty was that not only did she desire to be in control of her life, but also all of the conditions and circumstances of Nolayte's as well. Of course for her to be able to do that, she had to be able to control you and she finally realized that she could not. You, on the other hand got caught up in the pleasing game for a while in that relationship, and that in Reality only added fuel to the fire so to speak. On the occasion when you told her that you would not fulfill her next immediate demand, it was all it took for her to take off.

So you are now wondering what the Proper thing might be that one should do in such a circumstance? As I have told you, the answer is to simply Let Go, and then maintain complete control of oneself at all times in it. Remember, you have no right or responsibility to even pray for a change in her. More important is that you make sure you do not change or loose focus of your own Value System in some expression of contention or otherwise. You can be only rightfully in control of yourself and thereby the expressions that you make, and nothing at all other than that. As you are also aware Little One, Nolayte has his own Prayerstick and Plan. Even with all of the Imagined and Cosmic / Communal Self influences just mentioned, you will be in his life at some point and in this you can rest well assured. As you are also well aware, if you had continued to fulfill her immediate demands then, you would not be doing this now for Me, Nolayte, yourself, the All, and the Future. Such is the effects of one's use of the Sword of Choice, as you call it. Consequences, ho, ho, ho.

Of course that is what we are talking about here; just what can happen when one allows another Being or Thing to have some measure of Control over the life and expressions of oneself. From the example of your own experience, one can more easily understand how important this first step in the process of the Remedy of Control Issues is if one is to be able to realize any semblance of Real Success in life. Now then in this first step, it is not only important to Choose to accept the Reality that one is In Control of oneself and one's life, one must also Commit to maintaining that it stays that way. If one does not feel that such is the case, then the responsibility of each and all Beings and Things in such a condition is to choose to Let Go of the current and past conditions of oneself, so as to choose to establish such once again in the condition and life of oneself. Once done then one only has to step forward while maintaining that control over oneself and one's life as being most precious with commitment. And this leads us to the next step in the process, which is to:

Identify the associated illusion and Fear.

This is a necessary and fundamental next step to take, be it in being able to conquer addictions, complexes, or any condition of not being in complete Control and Balanced in that. Here it is important to understand what the source is of one's incentive to over-eat or engage in other types of self-abuse or escape such as with drugs, alcohol, or any other type of substance or Choice of expression, including sex.

Yep, Little One each of these behaviors and complexes are all in this category and they all have the same cause as well as Potential Remedy. You see, unless one can identify the Real Why and therefore Motive for such behavioral responses and expressions, one can only have a semblance of success in having to continually deal with them.

At this point, some might be using the old standby of excuses so as to not take total responsibility. After all, to do such would mean they would have to choose to have the ability to manage these expressions in themselves. Believe me little One, I have heard them all, Ha, Ha, Ha. I am not being insensitive to this distress in Beings, yet it is comical in a way. Certainly you would not be surprised to know of the diversity and magnitude of bequests from individuals that I magically change them and their lives in these regards. And as you also are aware, that would not be Proper for Me to do in most instances.

Yep, even the excuse that one's parents were alcoholics or obese, does not float here. Nor does the fact that one has a problem with a gland or the like. The reason that I say such and that you also know, is that each individual is in control of the operation and WellBeing of that part of themselves at all times. If one chooses to cause a condition in their bodyform that results anything at all, such as having an addiction or even being overweight, it is just a response and symptom of some greater issue, period. Also, if one chooses to incarnate in such a condition to experience it, who am I to intervene?

And as you are now surmising Little One, all of these are simply response expression Choices, usually by some influence from one's Bark on Tree and most often that of some type of an illusion. Therefore, one must first Recognize the illusion and Fear and then Desire, decide, and Choose to do something about it. Otherwise one will only continue to operate in that same manner. Of course if one chooses not to change anything in that respect, then they will only continue to experience the same experiences over and over again. So you can easily see how important this step is Little One and that one is completely Real and Honest in it as well.

Actually this step can be relatively easy to accomplish as all that is required is for one to identify the Need factor that is associated with one's conditions and responses to stimuli. For instance, why does the alcoholic choose to drink? Why do certain individuals choose to over eat or develop certain responses to food? Why does a person choose to use drugs? As you can easily recognize, I do mean Choose here. No one is Really ever born that way. Nope, all Beings and Things incarnate or are born in Have, not Need mentality. So the real source of these types of conditions is nothing other that taught behavior of some type that results in certain choices being made by some individuals that favor one behavioral response over others in response to some type of stimuli. Actually the stimuli can be of a general or specific nature and is not the Real issue at all. It is not important to consider the Why it is that one continues to choose such behavioral responses to stimuli here at all. It is however, Real important to determine Why one started or Chose to express such responses in the first place.

To do such is simply to answer the question of: What is the illusion and Fear? Did one first try drugs or alcohol because one wanted to be accepted by others that were doing it? Does one eat something because they Fear that they will not be fulfilled in some capacity? Does one feel poorly about oneself because someone else said that they were ugly, fat, skinny, have a big nose or have large or small breasts and so forth? Or did someone call oneself clumsy, untalented, uneducated, stupid, and on, and on, and on? And of course the worst perhaps has to do with performance, like making straight "A's" as you know, ho, ho, ho. It should be obvious that without someone else being in one's life whereby such were considerations at all, none of these things would ever be considered at all about oneself. No one is born caring about any of these things. It is from some or all of these behavioral expressions from other people in one's life that eventually result in choices of personal behavioral expression responses that fit into this category. Of course the tricky part to this step is also the mechanism that makes it relatively easy to do. As you are now rightfully surmising Little One, the tricky part of this condition and step is that these behavioral expressions can be operative in any type of Self, except one's Real Self and one's Primary Cosmic / Communal Self. In most cases, with addiction specifically, the causative agent in one type of Self will typically result in the manifestation of a Projected Self in order to maintain as well as expand support to that expression and experience well past its genesis. In this I mean that the individual that started out "experimenting" with drugs because they wanted acceptance from individuals that were practicing such behavior themselves, did not incarnate with a Drug User Projected Self. However, some individuals will in time possibly express such a Projected Self if the experience is of a certain type of reward or fulfills a specific need. And of course once it becomes established, the Projected Self will then keep issuing forth Imagined and Cosmic / Communal Selves in order to continue or expand such experiences *and expressions in one's Life. Of course the same holds true for the individual that becomes the police officer, the fireman, or any other type of occupational identity. Actually, it is this very methodology of Selves that effects any and all experiences and expressions of some type in one's life. Therefore, the easiest method to identify the causative agents is for one to strip away all of the multitude of Selves that one has expressed past one's Real and Primary Cosmic / Communal Self so as to evaluate the Real Motive and resulting effects of each leafy branch of such. The child that is in a gang and stealing to get money for drugs is not doing such simply because they are in a gang. On the other hand the Real reason and Motive that the child is using drugs, is the same as why they are stealing, which is the same as why they are in a gang in all cases. Therefore as regards behavioral responses in the way of addictions, complexes, and so forth, one will find that the Motive that started any of these types of behavioral responses to external stimuli is the same one that keeps them in operation so to speak. Once the Real Fear and illusion is determined regarding such behavioral response choices, then and only then can any individual take the next step which is:*

Choose to Commit to Change.

Yes Little One, each and every Being and Thing has its own unlimited supply of the Essence of Change and thereby always maintains the ability to experience and express that in itself. But in this step We are not talking about any halfhearted Desire. Nope, here We are speaking of Real Commitment. As you are aware there is what is called an energy of inertia and momentum. It is the Reality of this energy that makes it seemingly harder to stop something than to start it. Actually, it is not the condition of things at all. The Real condition is that the energy of inertia and momentum can be considered to be a subset of the Essence of Change and it is simply one of the inherent qualities of it. Clearly it is harder to change directions quickly because of this energy. However, once one does commit to start changing, it will facilitate one to easily continue in that new direction as well. Therefore in all cases and conditions, it is as simple as making a Choice, and then following it with Commitment.

Oftentimes you have likened habits to be the keeping of a pattern of behavioral expression at the top of a stack of such things, and continuing to use that one as a response to stimuli. This is not too far off the mark, as some say. However, in Reality one always and in all ways, has limitless Potential, including that to choose different at any moment. Yet for some individuals the more appropriate response to a given stimuli may not be so apparent. As you now also recognize Little One, all of the conditions in this group result from some form of Self-image condition, and one's Image of Self is the target that one must Really Focus upon changing in this part of the process. And again, if one does not Really Desire and Believe such is possible, then it will not be for oneself, period.

Once a Real commitment to change is made, then the next step is:

Reclaim Control of one's Life and Self-image.

Here again, this step requires Real commitment as well. In this part of the process, one must recognize that they do Really and at all times, possess the power of their Sword of Ability, and continually choose to use it. As you are aware and have oftentimes said Little One, many if not most in the prevalent society are taught to only see themselves in the reflection of the eyes of others. In some, if not most instances this may be Real and true. However, even though it gives rise and cause to Self-image problems, such as are causative to the behavioral expressions of this group, it is relatively insignificant as relates to their solution.

I say this now Little One, for the simple reason that for any and all Beings and Things to effect a Proper and Positive Image of themselves, they must detach the hoses of their Care Essence-Operative as you call them, from all others for a period of time so as to effect the Real change that is involved in it. Another way of describing this process is to detach from all of one's Projected, Imagined, and Cosmic / Communal Selves. To reclaim one's life and establish a change in one's Self-image that is Real, one can only be alone in it for a period in order to do such for oneself. Any efforts other than that, and in Honesty, will be fraudulent to some extent. Also, while one can and should maintain one's respect for other Beings and Things in this regard, it should not have Any bearing upon the outcome. And the question as to what is a Proper Image of Self is easily answered in ones Lists, Resource Wheel, and Hero definition. Also, those that have any cosmetic or weight issues may in fact find that the "Ideal" weight and bodyform configuration for themselves might be perfect already. Should anyone Really desire something different, then that change can and should become a part of their new *and Proper Image of Self and they should then take the necessary steps to change into it.*

And the final step in championing the expressions of this group about Control issues is:

Commit to that Change in Self.

This is as easy to accomplish as by making Conscious Choices that result in one's doing nothing from this point forward that will cause one to not be of one's new Self and Self-image thereof. Of course, one will also have to introduce this New, Complete, and Real Self into the activities and associations of one's daily life and learn new ways to respond to stimuli that support the WellBeing and continuance of it. Yet this is as easy to accomplish as reflecting upon the things in one's Lists, in one's next and Future Choices. Of course, if one Chooses to empower others again from that point on in one's life and Future, then starting over at step one will become necessary."

At this point, noticing that I had finished my treat, Great Pop handed me another and sat back to see what I might next say or do. Probably to the surprise of both of us, I chose to reflect upon what Great Pop had just shared with me. Much of what He had just explained certainly hit home. It seems that in some capacity or another because of the influence as well as requirements of the current prevalent society and culture, I seriously doubt that any single person has escaped all of the complexes and so forth that it not only fosters, but also outright promotes.

Anyone can easily understand Why I might have grown up with a certain sense of inferiority, considering the Reality of my early time. And like Great Pop explained, that is insignificant as regards the Potential remedy of such. Also, as of late I have been examining my condition to alcohol as well. It was an ever-present thing in my early years. As a teenager, I learned early on how to "hold my liquor" as some call it. As a young adult, I learned how to metabolize myself in response to it, because that was what was important to the peers that I then had. In Reality, I now do not like even the taste of it so much anymore. At this point in my life, I might drink a beer now and then but oftentimes I do not even like the after effects that one or two of those has upon my biology and consciousness.

Actually, the Real reason that I ever drank any form of alcohol can be, simply put, so as to be accepted, belong, or to in some manner, fit in. The Real reason that I went to nightclubs so frequently and for so long of a time was not even to drink alcohol there actually. Nope, it was to be with people and perhaps find some acceptance there. I also feel that I was doing all of this partly so as to either keep Jack alive that way, or perhaps to find some other person to fill the void in my life that was resultant from his exit so very many years ago.

I was next given to consider some of my experiences with some people that belonged to the program that they call AA. In going there, I quickly recognized that it was little different than the programming method and morays of the prevalent culture in that it was predominantly Fear based, and Need driven. It did not take much to recognize that while it was an alternative for some people, it also fostered dependency and co-dependency to a great degree. I even recognized that for some of the participants, it was just a replacement so to speak, of an addiction to alcohol with an addiction to going there to the meetings. It was at this point that Great Pop began His discussion again with:

"Ah Little One, that brings us to our next topic which is:

***

How to Experience Renewall (Versus Recovery), and Healing.

Yes Little One, in Reality it is as you have oftentimes mentioned, all conditions of physical disease, discomfort, or anomaly are resultant from Spiritual issues. Yep, in a sense one can accurately say that the Spirit, and thereby one's Real Self, defines and drives all of the experiences and expressions of one's physical form in all instances. Unlike what some are led to believe, physical incarnations are not meant to develop, mold, or do anything to one's Spirit at all. And as you are now also recognizing, growth is not any objective except as an individual Free Will choice of experience and expression. Actually growth is not even a consideration as to why I made the Physical realm. Nope, I did such only as a means of providing a self-renewing and perpetuating, ever-changing theater of Potential experiences and expressions. In a nutshell, the many arenas in the Physical realm are provided simply as places for Spirits and thereby outwardly expressive Potential to go so as to experience and express being themselves in.

As you are also aware Little One, not only is one's Bark on Tree of Ego associated and involved in these experiences and expressions, but also one's Emotional Body, Wills, and Attitudes. Needless to say, this only happens in the incarnated condition of being. As you are now beginning to realize, it is because of the participation of these other elements of one's Personal Structure that the other types of one's Selves become involved as well. It is as you are now surmising; one's Projected, Imagined, and Cosmic / Communal Selves in most senses serve to facilitate the operation and expression of their related components of one's Personal Structure.

Perhaps the best place to start with in describing what is involved in the process of this subject of healing, is what one's condition is before one incarnates. Before any Being or Thing incarnates it is a Potential that exists inside of My Essential Will and can be considered to have and operate with a Personal Structure that is in True Spirit Form as shown earlier. Also in that condition and place, one has a Real Self as well as a Primary Cosmic / Communal Self that one uses to experience and express that form of one's Personal Structure with. As you have learned and experienced many times by now, when a Being or Thing chooses to experience a sojourn outside of My Essential Will, there are many places for such to occur. Yet if the targeted place is within the arenas which I developed and can be considered as being the Physical realm, then the process of incarnating is much the same as exit, meaning that one goes through a tunnel and process of Transition to get there or return. As you also know, it is during the Transitional process of incarnating whereupon one's Personal Structure receives the alterations and additional elements that result in one having the incarnated form of it. This means that while incarnating, one's Personal Structure is amended by receiving an additional Heart Will operative and its associated Attitude operative, an Ego operative with an associated Fear pseudo-essence, and an Ego Will operative and its associated Attitude operative. As you also know, these additional elements will be removed in the return process of Transition, including the connectives that facilitate expressions though them to the other parts of one's Personal Structure when it becomes once again in True Spirit form. In this return process of Transition not only are these elements removed and remain with one's physical body, so also are any additional Selves that one has chosen to express and associate to one's Real Self and one's Primary Cosmic / Communal Self. Also, the Transitional processes of getting to the Physical realm as well as that of returning to My Essential Will can have no anomaly or malfunction by My design. Whatever occurs between these two processes is chosen and manifested by each individual Being or Thing that incarnates and exits. It occurs as a Free Will expression of Self-determination and can be considered as being a physical life experience and expression. Even for a Being or Thing to choose not to immediately return to my Essential Will and remain in the discarnate condition of Self in what you call the Zones for a while, is simply another Free Will, Self-determined choice of experience and expression.

So Little One as you know by now there is no condition of being that is not in some way chosen if not also self-manifested. In this I mean that if someone cuts one's throat or arm off, while one did not personally do that to oneself, one did choose to place oneself in availability for such a possibility to occur. As one also knows, at a certain level of consciousness each and every Being and Thing does always know of such potential before it does finally occur. Simply put, any and all other conditions of being and being in life can in fact be considered as Self-chosen as well as Self-manifested. This reality does even include those conditions that are considered as being birth defects. While the loss of a limb or organ, or the experience of some type of birth defect is not a condition of which one can remedy in the physical sense of such, the remedy to the Emotional Body and Real Self in those instances and conditions is the same as for any other type of physical anomaly. Therefore these particular conditions and circumstances are also to be considered within the process that is being described in this section.

As you are now surmising, yes Little One any and all types of physical infirmary or anomaly are direct manifestations of one or more of the components that are added to one's Personal Structure during the incarnating Transitional process. In this I mean to say that these are the elements that operate through one or more of one's additional Selves and manifest any problems in the condition of Balance and WellBeing of the physical form. And while in most instances, the dilemma or anomaly in the physical form is temporary, it can and will oftentimes recur until the Spiritual issue is dealt with. This is especially true for allergies and the like, which always develop as response expressions to issues of Control. Also as you are well aware Little One, there is a great difference between Renewall and recovery. And while attempts in the Mind-set of and practice of recovery might realize certain limited results that most likely have temporary benefits, only Renewall is what is to be considered here. Therefore the first step in the process of Renewall, and Healing any condition of oneself is to:

Take a Personal Inventory of Selves.

Little One, this is necessary so as to determine the Real causes of the symptoms that are being manifested in the physical body. While Renewall can and should be considered and chosen as an expression for many purposes in one's life expression, I will discuss the process entailed in Realizing it to oneself in this topic. So, just how does one go about taking this personal inventory of Selves? Actually, it depends upon the status of one's lists that have already been made. In this I mean how recent, honest, and accurate they are at the point of dilemma. If they are relatively current, then the work is pretty much done in this regard already. And if not, it is as simple as for one to make new ones. In addition to those lists one can and should also make a chart or map of one's current Projected, Imagined, and Cosmic / Communal Selves. Start with one's Projected Selves as follows:

	Real Self		
	White Eagle		
Projected Self	*Projected Self*	*Projected Self*	*Projected Self*
Poh Tika Wah	**Family**	**Occupation**	**Person**
Imagined Self	*Imagined Self*	*Imagined Self*	*Imagined Self*

259 Selves – Vol. 1

Then expand each of the Imagined Self branches:

Real Self

White Eagle

Projected Self

Poh Tika Wah

Imagined Self	Imagined Self	Imagined Self	Imagined Self
Author	Visionary	Healer	Priest
Cosmic / Communal Self	*Cosmic / Communal Self*	*Cosmic / Communal Self*	*Cosmic / Communal Self*

Projected Self

Family

Imagined Self	Imagined Self	Imagined Self	Imagined Self
Child	Parent	Husband	Relative
Cosmic / Communal Self	*Cosmic / Communal Self*	*Cosmic / Communal Self*	*Cosmic / Communal Self*

Next expand each of one's Cosmic / Communal Selves:

Real Self
White Eagle
Projected Self
Family
Imagined Self
Parent

Cosmic / Communal Self	Cosmic / Communal Self	Cosmic / Communal Self	Cosmic / Communal Self
Heath	**Jacki**	**Nolayte**	**Another?**
Status -	*Status -*	*Status -*	*Status -*
Feelings -	*Feelings -*	*Feelings -*	*Feelings -*
Desires -	*Desires -*	*Desires -*	*Desires -*
Cares -	*Cares -*	*Cares -*	*Cares -*
Ambition -	*Ambition -*	*Ambition -*	*Ambition -*
Fears -	*Fears -*	*Fears -*	*Fears -*

Of course this Family group for you would also include entries for TohNaWah, Miss Nikki, and Lil' Bit Sundancer under the Imagined Self of Relative. These listings will define and include the current expressions that are ongoing in one's relationships and current endeavor of goal attainment and Potential Fulfillment. Again, Honesty is the Key word and necessary requirement here. As one describes one's goals and relationships of involvement in that part of the process, one is to also rate one's current position as well as progress and constraints towards one's Fulfillment in them. Once this first step is complete, then the second step is to:

Redefine Oneself.

In this step, one is to consider what it is that one Really Desires to Be, Now and in the Future. Also it is important here to first Give Away all of the conditions of the Past, period. It is important to know the source of any of one's condition of imbalance only in as much that one can now Choose to no longer participate in the experience of it anymore. At this point one can start their definition of their New Self with that of being in a condition of Reality, Balance and WellBeing, both physically and Spiritually. Needless to say, in this process of one's redefinition of oneself, one should start with the top items in one's current Value System list. It is most important to be not only Honest, but also Realistic as regards one's Real Potential to achieve such. In this I mean that if one has chosen to experience not being able to walk by loosing a leg, then it is not Realistic for them to expect and therefore Desire, to grow a replacement one. However, in such a circumstance it is Realistic for them to be able to walk or even run, as some individuals have shown in their choice of an expression of this process. These new definitions should be now included at the top portion of the lists that one already has fashioned in relation to one's True Desires and Cares. When that process is complete and Understood, then the next step is that of:

Commit with Passion and Focus, All of One's Wills to embrace Renewall and Change into the new pattern and Life Potential of oneself.

Yep, Little One, this part of the process is as simple and quick as one makes it. But here we are talking about Real Commitment and expression of Will and Desire. Also, it is important that no energy is applied in any fashion to things other than the Fullest Realization of this Desire, and Renewall to it in and of oneself, period. This is also the way of Miracles as you well know, and the All of the universe can and should be called upon in one's experience and expression of it. Then in the very next moment of one's life, one is responsible for maintaining the Transformation that if Honestly sought will be then Realized. Also, at this point, one will Realize the greatest ease and Success in life from this moment forward by remaking their Resource Wheel. By doing this, they will thereby define their next New Real Self, and then can and should, maintain Consciousness and Focus upon it in their daily lives and Future. *As you are now wondering Little One, I have purposefully not mentioned anything about the healing of any specific disease. Instead I have only provided a means to identify and remedy any and all causes of such. At this point, any of the means and methods found available to treat any specific physical malady or disease should be consciously employed with one's Focus of Will and with an Attitude that reflects the New Self that is established in this process."*

Next, Great Pop once again excused Himself and got up and left the room for a bit. He had left the little box on the table, probably knowing that it would pique my curiosity. As I was considering that maybe I might take a peek inside of it, Great Pop then told me to include the material on Renewall from the Proper Way at this point, so here it is:

RENEWALL PROPER - *Renewall is a process provided by The Creator by which any and all can make a fresh new beginning and start in their expression of Being, and being in life. To Be in the Way of Renewall Proper, one must embrace to one's Consciousness the true condition of one's Ego and all of the desires and controlling mechanisms inherent in it, such as one's Fear, doubt, vanity and so forth. This is necessary as these are the things which have lead one to one's own illusionary perception of oneself and one's idea of Being, and being oneself. To be in the Way of Renewall Proper, one is to then express a Desire for Change and Renewall. Once chosen and accepted, one is to then embrace it to one's Heart and beg for Grace and Mercy from the Creator in one's best effort and Endeavor of Humility Proper through giving it and all else in one's limited perception and consciousness away. Renewall Proper is then realized by one's asking the Creator to make oneself over so as to be of Renewall, and thereby Renew All aspects of one's Being, conscious and otherwise, to His Idea of oneself. In this act, one will thereby replace the old distorted pattern of oneself that one has made as the image of one's Ego of Self, with a new and Proper pattern of His Idea of oneself. Renewall Proper is further realized by again expressing a Real Desire from the Heart of oneself, and then surrendering oneself to it so as to become the vessel of oneself that is truly the channel of His Light and Love and Benefaction to oneself and all other Beings and Things of His creation. As one certainly cannot change one's past as it is over, one can through the Realization and expression of*

Renewall Proper, leave the influences of one's past behind so as to become as Born New in Renewall. The Expression of Renewall Proper is than realized in oneself as one begins again to walk one's path of experience and expression of life as the Renewed and bettered pattern of oneself that He is ever so willing to provide to oneself. The Creator is most willing to support all Beings and Things in this manner at any instant in one's life, and as many times a day as is necessary so as to ever be embraced, supported, and Loved by Him. In the process of Renewall Proper, it truly is a New plan and agenda in life that one seeks as the Creator provides all of the tools necessary upon each and every step to make ease in the expression of one's being one's Real and complete next new Self. Renewall Proper is easily realized through one's Prayerfully and Meditatively looking to the Heart of Self for direction and guidance from the very best Source of such, which is the Creator. Renewall Proper is much like the wonderful process that the caterpillar goes through. The caterpillar goes into and emerges from the cocoon so as to experience and express Renewall. The once self-indulgent and needy consumer of plant material, Renews All so as to become a beautiful Supporting and Benefacting Caretaker of the Plant Spirit kingdom in a Renewed form of a Butterfly. Yes, instead of continuing it's previous limited idea of Self as a ravaging parasite that preyed upon the plants, it chooses different, and Renewall is the process that such change can become Realized in itself. All Beings can also choose to become a Butterfly in oneself, through continuing the process of Renewall Proper in oneself at any moment and as often as found necessary so as to bring forth the Greatest expression of the Creator's Idea in and of each Self.

In what seemed like only moments, Great Pop then returned and again made Himself comfortable at the wonderful table of Understanding. Knowing that I had kept restraint upon my curiosity as to what was in the box on the table before us, He then began speaking on these subjects again with:

"Well Little One, I see that you are wondering what is in that box. In a little while I might just show you, maybe, ho, ho, ho. This next topic might seem quite broad in scope as it does in fact cover many things as relates to what one might express one's Care about. This topic includes the loss of a Loved one, divorce, loss of a job, or any type of events or developments that occur in one's life that have immediate impact upon one's sense of Self and one's balance therein.

So for simplicity, We will just call it:

***

How to Champion Personal Issues.

As you have figured out by now Little One, all Care expressions of a Being or Thing result and operate in Cosmic / Communal Selves, period. In actuality, even the maintaining or Care of one's physical body when incarnated, is expressed and experienced in just such a Self as it were. That is the reason that I defined the process of any remedy or Renewall of such in the previous topic. As We have already discussed the Cosmic / Communal Self in detail, I will only remind you here that it is in these types of Selves that one actually interacts with other Beings and Things. This includes one's profession, spouse, parents, automobile, employer, and so forth. These are also the most extended Selves as regards their relative condition to one's Real Self. While the Potential developments that might give rise to one having some type of difficulty or negative reaction to some condition or experience in them might seem diverse, in Reality it is not. Therefore, while the symptoms might seem to vary, the Real cause and remedy does not. In fact and Reality, the only condition of imbalance and dilemma that can arise in a Cosmic / Communal Self is that of what can be called one's own Failed Expectation in such. So with that understanding then the first step becomes:

Identify the Expectation and Loss.

In all cases one operates in a Cosmic / Communal relationship with another Being or Thing as a result of one's Choice of Care and Desire to experience and express oneself in it, in some fashion of form. Therefore when difficulties, imbalance, or problems occur within one, one only has to determine What has changed that now makes such to no longer be a viable condition for that Care and Desire Potential to be realized or continue? Also, it is important to identify what one Really expected to happen, versus that which in Reality now has developed. Little One, you knew that there was a Potential for Jack to exit when He did, in the beginning of that Cosmic / Communal Self that you both shared. The same holds true for many experiences of loss, like that of your mother and earth father. Yet you also maintained Hope, as well as an expectation that you might continue to operate in those shared Cosmic / Communal Selves with them for a period of time that was much longer than was realized.

Therefore, in these particular experiences and expressions, in Reality at some point you did have to face and recognize your loss of Hope and Potential in these shared Cosmic / Communal Selves. This is the same for any loss or disappointment that one might experience and express in one's life. One's facing and accepting Potential loss or failed expectations is also an important part of maintaining Consciousness and Focus of Perspective to Reality. Therefore Little One, as you now understand, this makes for a condition that one must be Real and hence completely Honest in this important first step.

Once this first step is complete and one's feelings are understood, then the next step is:

Recognize and Realize the actuality of one's Success.

Little One, as important as the recognizing a loss and mourning it is, so also is the Realization that one indeed did have a great Potential realized in the Cosmic / Communal Self that was shared with that Being or Thing. This is Real and true as well as is always the condition and case no matter what actually occurred in it, period. Also, if a Potential is Realized in any fashion or form, then that is by definition a Success. This actually is the difference between operating from Need mentality versus Have mentality in one's Perspective and Attitude. You see Little One, even Cosmic / Communal Self-expressions and experiences that embody dysfunctional relationships are in Reality always successful. And, once the success has become understood, then the next step is to:

Inventory what one Expressed and Experienced.

Yes Little One, you might liken this to being the West activity of the Medicine Wheel of expressions and experiences in Cosmic / Communal Selves. The relationship and Potential that was embodied and experienced in the Cosmic / Communal shared Self, as well as all of the preceding steps, can be considered as being South activity. This "West" step is where, through introspection and "looking inside" as you call it, one realizes one's participation and thereby Potential. In doing such a review and inventory of one's experiences in total Honesty, the greatest measure of profit can be realized from any experience, period. This is also the place of the Give Away and one's Real mourning of the loss should in fact be expressed and understood to completion here. Actually, one might liken the experience of this process as being the arrival of oneself after withstanding the rigors of a long trek or journey. Once one has arrived at a new destination, it may not have been so easy or be entirely what one expected. Yet in this review of one's participation in it, one will always find the potential of one's success in it no matter what outcome actually developed. Once this step is accomplished then the next step is to:

Reclaim that Cosmic / Communal Self.

Little One as you are now beginning to realize, each and every Self that is expressed from one's Real Self requires continuous maintenance and energy. This is Real and true in all conditions and circumstances. Therefore if one Really desires to Realize the greatest Expanding Potential of Real Success in life, it is very important to reclaim any Self that is expressed from the Real One when the Potential in it is no longer to be considered as being viable or possible. This step can also be considered as the North position as relates to the Medicine Wheel of expressions and experiences, and hence it is where the Real work is s accomplished. As you like to say, this is the time and place to retract and clean up one's Care hose that was extended into that Cosmic / Communal Self in support of it. If this process is done with Real Respect and Value, then one will naturally embody as much expansion as is possible from understanding all of the experience. In this step one is to not only let go of that relationship and Self which no longer is viable or potentially fulfilling, but also one is to reclaim and hold as precious, the openness, desire, willingness, care, and trust that one offered in it. Once complete, then the next step is to:

Integrate one's feelings about the condition or situation.

Yep Little One, this is the East work of the process, very good! Yes, in this part of the process, it is recommended that at Proper times and in Proper circumstances one describes and discusses one's feelings about the experience and expression. Through the integration of one's feelings in this manner, one can again regain a Proper sense of value, completeness, balance, and control, especially in regards to one's Bark on Tree, Ho, Ho, Ho! Also Little One, it is important to be

Honest here as it is not to dwell too long upon any loss or other negative conditions that might have been resultant from the expression and experience. The means to effect such integration is to let go of the past and simply choose different for the Future. Remember here, Little One, Real Success in life is not about winning or loosing like some are led to believe, it is simply the realization of some Potential through one's personal experience and expression. Once this step in the process is complete, then the next and final one is to:

Become one's next new Expanded Real Self.

As you now recognize Little One, this is where one again begins in the South of the Medicine Wheel of expressions and experiences. The important thing to consider and remember here is that at any point one can and should Choose to become one's next New Real Self. Also, at any point one can choose to again experience and express one's Desires and Cares through experiences and relationships with other Beings and Things in New Cosmic / Communal shared Selves. Another important thing to consider here is that one should endeavor always, and in all ways, not to become the product of one's past experiences and expressions. Instead, one should direct as much openness, focus, and energy as is possible towards the Realization of one's unlimited Potential of one's Real Self in one's next expressions and thereby Future."

Having once again completed a topic as it were, Great Pop signaled such to me by again leaning back in His chair to see what I might do or say next. Having now gotten a little more at ease and used to being put on the spot so to speak this way, I thought to try and relax more as well. I was then given to consider my situation as regards my children and also the marriage that I had experienced with Nolayte's Mother. Clearly, these Cosmic / Communal Self-expressions of mine and thereby Relationships, seemed to fall within the previous category and topic to some lesser or greater extent.

My marriage to Nolayte's mother certainly could be considered as being dead now, just like Jack. While that is Real and true, I still feel that there still remains a Potential that if I can get the resources and funds necessary at some point, then I can be in Nolayte's life some way and even perhaps in the lives of my other two children as well. Then I was given to remember the saying that it takes the effort and desire of two to make and keep a relationship, and only one to destroy it. Thankfully, Great Pop saved me from myself again with:

"Yes Little One, even a situation whereby one is being bullied or abused by another Being or Thing is a Relationship that is being expressed and experienced in a Cosmic / Communal shared Self. Naturally this will be the subject of our next topic, which is:

***

How to Realize Success in all Relationships.

As you are now aware and have experienced, there are limitless possibilities as to what one can experience and express when one is in a relationship with another Being or Thing. We actually could write a whole book on this singular subject, especially with regard to what one should do in certain circumstances in them. Even so, there are certain things that one can and should do in order to realize some measure of success in all of them, and that is what is going to be described herein. Previously, I have given you the definition of what is Proper in regard to Relationships, and I Desire that you present it here at this point for reference."

So here it is as follows:

*****

RELATIONSHIP PROPER

The way to be in **RELATIONSHIP PROPER** as given by the Creator in the Way to walk one's path of life is defined as being:

The Respectful Sharing of the Experience of the Expression of Being, and One's Allowing for Others to experience and express being themselves in ways and means of their own choice which Walk in Balance and with Harm to No One Being or Thing and are most comfortable to themselves.

In Reality, the All of the Creator's creation is in some condition of being in a relationship to each and every other part of it as well as to Him by the very nature of His design of it. Therefore, what is given to be expressed here is the Way to Be Proper in the expression of one's individual behavior of Relationship Proper in the network of the structure of the Great Web of the All of Creation, as is also designed by Him. The key words in the Relationship Proper definition are **Respectful** and **Sharing**. If the condition of the experience of the interconnection of one's Care in relationship to any other Being or Thing of His creation is truly not that of being of Respect Proper and of Share Proper, then indeed that relationship is not to be considered as being Proper. It is stated in this manner because the interconnection of Care must facilitate Flow in both directions so as to be able to give and receive at the same moment, which is to Share. One can in fact be of respect or share to a certain Being or Thing without there existing a Proper Relationship, which in all cases requires both to occur in evenness. Truly the cause and cure for any problems in relationship is manifested in the process of communication and the interaction expressed thereby.

If any relationship is found to bring forth any cause or condition of imbalance to oneself or any other participant of it, then it is not to be considered as being Proper. Nor is any relationship that is found to not be in the nature of Equitable Sharing and thereby supporting to the Attainment Proper of each individual part in it, to a common goal or ideal. Any relationship that restricts the Freedom, Expansion, Expression, or Wellbeing of any single part of it, is not Proper. If anyone is found to have become in such conditions, the Proper Way of Relationship is for one to then seek and see through Prayer and Meditation the purpose of one's desire in bringing forth consciously or subconsciously that condition of abuse to oneself or any other, and then learn the lesson in it. In Reality, one can only learn and thereby experience one's own expression of expansion through Understanding. Also, it is in relationships by which any and all understanding is achieved or developed. This is Real even if that relationship is simply that of oneself with oneself.

The Real and true condition of being is that of everlasting life. Also, each Being and Thing chooses to incarnate into the Physical realm to experience something. That something can be, but is not restricted to, growth or lesson taking. However, growth in the form of Expansion is an inevitable condition as well. Also, the roundest expression of growth should be the only measure of it to consider as being Proper. Of course the roundest condition of growth is always manifested through one's experiencing and expressing unconditional Care, which is Love. Therefore, one can make a positive experience from any development in any kind of relationship, be it Proper or not. In the condition of a relationship that is not Proper, one should recognize the true perfection in it, Love it, and then abandon it. Then one should spend time reflecting upon what one truly does desire in the condition of a Proper Relationship.

The very most important and enabling relationship that one should ever endeavor to Become and Behave most Proper in, is one's individual relationship with the Creator. This is so as to become an ever more Proper and expanding expression of His idea in oneself. To do such, one will then have more of His idea of and in oneself, to share with the All of His Creation in the Relationship Proper Way. If one is of Relationship Proper, then one will value that relationship with such regard and respect so as to do nothing to cause harm to it by any thoughtless or self-serving act of behavior of oneself. To express Relationship Proper is to Caretake for the relationship, like a precious flower or plant of great value and beauty. One does this by nurturing it from time to time as is required and requested, and then with Faith, Trust, and Patience, watches its beauty and benefaction increase as it teaches one how to share in the Brotherhood experience that is the Earthplane.

*****

Great Pop then began again covering this topic with:

"As you recall Little One, on many occasions now I have given you the Proper Way to deal with problems that might arise in relationships. At this point, I will only remind you of two of them. As was given to you in the material of The Plan, the first recommendation relates to problems in Tribe or family. In these instances, because of the closeness of the individuals involved in the situation, it is recommended that they employ the assistance of an intermediary. The intermediary should be an individual that is impartial to the individuals involved and can provide the necessary support while maintaining their own Balance, Focus, Objectivity, and the Proper Perspective to all that is involved in the situation.

The second recommendation relates to problems that arise from some individual operating in the manner of being a "bully" as you call it. In this condition, one is to simply detach one's Care and then simply walk away if at all possible. If that is not possible, then one is to find some means to do such as soon as it is possible. In the mean time, one is to do no single thing to aggravate the situation or add any type of energy at all to it. Furthermore, one is to do these things with one's Attitude and Perspective being centered in one's Real Self and thereby one's own True Value System. This is important so as to preclude any involvement or take over from one's Bark on Tree of Ego as you can now realize. You see Little One, to be able to experience the greatest Expanding Potential of Real Success in life, then one must at all times be one's complete and Real Self in it as much as is possible, at all times, period.

With that having been discussed, let Us now turn our attention to what I really desire to talk about in this topic. As you are now aware, all relationships are simply conditions that exist within chosen and shared Cosmic / Communal Selves. In Reality, one actually is involved in some type of relationship in all of one's types of Selves. However, only Cosmic / Communal Self relationships are external, as the rest are internal. While Cosmic / Communal Selves do facilitate internal relationship interaction as well, they are the only type that also facilitates external ones. The reason that I am mentioning this at this point is that in Reality, the issuance of a Cosmic / Communal Self-expression is always and in all ways, a response to a choice that was singularly made as an expression of some Will of oneself, no matter what. Also in Reality, is that a relationship can only exist for one to become involved in, if one issues forth a Prayer of Desire for that particular Potential to become Realized in one's life experience and expression. In this I mean that even if one does not originate the Cosmic / Communal Self relationship, one does always pray for it in some fashion before one can become involved in it. Of course in the mechanics of such is that when one sees a Cosmic / Communal Self that they wish to join, they can only do such by issuing forth another Prayer of Desire that results in a Cosmic / Communal Self of their own with which to join the other one with.

Also Little One, just as much as one is always born with unlimited Potential, so also can be all relationships. However, many times relationships are resultant from a wrongful idea of oneself or another Being or Thing. In this regard, I mean to say that some relationships are entered into by individuals which are not always Real, complete, and balanced in their own image of Self. Most times this condition occurs as a byproduct of Need mentality. This circumstance is always resultant from some type of Fear, be it of loneliness, of not being valued, of being abandoned, and so forth. Of course when one honestly owns one's participation and choice in this way, many times the relationships that one considers as being horrible failures are found to actually be Really great successes.

Therefore the most important first step in ensuring the greatest Potential of Success in all Relationships, is to first:

Make Certain that one is Real, Complete, and Balanced in oneself, period.

This means that one is of Have mentality, is in Balance and of the Perspective of being unlimited in one's Potential and capacity of fulfillment within what one already has in oneself and one's being in life. As you have come to realize Little One, this is Why your relationships with Jack and so many other Beings and Things have worked so well right from the beginning and stayed that way. When individuals seek to get something from a relationship or operate from any mentality other than Have, then there can be no Real Success, Balance, or Fulfillment for all of the participants in it. Therefore when one is certain of this condition in oneself, then:

Consciously, Define one's Real Desires and Motives for the new Relationship.

In this step, one is to determine and choose specifically what one does in Reality, Desire to Realize as well as offer and Share in one's participation in a new Cosmic / Communal Self Relationship expression. Here is where the important design work both begins and ends. For Real Success to be realized, one's total honesty in this step is mandatory. Also, the key word and consciousness to include in this step, is that of Flexibility. In this respect, I mean that one is to expect any and all individuals that become operative within the new relationship to Change to some extent during the term of it. Therefore one certainly should be flexible and even plan for that to occur. It is equally important not to expect them to change into one's own image and idea of them, but instead to support their becoming their own roundest and most complete and balanced idea of themselves. And once one has clarity of one's desire and thereby design, then the next step is to:

Call Forth that Potential into One's Life.

Yep Little One, here is where one's real Openness and Desire is expressed. As you are aware, I have given you the manner and method of a Spirit Calling Ceremony in the material of the Proper Way. However, I will only mention that this is what always does Really happen and is what causes any condition of relationship, especially for new ones to develop. And while this process and step is not always done in a ceremonial manner, even the issuance of the simplest Desire Prayer with Passion will always affect a similar result. Here one is to be as specific as possible as to one's Real desire. As you well know, if one does not ask for something specifically, then it is much more difficult for that unique Potential to respond. And when that is done, the next step is to:

Accept no Relationship condition that is less than that of one's Real Desire.

As you are aware Little One, here is where most individuals have trouble and usually it begins by not being specific enough in the previous step. Also, if one does not Really Believe a thing possible, it will not be for them, period. As you also now realize, the more specific that one is in one's design of such, the more difficult it might seem to become realized or perhaps longer that it will take. Also, just because some of what one desires does at times come along, one will only have the greatest Potential of success if one waits until the Real answer to their Prayer of Desire is presented. This means that if one takes less than that for which they ask, not only is it usually not for them to begin with, most oftentimes it will slip away anyway. Actually it will rightfully do so in such circumstances so as to realize its fullest measure of Potential elsewhere. As you also know, herein lies the Real source to most problems in relationships in the way of disenchantment and failed expectations. These conditions result in most instances simply because individuals compromised the Potential of their success and fulfillment because of impatience and the lack of Trust and Faith. Many times individuals will enter into unfulfilling or compromising relationship situations simply because they lack Trust and Faith that I Will Provide exactly that which they ask. As you know when you called forth the greatest Love that you have ever known, the Cosmic / Communal Self Relationship of the Potential of it was provided. As you also know, it was provided rather quickly, simply because you honestly were prepared to wait several lifetimes for it to be realized. Because of your experience of that, you only now are prepared to call forth and experience the Potential of the greatest Love possible for you in your current sojourn. Only when the Real answer to one's Prayer of Desire for such a relationship Potential experience and expression is presented, then the final step is to:

Behold it as a Precious Gift and Nurture it.

As you know Little One, most oftentimes relationships are not as successful as they might be simply because individuals fail in this step and process. However, it is also important to realize that all Cosmic / Communal Self-expressions and the relationship within them are of a somewhat temporary nature. After all, there is a relatively short term Potential within any incarnated experience anyway. One can see how this is Real and true when one remembers that each individual Being and Thing that is incarnated, is only visiting. As you also know Little One, even an automobile requires periodic attention in the manner of maintenance if it is going to function well, or for a very long. Most assuredly one can consider this maintenance to be energy in a sense. It is this energy that is also necessary to keep any relationship alive and healthy. Therefore the necessary thing that will realize the greatest Expanding Potential of Success in All Relationships is the periodic application of the energy of one's Care, attention, Openness, Value, Support, Understanding, and time. To realize the greatest measure of Success and Fulfillment in any Relationship these are the ingredients of the food that is necessary to maintain it. Also, one will never be of any semblance of success in any experience of relationship if one is not completely and always one's Real Self at all times in it, period."

With that statement, Great Pop again paused. I chose to then sip on some of that elixir while "digesting" what He had just given for me to understand. Over the years, I have had quite a bit of exposure to the subject of success or failure in relationships both inside and outside of my own experiences of them. In part this is due to the counseling work that I have at times been called upon to do as a PohTikaWah. Of course in doing such counseling, the greatest single resource that I have had to draw upon has been Great Pop. Clearly this is especially true in what He has given for me to understand in the development of the material in these books and in this, I am most blessed and thankful. Of course that in itself does not mean that I am any sort of expert in success or relationships. Yet one could rightfully consider that I do have the knowledge of some if not most of the things that are required to achieve success in relationships. And this is Real and true even if I haven't applied it at all times in those of my own. While some of what Great Pop just elaborated upon is not new to me, some of it was. As if to reinforce that realization, Great Pop then began again with:

"Yes Little One, I recall many times that you have told others in your counseling efforts to do as you say, and not as you do, Ho, Ho, Ho. As you well know, there can be many different sources to problems in relationships. As I also have given you to understand, communication is both the source and cure for any of them. While communication can be called the tool of cause and cure, one or more of the many faces of Fear is in all instances the prime motivator for any such problems to develop. So, since Fear is one of the primary issues in relationships, the focus of the next topic is:

***

How to Champion Anger and the other many faces of Fear.

"As you well know by now Little One, Anger is just one of the many faces of Fear that one's Bark on Tree likes to use to cause imbalance so it can take control of situations. As with fear, anger is also of My design and in Proper application it too is Perfect. Ah, Ha! Now I see that you are wondering as to what would be a Proper and good thing to be angry about, as well as just How can it be considered as being perfect? Well, since anger is fear and in most instances has to do with Control issues, you have your answer. Try to think of something that you have been angry about which did not have some association to an issue with control in some manner. You see, you cannot. Even when you get angry over what someone has done, or when you mistakenly hit yourself when using some tool, it is all about control in some manner. Like fear, anger has a time limit as well, and in that it is perfect. It is perfect you see because anger is designed to motivate one to action just like fear, and many times that action is to be more careful in what it is that one is attempting to accomplish.

However, like fear, anger can at times motivate one to make improper expressions in response to it. Yet, one can learn from all of these types of choices of expressions, hence in that manner it is most perfect. Have you not kept attempting to do something that continued to make you angry as to the outcome of your efforts? The harder that you try in such a condition of imbalance, the worse it seems to get in fact. Of course when you do finally give up, then the perfection of My design of anger is actualized in the process. You see that is Really the Why it is that I made anger in the first place! Now I see that you are recalling the time that I was trying to move when I first became My individualized persona in The Great Void. As I had you experience and describe in Origins, that is the event which actually lead me to originate anger. Very good Little One! Yes Little One, in that event I was stuck. I kept trying to move and would still be doing just that if I had not realized that I should stop and attempt doing something else. Of course I was not angry in the sense that some might think, because as you know, I have no Bark on Tree, Ho, Ho, Ho.

As you watched in that event, I did in fact ultimately devise a means by which I could situate myself in a different location, but normal movement was My Real objective and I knew that there was a Potential for such. This is pretty much the same condition that We discussed in the previous topic. If I Chose to accept less than I Really Desired in that condition of Myself, and was not patient enough and had Faith and Trust that I would ultimately find and resolve the problem, then much of what has occurred since would have not happened. I finally chose to simply accept that stuck condition of Myself. Yep, I finally chose to quit trying to make something happen outside of Myself and began making things happen inside instead. As you also experienced in Origins, this happened many times about many different things. Of course I saw a great benefit could be ultimately resulted in these "Failure" episodes. It actually was with that inspiration and motive that I ultimately made both Fear and Anger so as to be used in experiences in the Physical realm.

You see Little One the obvious circumstances that most oftentimes result in expressions of anger are about outcomes, and thereby failed expectations, just like you are at times with someone else. Here we need to consider basically two things, one's feelings and one's expressions. Both Fear and Anger can be internal or external expressions, yet most often Fear is internal and Anger is external. Both are pseudo-Essences that can be considered as a type of energy that one has available to express personal responses to stimuli in some fashion. And yes Little One, circumstances just like My being stuck for a while in The Great Void is in fact just such a type of condition that can be a stimuli. If being stuck was a real desire and condition that I sought not to change, then it would not be a stimuli and that is a pretty good way of determining what a stimuli is. Yep, one can consider all stimuli to be associated to Change and Desire in this fashion. All Cosmic / Communal Self Relationships embody these things as well, meaning conditions, stimuli, Desires, Change, Feelings, and expressions. I designed it this way so that one can choose to experience expressing oneself with one or more of them. As you now recognize, choosing not to do anything about a condition in a relationship is in fact one of them, just like my being temporarily stuck in The Great Void. Very good again, Little One!

Little One, to really get to the source of a condition in a relationship one must always consider what was desired in it by all participants. This is the only way that one can be centered and of proper perspective and therefore not become put out of balance by things that occur or conditions that develop in them. Also one must separate one's feelings from one's expressions, which is as simple as maintaining one's Focus of Perspective and objectivity. If these things are done, then whatever does occur in a relationship can only be considered as a success. Otherwise, one will continue to be stuck in repetitive experiences of failed expectations and the many faces of Fear such as despair, disappointment, resentment, and so forth. And as you are now surmising Little One, yes these are internal feelings that are also some of the many faces of Anger. In fact there are all kinds of expressions and behavioral patterns that can be considered as being different faces of Anger. Hate and rage are the obvious ones, but also is resentment, anxiousness, despair, disappointment, and so forth. And while anxiousness might be considered to be worry and thereby another face of Fear that way, it is in fact worry with disappointment included, and thereby can be considered as being Anger as well. Yep, one can only be anxious over something that one is also of some disappointment that it has not been Realized already. Actually anger can be real subtle in its guise at times, such as when one feels left out or excluded from something. This type of response and expression which some might consider as being let down, disappointed, or hurt is just Anger and thereby it is simply the result of some type of Fear.

So the first step in the process of Championing Anger and Fear is to:

Quit It Now!

Yes Little One, when one is in this condition of Self, one must stop doing something before they can start doing something else. Of course I am not implying that one should immediately stop being afraid or angry at all. Nope, I am saying to quit doing whatever it is that is the Cause of such a choice of behavioral response, just like when I was trying to move way back when. This is a most crucial first step Little One. And the reason is that unless one stops attempting to do whatever it is that is resulting in these types of responses, then the Attitude of Fear and Anger will become spread and multiplied throughout one's other expressions and activities. Yep, it will spread, much like the spreading of a virus through a computer network and the like. Also, if one is not certain as to the Real source and issue, then one should stop and detach from any and all interactions and activities until one is consciously aware of the Real culprit so to speak. Once the source of the failed expectation is identified and one has detached from it, then the next step is to:

Physically Express and Release one's Anger or Fear.

As I have oftentimes told you Little One, the simplest way of regaining one's balance over any issue that results in Anger is to make some type of physical expression. Such expressions might be to yell loudly, strip Bark from tree, throw pebbles into the water, or any other type of physical activity that brings harm to no Being or Thing at all. Any such physical activity and hence expression, will serve to deflate the condition of expansion and heightened sensitivity in one's Emotional Body that is always resultant from Anger and Fear. This crucial next step of the process is designed to facilitate one to return to a Balanced condition of oneself. All Anger and Fear conditions are in Reality simply Choices of Behavioral Responses to stimuli in the Physical realm, no matter what. As you are also now aware, one has to keep applying energy, usually in the form of Thought, to stay in a condition of Anger or Fear. Of course this is because of the time limit that is a part of their make up. Therefore, since I made these things so as to motivate some type of physical response, the Proper first response is that of a physical expression of some type that Walks in Balance and with Harm to No One Being or Thing. Yep, the Way to Real Success in life is not to avoid getting afraid, sad, or angry, but instead it is to make optimum utility of such expressions when it is appropriate. You see it is like in falling off of a limb of a tree that one was sitting on - one's Balance must first be returned before one can effectively do anything else. Again I will emphasize that in such a first and physical response, one is not ever to cause harm to any Being or Thing including that of oneself, period. Once one has regained one's balance in this step, then the next step is to:

Take an Inventory of One's Personal Assets again.

Yes Little One, this reflects the response that I finally chose to make when I could not move in that early event. In this step, one is to Realize and retrain one's Focus upon what one has and can do, and no longer upon what one does not have or cannot do at this point in one's life. To do such will naturally result in a Renewall of Focus and Perspective. As you now realize little One, Focus and Perspective are critical to realizing Success. Therefore, this process will enable the Potential of a Change in Attitudes that is necessary for one to be able to then again attempt and Succeed in one's subsequent expressions and experiences. The final step of this relative short yet important process is to then:

Simply Choose Different.

As you recall Little One, when I was basically stuck and could not move or do anything outside of Myself, I chose to then do more of the things that I could then do inside of Myself. This is where the tools of one's Lists of Values, Cares and Fears and Resource Wheel can be employed and are invaluable in assisting in one's next choice of personal expression and experience. Also, just because something happened that one became of Fear or Anger about in the past, does not mean that it will always be of that same result in the Future. In this I mean that one should not color or limit one's Potential of experiences and expressions of the Future based upon one's experiences and conditions of the past at all. This is Real and true and is evidenced by the simple example of My now being able to do many things including that of moving freely about, you see. And this brings Us to the next topic which is that of:

***

How to Realize One's Objectives in the Medicine and Proper Way.

In this topic I am speaking now in terms of objectives versus that of goals, as the two are really two different things in most senses. Little One, any form of Real Success is not the realization of a specific goal at all. Nope, real success is realized in the Manner as well as Motive of any single or multiple expression of oneself. One might liken the difference between these things as to when one chooses to participate in some activity such as playing a game. You see, one is really successful when one plays. One is not of any particular real success simply because one wins, actually one can be of real success even when one looses. I remember many times that you have purposefully let someone win a game so that they would build their confidence in being able to do such again. In a certain sense you might consider that to be of a greater nature of success than when you have won over someone that was not as able as yourself in a certain type of ability or expression. Of course success can mean many things to different people, as is the case with the word called Love. Therefore in the discussion of this topic We will limit the idea of the word success to being that of Fulfillment.

As you are aware by now Little One, at all times there are in most instances many ways to do a single thing. Also, there is no right or wrong, good or bad, evil or sin and such. As I also have told you, there can be a huge difference in the impact that any expression that one chooses to make can have as regards the condition of WellBeing and Balance in the All of the Great Web of Creation. Any and all choices of expression that consider and support WellBeing and Balance can be construed to be in Conscious Respect and regard to such Potential. These choices of expression are thereby In Medicine With the All of Creation as well as being considered Proper.

As you recall Little One, many times I have told you that the most important thing to consider in any expression of oneself is that of one's Motive. Motive is much more important to consider than one's objective, or even the methodology that one might consider employing to realize it. Therefore, the first step to achieve Proper Fulfillment and thereby real success in the realization of one's objectives in life is to:

Become centered and of Clarity and Balance in one's Perspective.

As you well know by now Little One, one's lens of Perspective is the primary tool that one has to restore Balance. It is also the most effective tool that one has to effect changes in attitude as well as to regulate the effects of one's Bark on Tree. In a sense, this first step is of the same nature and purpose as that of the previous topic. Oftentimes, many individuals have not been able to realize any semblance of success in life for the simple reason that they have become imbalanced from some condition or stimuli. In this condition and regard, they are pretty much just reacting and thereby behaving in the same manner as a runaway train. Actually, many individuals have found that they have been able to accomplish more in life by doing less, and this is the reason for it to occur that way. How many times have I told you to do nothing at all about a condition or circumstance, Little One? Yep, this is the reason and Why of that. Yes, to continue to pour energy into conditions and expressions that are not in Medicine and Harmony, only serves to continue them. When that occurs, it maintains their disruptive influence in one's life and upon the Great Web. So in simplest terms, before one can start doing something that has any Potential of success, one must first stop all activities and expressions that do not. And however long this step might take, when one is complete in it, the next step is to:

Examine and Consolidate one's Resources in Self.

Little One the very first things to consider in this step and process are one's Consciousness, Balance, Openness, Objectivity, and ability to Focus. These are crucial to one's being able to make a true and Proper assessment of one's condition as well as Values and Desires. In this regard, if one is currently making expressions that are of any type of debilitation or can be construed as wasteful in any manner, such as of one's energy or time, they should be ceased immediately. Also, one is to regard sufficient rest to be of a priority here as well. Sufficient rest is important to one's WellBeing and Balance, as well as mental, emotional, and physical health.

As you know Little One, many times one does issue forth many different and diverse expressions of Selves. Therefore to be of the greatest expanding Potential of real success in life, one must periodically examine and consolidate one's resources in Self. As you are now aware, any type of Self that is expressed outside of one's Real Self and one's Primary Cosmic / Communal Self requires maintenance and energy from them, period. This maintenance and energy can in reality be very productive in some applications and not in others. As you have experienced, there is only so much one can do in any moment and this is the Why of that. Actually Little One, the way that it works is much the same as that of a tree. The more branches and leaves that the tree makes, the more energy is necessary to maintain the system of such. Also, as soon as any branch or leaf grouping becomes debilitated or looses its Potential, the tree ceases feeding energy to that part of itself. So you can see Little One, one's Potential of real success is at most times dependent not so much in how well one is doing in the Fulfillment of any single expression as it is upon how one is doing in all of them at a given moment.

Yes Little One, the more that one puts upon their plate at a time, the more energy and time will be necessary for one to eat it all. Also, if one puts things on their plate or allows for others to do such that one does not Really desire for oneself, then there is no Potential for one to realize the greatest expanding Potential in a meal, and so also life. As you now realize, one's Lists and Resource Wheel are the perfect tools to accomplish this step. Once a clear definition is realized, one is to prioritize one's real life objectives here. It is also important to classify each objective as being of a near or long-term nature. This classification will assist not only in one's prioritization, but also one's energy and time management as well. This step should be repeated periodically as some long-term objectives can and will become near-term. Also, in the process of one's realization of some near-term objectives, new and more objectives will automatically become manifested anyway. Just like the tree Little One, in this step one should give away or consolidate as much as possible any and all of one's Selves that are not in orientation to one's current real life objectives of one's Real Self. Once one has completed this step then the next one is to:

Take Action with Focus and Perspective.

Little One when you asked Me about life, I told you that it was a doing thing. Therefore, one can consider that to be of real success in life, one must be not only Conscious, but also Active in it. The key ingredients to real Success are both Focus and Perspective. Even with the map of one's Resource Wheel and tools of the Lists, both Focus and Perspective are the necessary additional things that one must employ in the realization of Real Fulfillment and thereby Real Success in life. Action without Focus and Perspective will certainly keep one busy in life, but in most instances it will be only counterproductive due to the expenditure of one's time and energy. Perspective is necessary in as much as it facilitates Openness as well as the ability to see and recognize Potential when they do appear. Perhaps even more important than that, is that Perspective is crucial for one to be able to recognize if and when one's real objective has been realized. If one's real objective was to play, then loosing a game with Proper Perspective will not preclude one having a future winning experience as well. Of course if one's real objective was to play, then whether one wins or looses is of no consequence to one's real success at all. Obviously one's Focus is necessary, so as to not waste one's resources and especially those of one's time on any other things. Needless to say in this step, is that The Medicine and Proper Way of any choice or expression is that which Walks in Balance and with Harm to No One Being or Thing. And when complete with this step then the final one is to:

Accept and Embody the Fulfillment in a manner of the Expansion of one's Real Self.

As some say, "the job is not finished until the paper work is done" Ha, Ha, Ha. Actually, the same condition is real and true here. Yes Little One, it is as you are now surmising, an incarnated life is a sequence of experiences resultant from one's personal choices of expressions. As I have often told you, one must give something away before one can receive anything else. Also, I have oftentimes reminded you that one should not judge or measure oneself in the physical condition of being in life. This is because one will always become influenced in such by one's Bark on Tree. Yet, one can and should receive to one's Real Self and Heart, the greatest measure of esteem and rightful pride when one realizes even the simplest objective. To do such will also realize the greatest expansion of one's Real Self, period. To hold one's success and thereby fulfillment as dear and precious is to give back and away something to it that adds value to the Potential of that objective. Of course in the action of this embodiment and give away, one does also make room for more Potential success to be then realized to oneself in the Future.

Yes Little One, life is a doing thing you see. As you also now realize, pretty much all that one really does in life is to make choices about one's expressions of Care and Desire. By My desire and design, each individual Being or Thing is not only in charge of their Prayerstick and Plan in life, they are at all times singularly responsible for the outcome of their expressions in it. As you have experienced many times now Little One, a complete and final Life Review does occur after one's exit and return to My Essential Will. And in that condition and expression of oneself, one is without any Bark on Tree.

Periodic reviews and assessments as to one's progress towards any or all objectives can and will be very productive from time to time during a life expression. However, one should not judge anything in it lest one restricts the limitless possibility of one's Future. In this I mean that one is to review with openness of Heart and Perspective, not so much one's successes or failures, but instead one's experiences and expressions. Periodic reviews should definitely be made from time to time so as to be able to continually and periodically consolidate one's resources in Self. You see Little One, one's greatest Potential in life can be and oftentimes is realized by choosing to make fewer and more balanced and meaningful expressions, than from making many more complex and difficult ones."

And with that statement, Great Pop again excused Himself as He got up and left the room. I was quick to notice that this time He was carrying the little box with Him. I was then given to consider the many things that have caused the present conditions of myself, and the Real desire expressions and Prayers that have been answered to make them as they are.

I next thought about the manner in which I met Nolayte's mom for the first time and what happened after that. When I was in Texas several years prior to that time, a psychic had told me there was a Potential that I would become involved with a younger woman who would want to have a child with me. This psychic said that this would, in a sense, serve to distract or prolong the time that it would take to realize a certain goal or success in life and told me of another woman that was considered as being more "right" for me. To the surprise of some perhaps, all of this did not make me start looking for either one, yet it did cause me to consider trying to be of some success in a family condition again. I pretty much put all of it on the back burner or on a "Wish List" of sorts, which we all have and maintain to some degree.

Several years later while I was still in Texas, a young woman told me of her desire to have a child by me with certain conditions attached. After that did not happen I pretty much forgot about it all. Throughout this period, I had already given my life over in service to Great Pop's Will and about the time of the reading, I had finally chosen to be openly expressive as a PohTikaWah as well. By most standards, my life was "Not Always So Easy". In fact, at times it still is both scary and tenuous. I got to North Carolina basically homeless and once I arrived things were still day-to-day existential living in the most part. It has been almost a decade now since I arrived, and there has been no change in that regard. Even so, the work on the books still continued, and in that I feel most successful. I even made another start on establishing a church and tribe on a couple of occasions and they were operational to a certain degree for a while.

When I first met Nolayte's mom, I had been in North Carolina for a few months and it was the start of my first summer here. I had gone to a comedy club and she was a waitress at the table that I shared with another woman that I was involved with, initially in support of her efforts to heal herself in a certain way. Anyway, I did give Nolayte's mom a Medicine stone and perhaps one of the cards that I had at the time. Soon after that first meeting the other woman and I went to Mexico for a certain treatment for her illness. I left North Carolina planning to be away for a few weeks, which turned out to be several months of what for me, was pretty much a trip into Hell. This is because when we finally left Mexico we went to where I used to live in Texas and upon arriving there, I was literally dumped at the side of the road with my belongings, ending my relationship with that woman. Subsequently I was offered a place to stay with another woman. This woman desired to have a baby by me, but this relationship ended when she also dumped me on the side of the road after stealing what personal belongings I had managed to accumulate.

After a couple of weeks of doing readings and so forth, and with the help of a couple of angels, I was able to get a bus ticket to North Carolina. The return trip took twenty-five hours and I arrived home with twenty dollars in my pocket. I was now several months past due on my rent with no clue as to how I was ever going to continue in life. During the trip I had even wondered about the wisdom of returning at all. On the other hand, I knew for certain that I would rather die on the side of the street anywhere in North Carolina, than spend one more moment in the Hell that I had just left in Texas. Needless to say, I spent much time in thought during that bus trip home. It was actually when it was almost over that I made a Prayer of Passion. I told Great Pop in this prayer that I did not care if it would take many lifetimes, I would not honestly even consider getting involved with another woman as a mate unless they were of very specific qualities and characteristics. In this Spirit Calling, I did in fact unknowingly describe most of the qualities of Nolayte's mom.

A few weeks after my return, more angels in the form of another couple had loaned me a car to use to get some work with. Late one evening, after working on the current book project of that period, Great Pop had me use the little white pony as I call it to go to a place that I would not normally consider or frequent. Upon my arrival, I opened the door and noticed there were only two male patrons and they were vying for the attention of the young female bartender and another young girl who was seated at the bar. I thought that the girl at the bar was somewhat attractive as well, and understood their attention. For some reason she looked a little familiar, yet I was not sure why. Then she asked me if I remembered her and you guessed it, it was in fact Nolayte's mom.

As it was Great Pop who had sent me on this "Walkabout" as I call it, I asked Him what I was to do or say. I was told to give her another card with my phone number on it. I do recall telling her that the phone would be working again in a week or so due to my conditions with funds. I also remember watching her with the other guys through the open door, when she left and walked to her automobile soon after our brief conversation. I did find her to be captivating in a way, but I certainly did not expect any other type of involvement and I left soon after that myself.

On countless occasions Great Pop would have me go to such places with no particular motive or intent other than do what He would tell me to do when I got there. I do realize that many times the stones that I might pass out or thoughts and insight that I might offer was the specific reason, and that certainly was enough for me. On such occasions, I never have asked why, I just do, and this was just another one of those occasions for me.

After returning home, I resumed my normal activities of trying to figure out how to continue in life, while also working on the material of the book that Great Pop wanted me to write at that time. I certainly did not expect her to call in the wee hours of the morning after only a few days. I had just gotten the phone working that afternoon and I was working late, as usual, on the material of The Proper Way. Nolayte's mom had an ever so sweet voice on the phone, and we talked until dawn. She had called to set up an appointment, and so we met the following day. It was in that meeting that I started to realize that we were both resonant to something. Yep, when Nolayte's mom did arrive and I looked into her deep blue eyes, I was hooked. In my Spirit Calling, one of the criteria was that of a much younger person to carry forward the Medicine Way past my exit, and one that would never leave me. And just like that part of my Spirit Calling, she basically never left except at the end when she took Nolayte.

I then was given to recall that after being in that Cosmic / Communal Relationship for awhile, I never even wanted to die. And this was not because I feared death, it was because I was so much in Love and never wanted to be away from her. Now that I think about it, I Really felt that Great Pop had given me a great blessing in having her in my life, and I did so cherish that and never wanted to be apart from it. In thinking about all of this, I was given to recognize just how very much of what Great Pop has given us in this material is so very Real and perfect. With that realization, Great Pop returned to His chair and continued His explanation of these things with:

"Yes Little One, when you asked me if Nolayte's mom was the person that you prayed for, I said she was, and that was Real and true. Also, you said that you did not feel that you were ready to be with her because of your insecurity over finances at the time. Yet, that condition of yourself was of no consequence at that moment, even though her insecurity over just such a thing would be the reason that she would use to justify her ultimate Choice and behavior in leaving. Therefore, your Prayer of Desire was answered and the Potential was Realized with regard to that Spirit Calling experience. You see Little One, no matter how one looks at it, that episode and experience was a Success and thereby the Fulfillment of an objective even though it was relatively short lived. Naturally this brings Us to the final topic, which is:

***

How to Live Life more Fully, and Stay Oneself in it

As you by now are most aware Little One, each and every Being and Thing that incarnates into the Physical realm is a Potential that does so of its own accord. Each incarnated Potential and thereby Spirit, is also singularly responsible for the consequences of its choices. This includes any actions as well, which are just expressions of one's Free Will Choice. As you have experienced, upon one's return from an experience outside of My Essential Will there will be the Reunion and then a personal Review. As you also know, it is oneself that does the Review, and in that condition of oneself there is an absence of Bark on Tree. The actual purpose and intent of the Review process is not really to be of any type of judgment, as some individuals are taught to believe. The Real purpose of the Review is actually so that one can more fully realize and understand all that one has experienced in one's experiences and expressions, and it is little more than that. It is in this process that one does in fact and Reality see the big picture. What is to be gained in this Review process is not only a greater understanding as relates to cause and motive, but also what all is effected by one's expressions as well.

Therefore, for any incarnated Being or Thing to try to keep a running tally or scorecard of what they consider as successes while incarnated would be not only impractical, it would yield unrealistic results anyway. Of course one's Bark on Tree when incarnated does oftentimes try to make one think that one should and that any results or assumptions so developed are Real and even matter. Even so, there are some things to consider doing in one's incarnation experience that can and will assist one in living life more fully. And if one lives life more fully, then one will naturally realize more Real Success in life. Hence, the first thing or step in the process of this objective is that of:

Be Conscious.

While the importance of Consciousness might seem pretty obvious, many individuals in fact do many things during a sojourn that serve to either impair or distract the Consciousness of themselves. While drugs or alcohol might be some of the obvious things that some individuals employ, there are in Reality a myriad of other escape methods and mechanisms, including watching sports or movies and listening to music. This is certainly not to say that these things are bad, or even that one should not from time to time do such at all. Yet even in these choices and types of expression, one will always benefit from maintaining one's Consciousness when doing them. Whatever causes any distraction or impairs one's Consciousness in any manner, essentially puts one's being in life on hold, like some individuals do when using a telephone. Yep, Little One being Conscious is "Numero Uno" as you call it, as far as the recipe for Living Life more Fully, and for obvious reasons. In a nutshell, the more Conscious that one is throughout all of one's lifetime and experiences, the more fully one will have lived it. Clearly to do such will obviously facilitate one to be able to experience and express a greater Expanding Potential of Real Success in life as well. The next thing or step in this process and recipe for Success is that of:

Simplify and Focus.

As you are now wondering Little One, I have defined this step in the "dual" sense in a way, because these are actually conjoined expressions and thereby Choices. In this I mean that while one can consider focusing on something without trying to simplify it, in actuality to focus automatically effects simplification anyway. This is Real and true, because one simplifies and thereby reduces the number of elements that they should consider important and thereby embrace with their consciousness when they focus on something. Therefore, one cannot do one of these expressions without also doing the other at the same time. Now that I see that you have a grasp of that, I also see that you are now wondering as to what it is that one should Simplify and Focus upon.

The answer is simple Little One, it is: Focus and Simplify **Being Oneself in life**. Here you will recognize the many moments and amount of time that you have spent in dreaming up different scenarios, such as what you will do when you win the lottery and so forth. In Reality, to do such is no wrongful or improper expression per se. Actually, to do such can be entertaining from time to time. However, even a single moment spent in such an activity and expression can be used to make more Real headway in the realization of a more promising and tangible near-term life experience and expression objective. And as you are now surmising, yes Little One that is what one's Lists and Resource Wheel are all about and define. Certainly you should have fun in life, and if dreaming up such scenarios is one of one's Real life objectives and True Desires, then by all means simplify and focus on that. However, if other experiences and expressions of one's Care and Desire have a greater priority, then one's time as well as one's Focus would definitely effect more Real Life success if they are applied to those things. Now that We have Consciousness and Focus in the mix of Our recipe for Success, the next step and ingredient is that of:

Develop and Maintain a Real Self-awareness and Image.

As you are realizing Little One, I am using the term and word Real a lot in this material. As you know, what is true is conditioned to time and by definition what is Real is not. Life is Real more than it is true, even though in a sense it does seem to have an expiration date, Ho, Ho, Ho. Even after one exits a sojourn, or life expression, one's having been incarnated will continue to result certain continuing effects, no matter what. Therefore, if one is to experience even the slightest semblance of Real Success in life, it is and can only be one's Real Self that can accomplish such. This is a fact that is Real and true in any and all cases and conditions. As you are aware, some Beings and Things can and do primarily express themselves and experience life as a Projected, Imagined, or even Cosmic / Communal Self. As you also know Little One, these choices can and at times do support Possession and so forth to occur. Hence, for one to do anything other than being one's most complete Real Self at all times in one's life, would be simply the perpetration of a fraud. Now I see that you are remembering and thinking of the light at the end of the tunnel Little One. Triple Bingo!

Indeed Little One that is precisely the reason I put it there, and it works that way. By My design, the white light at the end of the tunnel of Transition erases one's memory of past incarnations in the most part when one incarnates, and restores it when one returns to My Essential Will. As you realize, one can only have a totally new beginning if one is totally new in it. In this I mean to say that I put the light there so that one will not try to be a past persona in one's next incarnated experience. That is Why this step and ingredient is so important. Even so, some individuals do choose to step out of the pattern of their Real Self so as to emulate the persona of one's past, or even that of others from time to time. As you know, to be able to begin *fresh and have limitless Potential, one must discard the past image and patterns of behavior of oneself, no matter what. Likewise, no matter how hard that one might try, one can only Really be one's Real Self, period. Also, being one's Real Self is the only way that one can have limitless Potential. Therefore, one can easily recognize that this condition is very important and it is fundamental to being Really in life. So once one makes a commitment to maintaining one's Real Self-awareness and image, it is facilitated in the next step, which is to:*

Identify and define Oneself and one's Life Objectives.

As I see that you are beginning to now realize Little One, this personal evaluation and definition process can and should be taught and done both early on and throughout one's incarnated life experience and expression. As it was in the establishment of the Tribes in the beginning, one's immediate family and associations should support this identification and discovery process as well. As I have given you the ability to Name individuals, you have realized how special and valuable such knowledge of one's Real and Essential Nature can be as a parent. This is Real and true because it gives those responsible for the support of the foundation of the child being in life, knowledge as to what is uniquely special in the persona of the child. Successful and Proper parenting and family occurs when that support is given in such a manner that the child then has a Real and unique identity and image of Self from which to build upon and operate with.

Whether one is founded in such beginnings or not, any and all incarnated beings should endeavor to establish and maintain such an image of Self in themselves throughout their life processes and expressions. While this is an individual ability and responsibility, support should be considered and maintained by all that are of any type of relationship with that individual, period. This is fundamental Little One, not only in being Real in life, but also if one is to Realize any of one's limitless Potential to a greater degree. So, in this step and ingredient, one is to identify and define one's Real Self, as well as one's Desires, Care, and so forth as is supported by the Lists and Resource Wheel part of this material. Once one is complete with this step then the next step is to:

Choose and Consolidate.

Here is where one does the important work that will make the most significant difference in the possible Fulfillment and Expansion of one's near and long-term Potential in life, period. Just as the preceding activity and step should be done periodically throughout a life experience and expression, if one is to realize the greatest expanding Potential of success, so also should one do this. In this step and process, one's objective is to reduce the number of one's associated Self-expressions as much as is necessary and comfortable. You see, by periodically pruning the tree of one's Real Self in life, one stimulates much more Potential for Future fulfillment and thereby the sprouting of new branches of experience and expression. I choose to use the wording of necessary and comfortable, as this is what matters most in one's capacity of realizing any Real expanding Potential fulfillment. Also the type of comfort that I am referring to here, is that of being at peace in one's Heart of Self as to one's choices being made.

Clearly if one has made too many Imagined Self and Cosmic / Communal Self-expressions that are draining the resources of one's ability in the way of time and energy, or taking one's focus and energy away from those of greater Priority as regards one's Real life objectives, then something has to change if one is to realize any of the latter. Here again, oneself is solely responsible for any fulfillment or outcome in life. It is your life Little One, and if you choose to spend it helping others instead of helping yourself in it, then that is perfect. However it is only perfect if helping others is your Real life objective and it has such a priority.

Yes Little One, this is a very important process and step, and it does not have to be of any discomfort or be unpleasant at all. And as you are now surmising, yes, to do such will again facilitate one to be aware of the Real objectives and priorities that will realize the fulfillment of one's Potential and objectives in the shortest time, and with the greatest ease. As you are also now thinking, yes, this is another place for the application of the Lists and Resource Wheel. Once one has defined and trimmed their tree of one's Real Self, then the next step and ingredient is to:

Do one's part. Take Action.

While many might in the conventional thinking of the prevalent society consider this to be the most important part of the process and recipe for success in life, it is not. Mind you it is significant, but not the most important part. As you also remember, when you asked Me, I told you that life is a "Doing Thing." Yet Ho, Ho, Ho, doing nothing can be also considered as doing something! Actually, Little One, what I am getting to here is that timing as well as motive are very important to consider in regards to the realization of Real success and thereby the fulfillment of one's life objectives and potential. As you understand and know, to plant seeds in the winter for a crop to be grown that will flourish normally if planted in the spring, will severely hamper the realization of the Potential in each of the seeds. Yet some individuals do just about the same thing in the guise of being "busy" at something in life.

And just like when you asked Me about taking action about realizing certain objectives that have a relatively high priority in your life and Plan, sometimes inaction is the best action that one can take for awhile. Actually, some Potential do not even need any action of oneself at all after one has issued forth a Prayer of Desire expression about such. Therefore, just to be stirring the pot about such Potential at times can hamper the speed or eventuality of such being realized. So you see, doing one's part can be and oftentimes is Really separate from taking action in most every sense. In this step Little One, one should also consider the employment of the Proper tools for each job, so to speak. An example of such is to use a precious and fragile object to drive a nail. All too often, individuals seem to consider that the end justifies the means without consideration to the damage that is effected upon other Beings and Things when they take action in pursuit of an objective.

Therefore, in this step one is to consider both separately and collectively the responsibility that is ever associated with expressing one's ability. Also, one is to consider the consequences of each Choice of Action that one takes, including both the near and long-term of such. Naturally, the test of appropriateness is found in the question as to whether it does in Reality, Walk in Balance with Harm to No One Being or Thing. If one does find such to be the case then by all means, to Realize Success in one's life then one can and should do one's part and take action accordingly. So Little One, once this step and ingredient is applied, the next one is to:

Share the Vision.

One has at times heard of the saying that no man is an island, and that certainly does apply here. Over the millennia, many a Being and Thing has wondered what it would be like to step upon the moon's surface. And not only have they expressed a curiosity about such, but also at times many have expressed Real Prayers of Desire of such an experience as well. Of course as you are aware, since the beginning many people such as yourself have journeyed there in the out-of-body sense. Yet no one had done such in the physical sense until recently. And the only way and manner that any such objective can be and was realized, was because some individuals chose to Share the Vision. Even if one person was able to accumulate the wealth and technology to do such a thing, they would still be on the launching pad in most senses, you see.

As you are aware Little One, the reality and purpose of the theme park of Mother Earth and the Earthplane is that of Brotherhood and hence, Shared experiences. Even in the aloneness of one's place of residence, whatever one chooses to do or not will affect and effect the All of the Great Web of creation simply and perfectly by My design and desire of such. Little One, as you well know, you alone are responsible for what is in your Plan and Prayerstick, period. Yet whatever is in it does effect and have an impact on the Potential for all other Beings and Things at all times as well.

It is for each and all to choose the What and When of their enlistment of participation in any expression of another Being or Thing, as well as of others into any expression of their own. Naturally as well, most individuals do find that a shared experience is more rewarding simply because of the companionship involved. Also in joint activities of personal expression, the capabilities of all Beings and Things that are involved are increased immeasurably. This is not only with regard to one's capability of action and response, but also in the broadening and greater depth and variety of Perspective as to all of that which is involved as well. It actually is in this step and ingredient that it is possible to leave behind the fruit of one's tree of life for others to come. For any Being or Thing to do such, you see, will benefit all in the Future from one's Being, and being oneself in life. Once one's Vision is shared then the next step and ingredient is associated with this one, and is to:

Enlist Others.

In every consideration Little One, no one is born alone and all that incarnate require some support from other Beings and Things during certain moments in one's sojourn. As previously mentioned, such was the condition and case for man to be able to physically walk on the moon. Yet there is a great difference to be considered in what is dependency and what is support. All Beings and Things should maintain a condition of sufficiency in Self as much as is possible. This should be done at all times and in all conditions and circumstances. As you are now aware, to be in accord to my Plan and Desire for an incarnated life experience and expression, no Being or Thing should ever create a condition of dependency in any others, either. Of course as you have oftentimes stated, as soon as the slave learns to love the whip then the slave becomes the master, and the master has to serve him. As you also know, neither condition should even be ever considered to realize any semblance of Real success in life.

On the other hand, much can be gained in respect to the realization of a greater expansion in one's Potential of Real success in life if one at times does Enlist Others to co-operatively share in one's experiences and expressions. In such a choice and circumstance of one's enlisting the participation of other Beings and Things, the Medicine of all Beings and Things that are involved become available, as well as the Potential pooling of resources and broadening of perspective. By enlisting the participation of others, one will naturally exponentially increase not only the Potential that will be available but also the expansion that any and all might realize from such a sharing of personal Medicine, expression, and experience. Of course one should be of Consciousness as to one's energy and time as well as that of others that choose to be involved in these Cosmic / Communal shared Self-expressions. If the expressions are Proper, then the All of Creation will be the ultimate beneficiaries of such a shared choice and expression, and not just the direct participants. Still, just like some things at times are best left undone, some things at times are best realized alone. Therefore the Real test and guideline to be considered here is one's motive, as well as whether the expression Walks in Balance and with Harm to No One Being or Thing either presently or in the Future. Once complete, then the next step and ingredient to the mix becomes that of:

Review and Renewall.

Yes Little One, this is where the real goodies are received in life so to speak. And just like Focus and Consciousness are so important throughout all of this process, it can be stated that it is most critical to employ them here as well. Also, here is where one can and should employ another element to an even greater degree, and that is one's Essence-Operative lens of Perspective. Obviously as well, this is another part of the project that one can at times enlist others, not so as to measure or judge mind you, but so as to have a broadening of Perspective so that one can be able to ensure Real objectivity. By Real objectivity Little One, I am talking about grasping the impact and big picture of the event and expression in the global and multidimensional viewpoint. It is one thing to make a park for one's children and the children to come to play. However, one should not do such if it impacts the Future of any other Being or Thing. If the location or condition of the park causes erosion, loss of habitat, or any of a multitude of conditions that do not Walk in Balance with Harm to No One Being or Thing, then it should be not considered at that location, obviously.

As you are now surmising Little One, yes this Review should be made relatively frequently and even monthly or daily in some instances. Remember here, this review is not for the reason of measuring or judging anything at all. Nope, it is primarily to streamline and to reinforce one's priorities and perspective especially with regard to one's true Desires and Values. Throughout this step one can and should make consolidations as seen fit as regards the expressions of the many Selves from one's Real Self. In this I mean that one should regularly trim away any Self branches that are not active or are counterproductive as relates to one's Real Desires and objectives. In addition to the trimming process, one should also regularly reinforce those Selves that are in support and alignment with one's Cares, Desires, and objectives as well. Also, one should regularly redefine one's Care, Desire, and other Lists as the opportunity and changes occur. Just as you do the East work of the day in review of it before going to sleep each night Little One, this should be likewise done quite frequently. To do such will facilitate one to be not only on track as relates to one's direct progress in the realization of one's Real life objectives, but also as relates to one's being in life and of limitless Potential in it at all times.

Little One, just as one should be of frequent Review, so also should one be of frequent Renewall so as to keep Expanding one's Real Self Potential in life. As you know Little One, what I mean here in Renewall is to make a fresh new beginning in life as one's next New Real Self. One can do such as easily as making one's Lists and Resource Wheel and stepping forward in the Self-image, life description, and Plan that are inherent in them. Of course to experience and express Renewall is to completely abandon and disregard one's past image and so forth in total, so as to become that next new Self. Yes Little One, as you now realize, each and all of these steps and ingredients enable and facilitate what can and should be considered as one's first and foremost Real life objective. This Real life objective and Potential for each and every Being and Thing is that of the last and final step which is to:

Keep Becoming One's Next New Self.

Little One, as you well know, you are not presently the person that you were in your last incarnated life on Mother Earth, nor the many life expressions that you had before that one. Nope, in all practical senses you are a different and New You and thereby Self. Obviously, that new Self has many different parts that We have described in great length and detail in this material. These parts all have direct impact upon your individual Potential and thereby ability to realize any specific goals or objectives. As you also are aware, in some senses you actually do carry forth some of the memory of your past with you into each new day, be it in the current experience or from any other incarnation. These memories can affect the Potential of one's being in life at the present, but only in as much or as often as one Chooses to allow for such to occur.

Oftentimes now you have Prayed for Me to make you over, and your life and Plan to be that of My Desire, Plan, and Will. I have and will continue to do so, as often and for as long as you ask Me to do such. But remember here, Little One, it is your life, not Mine! You do not have to do anything to please Me, and that you Desire to be of service is only significant to you. I do certainly appreciate your commitment in this way, but as you well know, it is not necessary at all.

Each and every Being and Thing in life does in fact have limitless Potential at all times, yet it must be chosen for any of it to be realized. You chose to be a PohTikaWah before you incarnated Little One, and in Reality you are actually in most senses very good at it! So in that sense, You are of a great Success in life so far, even though you are currently worried about survival, money, Nolayte, and so forth.

Now that we have that stated, we are pretty much complete with this material. So put in the last chapter, and when you finish that, there is something else that I want you to do for Me next, Ho, Ho, Ho.

Yep, you guessed it Little One! It has finally come time for you to write the material on Tribes!

FINALLY....

As I finally begin this last chapter of this material, I am almost overwhelmed in what has taken a period of only two short months for all of this to happen. I began this "Project" on December 11, 2001 and it is now February 11, 2002. Clearly, I have discovered so very much in the experience and odyssey of it, and I discovered not only so very much about myself, but also life in general. In the smaller picture of things, the circumstances of my existence have not changed all that much in a certain perspective. Yet in another way of looking at things, I have been endowed with tools that can make the Future much better in every sense and way. At this point, I still do not have my license to drive, and I must wait another two weeks to find out if that will even be possible in the near term. I do still have some food, and TohNaWah and I are both still healthy. The rent will be again due in a few days and I still have some resources that were to go to the car and drivers license project. Of course, I am also very reluctant to use that for anything else, yet I can if it becomes necessary which is part of my Eagle Medicine perhaps and "if push comes to shove" as some say, I may not have any options in that regard.

At this point I still do not have any immediate potential of work, even though the weather is starting to be better for doing outside activities again. Yet the Real work as relates to my life and Resource Wheel has been done quite rapidly and with relative ease, meaning the development of this material. In the process of it, this writing machine experienced Renewall and in a sense so have I. I do not know when or how I will be able to be in life with Nolayte, and perhaps even in the lives again of my other two children. Yet, because of this material my present Perspective and Attitude is more of Hope than Fear, and in that I am most thankful. As a result of this project I now know the answer to the question of the Who and What I Really Am, and I have received many tools to be able to realize a much greater Expanding Potential of Real Success in life. Yep, I have been blessed many ways in this short two-month period of my life! Also, I am most appreciative to those individuals that have shared their resources and support, which has resulted in the development and completion of this project and my continuance in it. Of course, and Finally, I am certainly most thankful of Great Pop's providing all of it.

Lately I have been considering my condition in life and what it so far seems to have been all about. In this I mean that I have been given to consider the reality of what happened when I drowned at the age of four, and many of the other significant experiences that I have had like that one. I realize now how each and all of them have served to influence some of my feelings, desires, and cares which have resulted in certain attitudes and issues to develop within myself at times. One of the things that seems to strike me as most significant in that drowning event way back when, was that no one in my immediate family seemed to care at all if I was alive or not. My parents were not conscious of my exit and the only person that even cared enough to pull my body out of the pool at that time was an absolute stranger to me.

It even seems ironically perfect that this is pretty much the same condition of myself now as regards my condition of being with or in a family. This is especially Real and true with regard to my oldest two children with whom I lost contact well over a decade ago. I have had such minimal contact with Nolayte now that I cannot say as to his feelings or care about me, or my being in life at all. Yep, in most every sense I really am pretty much alone in life at this time. I am very certain that my True Desire to be in Nolayte's life is not to get anything other than the joy of experiencing and discovering him. Actually, it really is more to give him something than to get something and the same holds true for any others, be they of immediate family or not.

Like all of the material that has been given for me to prepare, I get a little remorseful when I finally near completion. It probably is something like what they call "Post Partum" depression for women that have given birth. It seems that as long as I am working on these books for Great Pop, my life finally seems to matter. Also, I feel that somehow Great Pop will continue to provide for me to continue to be able to survive in it, as long as I am in the process of writing the material of these books. Even so, simple survival can be seemingly of little reward after a while. One of the many things that I have realized about myself from the experience of the odyssey of this material is that I am of a great passion. Of course this means that I am somewhat extreme emotionally in the ups and downs of the cycles of life. I get really excited and joyful, or really sad and even of a great anguish at times. And I would not want to change any of that about myself, else I would not be the real me, ha, ha, ha. Even in my sad times I can laugh, and in my glad times I can cry from the heart and soul of my Being. I also would never desire anything different in myself in that way because I have started to see life in a different way. When one lets go of the Fear that one's Bark on Tree tries to use to get control and sees in Perspective, life in the sense of existing is not all that there is. My Bark on Tree is always telling me all kinds of foolishness about life, and death. Of course my Bark on Tree is the only part of me that is lost and left behind with my physical body when I do finally exit and hence existing is real important to it.

Clearly we now have many more tools to use in Realizing Real Success in life, including knowing not only what Real Success is but also Great Pop's desire of our being and being in life. Clearly, life is or can be the facilitator of opportunity and thereby Potential. Life is also a doing thing as Great Pop explained. To me life gets more colorful with Passion and my periodic emotional swings can be quite positive. I would certainly not want to miss out, on any of the feelings that I have had in it, simply because they are what make me, me. Yep, without feelings, life to me would be in black and white and pretty much two-dimensional. Of course that would not be bad and might be a condition that is easier for some Beings and Things to operate in. But I Really Love color, and so I choose to feel all that I can with the greatest of Passion!

For many years now I have recognized the important role that Hope can play not only in one's Potential of life, but also the quality in which one expresses and experiences being oneself in it. In this I mean to say that if one has Hope in their Plan and Prayerstick, then their time in life has not only more meaning, but also greater Potential for Fulfillment past the conditions of the present. Like Passion, with Hope one's life has greater Potential and thereby more value that way. It is obvious from the elements in my Lists that there is a lot of room for improvement in my present condition of being in life in some senses. Yet like Great Pop explained to me, all in all, it is and has been most fulfilling and rewarding and hence a great success so far. I do personally feel that I have done the best that I can as regards what Great Pop has given for me to do, and in all of it I am most appreciative and thankful!

In the many summers now of my being in life, I have read many books. In most cases there was given an ending, however, as in the Medicine of Self and Life as well as this book there Really is no end, only endless new beginnings.

Finally....

I pray that this material brings

As Much Hope, Purpose, Joy, and Real Success

To you and your being in Life,

As it has brought to me in mine.

Sincerely,

And

Pusch Na Tu Ku Oayte

(I Love you with all of my heart soul and being Great Pop)

WHITE EAGLE

Note:

As I format this material for E-Book publication it is now July of 2011. I found Nolayte and my other two children not too long after originally writing it and we are in contact and all are doing well. Pretty much all of what I had listed as True Desires when I prepared this material has in fact occurred, which is a testimony to its effectiveness. I am still waiting on that "Big" lottery win though, so I am making new lists.

APPENDIX

SOME SUGGSESTIONS FOR LISTS

The following are just some of the things that one might consider including in one's own lists:

Of Note: Some of the entries in these lists may be so similar that they should be combined into just one for use, hence the multiple things to consider that are presented in some of them. Also, some of these suggestions may fit into more than one category. However, it is recommended that any single item be used only one time in one's Resource Wheel definition.

VALUES:

Being (Anything at all)
Love of God
Love of Life
One's:
Ability to Change
Ability to Learn / Grow
Ability to Support / Share / Help / Serve
Balance / Stability / Strength / Centeredness
Commitment / Word
Courage / Choices
Curiosity
Heart / Love / Care
Honesty / Sincerity
Loyalty
Openness
Passion / Desire / Hope
Potential / Openness / Perspective
Sensitivity / Compassion / Feelings
Trust / Faith

ASSETS:

One's:
Care / Love / Compassion
Conscience
Flexibility
Honesty / Integrity
Imagination
Openness
Perception
Perspective
Reverence / Respect / Value
Sense of Humor

Ability to:
Call things forth / Pray
Change / Heal
Communicate / Share / Teach / Guide
Figure things out / Logic / Learn
Fix things / Problems
Help / Support other Beings and Things
Maintain Balance / Control
Maintain Focus / Self Discipline
Share / Give
Talk With God
Talk or work with Spirits
Tell the Future
Visualize things

DESIRES:

A Car / Transportation / Mobility
A Career / Profession / Opportunity /
Greater Potential in oneself
A Home
A Mate / Partner / Some one to Care about - Love
Balance / Peace
Comfort / Ease
Enhancement of Sensitivity / Ability
Fame / Fortune

Family / Children / Friends / Tribe
Freedom
Fulfillment
Guidance / Support
Health / WellBeing
Joy / Satisfaction / Pleasure
Love / to be Loved – Accepted – Valued
Security / Confidence / Proper Self-image / Esteem / Safety
Vision
Wealth / Flow / Abundance / Supply / Money

FEARS:

Being Homeless
Being Incarcerated
Being Sick / Disabled / Dying
Being Taken Advantage Of
Being Uncomfortable for any reason
Being Unhappy
Being Unnoticed / Unwanted / Not Cared About
Being Unloved / Disrespected / Under Valued
Being with someone that you do not want
to be with, know, or dislike
Being Without Family / Friends
Being Without Resources / Poverty
Failure
Getting Lost
Having a Loved one exit / die
Lack of Opportunity to Express / Better oneself
Making Decisions / Changes / Choices
Not being able to see or be with those one Loves
Not being able to Control oneself, a situation,
or the outcome of something
Not being able to realize Fulfillment of one's Desire list
Not having one's Being, and being in life matter
Success
To Have to do something that one dislikes / Enslavement

CARES:

Being Able to do something / Play
Being Able to win / Succeed
Being Good at something
Being Healthy / Not Sick or Dying
Being Honest
Being Loved / Cared about
Being Self-sufficient / Free
Being a Success
Being Trustworthy / Dependable / Loyal
Family / Friends / Tribe
Having a Potential become Realized /
Fulfillment of some Desire
Having one's Life mean something
Helping Others
Honesty / Integrity
Joy / Ecstasy
Leaving things better that one Finds them
Loving some other beings or things
Making a difference some how in one's Being, and Being in life
Security / Safety / Comfort
Serving God first and foremost
Serving Oneself first and foremost
The Well Being of Oneself
The Well Being of the All of Creation
Winning

My True Values Worksheet

No.	Description	Rank

My True Desires Worksheet

No.	Description	Rank

My Assets Worksheet

No.	Description	Rank

My Fears Worksheet

No.	Description	Rank

My Cares Worksheet

No.	Description	Rank

Selves Worksheet (Example)

Self:	Status / Constraints
Real – White Eagle	Need Funds / Drivers License
Projected – In Family	
Imagined – As a son	
Cosmic / Communal - None	(Parents Deceased)
Imagined – As a brother	
Cosmic / Communal - Sister	Relationship is fulfilling for both / No change or energy is desired
Imagined – As a parent	
Cosmic / Communal - Heath	Estranged / Need Funds & Means to Locate
Cosmic / Communal - Jacki	Estranged / Need Funds & Means to Locate
Cosmic / Communal - Nolayte	Estranged / Need Funds & Means to Locate
Projected - As a PohTikaWah	
Imagined - As a Priest	Active / Need more Contact
Imagined - As a Healer	Active / No Need
Imagined - As a Visionary	Active / Need more Contact
Imagined - As a Writer	Active / Need Funds & Help editing and publishing
Imagined - As a Guide	
Cosmic / Communal - Others	Active / Relationships Are Fulfilling

My Resource Wheel

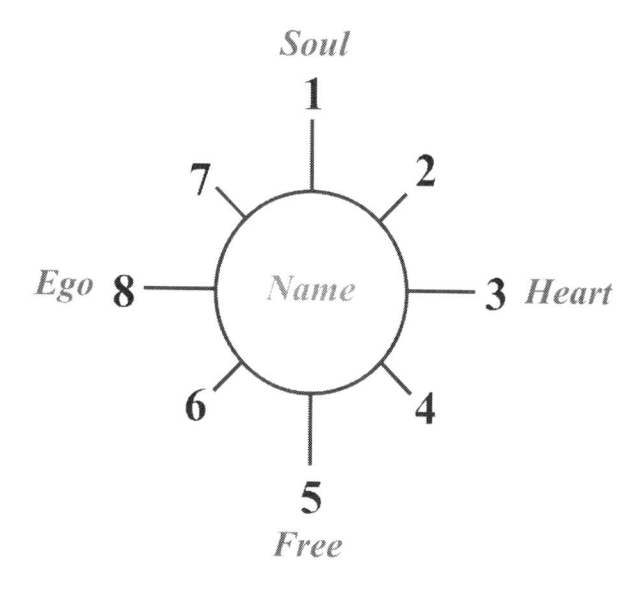

Soul
1

2

7

Ego 8 — Name — 3 *Heart*

6

4

5
Free

****

OTHER BOOKS
BY
WHITE EAGLE

At this time the following Books by White Eagle are also available:

The Medicine Way
The Proper Way
The Medicine in Names
The Medicine of Numbers

Origins -
Volume 1 - The Very Beginning
Volume 2 - The Beginning of Life
Volume 3 - Being Human
Volume 4 - The Future

The Medicine of Selves –
Volume 2 - Tribes
Volume 3 – Life & Survivor's Guilt

How To Make –
My Medicine Pipe
The Beaded Medicine Wheel
The Crystal Dew Claw Rattle

About –
Great Pop
Possession
Dancing With The Boogie-Man
About – 2012

****

****

I close with a special Thank You
To Susan "Speaking Wolf" McLellan,
For her editorial support of this material,
and to You for reading it.

****

Great Pop has gifted and blessed me with so very much and in so very many ways including being able to Name people.

Naming lets one know what one's Medicine is and thereby what is uniquely perfect about oneself and Why one likes or does things a certain way, which is invaluable.

To be Named please visit

ASpiritWalker.com

And click on About Naming

WHITE | EAGLE

Oayte, Pah Ay Kah!

(It is Good and it is Done, Great Pop,
Thank You for so very, very much!)

White | Eagle